THE PHONE BOOK

THE LATEST HIGH-TECH TECHNIQUES AND EQUIPMENT FOR PREVENTING ELECTRONIC EAVESDROPPING, RECORDING PHONE CALLS, ENDING HARASSING CALLS, AND STOPPING TOLL FRAUD

M.L. SHANNON

PALADIN PRESS • BOULDER, COLORADO

D1710463

Also by M.L. Shannon:

From Paladin Press
The Bug Book
Digital Privacy: A Guide to Computer Security

From Lysias Press
The Paper Trail
Vengeance Is Mine

The Phone Book: The Latest High-Tech Techniques and Equipment for Preventing Electronic Eavesdropping, Recording Phone Calls, Ending Harassing Calls, and Stopping Toll Fraud
by M.L. Shannon

Copyright © 1998 by M.L. Shannon

ISBN 0-87364-972-9
Printed in the United States of America

Published by Paladin Press, a division of
Paladin Enterprises, Inc., P.O. Box 1307,
Boulder, Colorado 80306, USA.
(303) 443-7250

Direct inquiries and/or orders to the above address.

PALADIN, PALADIN PRESS, and the "horse head" design
are trademarks belonging to Paladin Enterprises and
registered in United States Patent and Trademark Office.

Equipment photographs from the manufacturers. All others by the author.

M.L. Shannon is on the list of authors on the Paladin Web site: www:paladin-press.com

CONTENTS

Yes, Virginia, It's a Radio!
Myths about Cellular Telephone Transmissions

Vendors
Frequencies
Sets
    Voice and Data Channels
        Odd and Even Streams
        Page Channel
        Sites
        Control and Registration
        Handing Off
        Outgoing Calls
        Incoming Calls
        Borrowing Channels
        Reallocating Channels

The Law
Locating the Cell Sites
    Cellular System Maps
    Use a Radio
    A Field Trip
    FCC Records
        Write the FCC
        Visit an FCC Office
        PerCon FCC Database
        Scanware Associates
        Grove Enterprises
        Communications Engineering Technologies
    Finding the Latitude and Longitude

Channel Assignment
    Which Channels Go with Which Cells?
Programming the Radio
    Modify the Radio
    Use Two Radios
    Computer-Aided Scanning
Tracking
A Test Drive
Portable Monitoring

Controls
Particulars
Reaction Tune

Do They Cause Cancer?
     PCS and Ionizing Radiation

Easy to Monitor

Computer Hacking
     Physical Access
     Meet Dr. Van Eck
What Can You Do?

Intercepting Voice Pagers
Pagers and the Law
What Are the Frequencies?
Pager Intercept Systems
     The Beeper Buster
          Specifications
          Benefits
          Single-Channel Pager-Intercept System
          Multichannel Pager-Intercept System
     Power Fax System
     DataScope
     The POCSAG Decoder

How Fax Machines Work
Power Fax
A Homemade System
Securing Your Fax System

Subcarrier Extension Phones
Frequency Inversion Scramblers
     The Scrambler
     The TVS250
          Using the TVS250
          How Secure Is the TVS250?
          Conclusion
     The Motorola "Secure Clear" Cordless Phone
     Transcrypt International
900 MHz Cordless Phones
     Spread Spectrum Technology
          Technical Stuff
          How Secure Is It?
          Vtech

WARNING

ACKNOWLEDGMENTS

This book would not be possible without the help of the following:

Antique Radio Classified magazine for information on the history of radio broadcasting
David Banisar of the Electronic Privacy Information Center
Don Moser, owner of Motron Electronics, for information on the TxID system
Glen Roberts of *Full Disclosure* for permission to reprint articles from that publication
Joop Van Lingen, bon vivant at Viking International
Kevin Murray of Murray Associates for permission to reprint articles from his newsletter
Mike Russell, former owner of Sherwood Communications, now retired
Randy Roberts, publisher of *Spread Spectrum Scene*
Steve Uhrig of SWS Security for advice, proofreading, and manuals on his Beeper Buster
The equipment manufacturers who have lent equipment or provided manuals
The Internet and its users, the greatest source of information in the world
The reference staff of the new San Francisco main "bookless" library
The team leader of an unnamed countersurveillance company you will read about
And many others, some of whom are better left anonymous

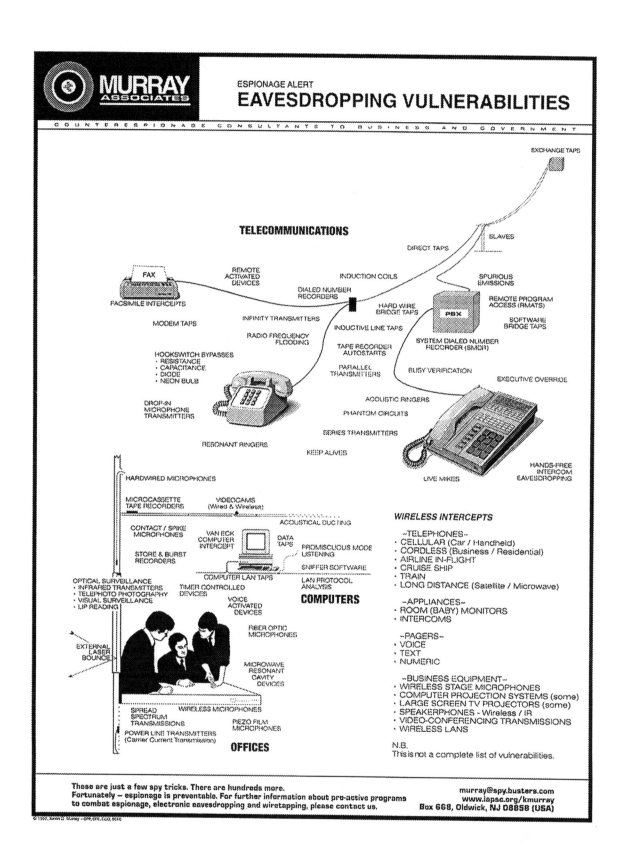

INTRODUCTION

When you had your telephone installed were you told how easy it can be for someone to tap your line? When you bought a cellular phone were you warned that your conversations can be monitored with an inexpensive scanner and that there are commercial monitoring systems that automatically "tap" you whenever you use it? That it is easy for someone to "clone" your phone's electronic serial number into another phone and make calls that you may have to pay for? That the new digital cell phone conversations aren't as secure as the vendors claim, and that they can be decoded with a home computer?

Are you aware that there are sophisticated eavesdropping systems capable of reading, from a distance, everything that appears on your home or business computer screen?

If you have a private branch exchange, better known as a PBX, system at work, did the company that installed it tell you that it may be very easy for "hackers" to break in and make long-distance calls that you will probably have to pay for?

Do you know that your cordless phone calls can be monitored with a $50 scanner from as far as a mile away? That your pager messages can be intercepted with a device that costs less than $50? That your voice mailbox and answering machine can be invaded and your messages listened to and even erased?

Are you aware of the "new" Clipper chip and the Digital Telephony Act with which the government would be able to tap virtually any phone, anywhere, anytime? With or without a warrant?

Do you know that the government is attempting to take away our right to send and receive confidential electronic mail or have private telephone conversations on the Internet? To dictate what we may or may not read and to whom we may or may not communicate?

In this book you will read, in mostly plain English, about all of these things and quite a bit more. You will learn about the technology used for electronic eavesdropping and how it can be defeated. You will learn what the government is doing to take away your privacy and what you can do to fight back. When you have completed this book, you will know a considerable amount about privacy and surveillance, and you will be able to use this knowledge to make your communications so secure that no one, not even federal agents, can eavesdrop on you . . . if you make the effort.

Also included are an illustrated step-by-step account of a search for eavesdropping devices by a team of experienced professionals, a source list for the products mentioned in the text, and an extensive glossary of the terms used in this book.

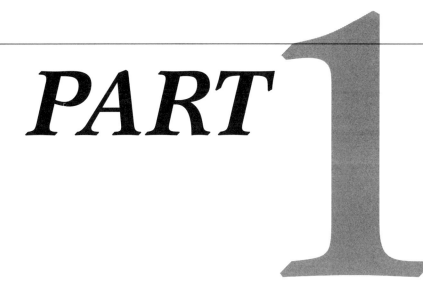

PART 1

LANDLINE TELEPHONES

"It is impossible to send the human voice through a wire."

—Unknown

ABOUT TELEPHONES

ANCIENT COMMUNICATIONS

Man is by nature a communicative creature. Since he appeared on planet Earth, by being created or having evolved from some primeval soup, he has found a way to make his feelings known to others. What began as a few grunts and screams (what would *you* do if a mastodon stepped on *your* foot?) naturally evolved into the spoken language. People had to be able to speak to each other if for no other reason than to say they weren't speaking to each other. This was done face-to-face, because there were no forms of long-distance communications; you wanted to talk to someone, you had to go visit him or her. Even after communication evolved from scribbling on cave walls to sending written messages, someone still had to hand-deliver them. This job was assigned to prehistoric snails, which in a manner of speaking it still is.

Many of man's greatest discoveries were made by accident; perhaps some ancient being became intrigued with the resonant sound made when he dropped his stone ax on a hollow log. Jungle drums or cave drums or whatever! This was probably the very first long-distance network. Some years later man learned about fire, and suddenly smoke signals began to compete with drums. One sunny day another cave person observed the light of the rising sun reflecting off a flat rock, and the heliograph was invented. Then there were three long-distance carriers, and the rates started dropping.

MR. MORSE AND HIS CODE

A few hundred years ago electricity discovered man, and while one may question the wisdom of flying a kite in a thunderstorm, this was the dawn of a new era. Then, in about 1800, Alessandro Volta demonstrated the storage battery, and, shortly after, the basic electromagnet was invented by Michael Faraday. This consisted of a coil of wire that, when connected to a battery, caused nearby iron objects to be drawn to it—which made a clicking sound. *Why couldn't these sounds be worked into some kind of code?* wondered Mr. Samuel Finley Breese Morse, who was born in April 1791.

Morse experimented with this idea, improved on it, and assigned a standard pattern of clicks to each of the letters, which became known as the Morse code. The instrument was perfected, and wires were strung 37 miles from Baltimore to Washington. Then on 24 May 1844, Morse sent his historical message to President John Tyler, "What hath God wrought?" I don't know what the president replied, but he probably assigned a Senate subcommittee to consider the proper response. Well, it wasn't long before telegraph wires were strung between major cities and eventually across the Great Plains to the still Wild West. It became possible for a person to send a message, relayed by dozens of stations, hundreds of miles and get a reply in hours rather than the weeks or months required by Wells Fargo.

MR. BELL

Some years after Mr. Morse had America clicking away, people started thinking that if it was possible to send dots and dashes through a wire, then why not the human voice? Alexander Graham Bell, a Scotsman and one of the most brilliant inventors of all time, decided that he would do just that. He described it as "a grand system whereby a man in one part of the country may communicate by word of mouth with another in a distant place." Such an undertaking required cash, something that Bell didn't have, so he went looking for investors, none of whom were impressed with his idea at the time.

Great spirits have always encountered violent opposition from mediocre minds.

—Albert Einstein

"Send a voice through a wire? Why that's impossible, and even if you could, of what possible use could it be?" was typical of the responses of people with more money than imagination.

Undaunted, Bell and his assistant, Mr. Watson, continued their research in the Court Street workshop in Boston. After countless hours of labor, they were able to send barely intelligible sounds through the wires strung across their shop, until that fateful afternoon of 10 March 1876, when Bell uttered the famous words, "Mr. Watson, can you hear me? Come here, I want you." The reason for Bell's urgency was the fact that he had spilled sulfuric acid on his pants while working on his primitive mechanism. Bell doesn't mention this in his writings; the account appeared in Watson's autobiography some years later. At any rate, Watson heard him clearly and rushed into the room. He repeated what Bell had said, indicating he understood it perfectly. The telephone was born, and the original patent was awarded to Alexander Graham Bell.

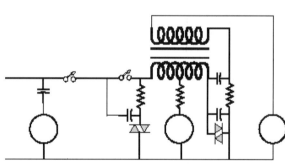

Schematic drawing of a simple telephone.

How Bell's Telephone Worked

The part of the telephone that converts sound to a varying electric current is the transmitter, a diaphragm filled with loosely packed granules of carbon. As they were vibrated by the sound of a voice, their resistance changed, which was how the current was varied. This sound was sent to the earphone, or receiver, on the other end, and a small amount of the transmitter signal was fed back into the talker's receiver. (This is called the *sidetone*, which is generated so that a person can hear his own voice from the receiver to determine how loudly to speak. The sidetone must be at the proper level because too much will

Some of the phones used in the days of the "party line."

Top: One of Bell's earliest working instruments.

Middle: An early "party-line" phone.

Bottom: Close-up of the center phone. Note the crank on the right side.

cause the caller to speak too softly to ensure good reception by the called party. Conversely, too little will cause the caller to speak so loudly that it may sound like a yell on the other end.)

Watson was able to hear Bell when he spoke into the instrument because he was standing directly beside it, and this was how in the first years of the telephone one person was able to know that another wished to communicate with him. There were no ringers, no way for one caller to let the other know he was being called, other than by picking up the instrument and shouting into it. If the called party was close enough, he might hear the tiny metallic voice and answer. Something better had to be devised, and two years or so later Watson invented the ringer and patented it in his own name. It consisted of a bell and a magnet that was cranked by hand. Since the ringer was loud enough to be heard at some distance, the problem was solved. That is, as long as only two phones were connected together.

The Party Line

With several phones on the same pair of wires (the party line), if someone activated the ringer by turning the crank on his phone, all the other phones rang—and all the other people answered. After everyone had finished shouting hello and calmed down a bit, the "parties" sorted it out, and the right two parties were left to communicate in peace—except when someone was listening in, and on party lines everyone did at least once in a while. There had to be a better way to communicate, so someone came up with the idea of using different patterns of rings.

"Uh, hey, Marge, was that our ring?"
"No, Chester. Ours is two longs and three shorts."

As with anything else, when one person has it everyone else wants it, and soon the telegraph pole became the telephone pole. Wires were strung everywhere, and by 1886 there were some 26,000 telephones in the United States. This was all well and fine, but it created another problem: the ringing system was just too much to deal with.

"No, Chester. Ours is 17 longs and 43 shorts, followed by . . ."

So the switchboard was created. This was back in the days of craftsmanship, when people took pride in what they built and used the finest materials. Switchboards were sometimes made of hand-rubbed hardwoods with ivory inlays and brass fittings. Across the top were several rows of jacks, and at the bottom a line of plugs connected with cables to the incoming lines. Each jack had a light below it and was labeled with the subscriber's name. When someone wanted to make a call, he turned his crank. A bell rang on the switchboard, and the operator would look up to see which light was turned on. That way she could greet the subscriber by name.

"Operator. What ya want, Clem?"
"Hi, Norma. Say, would you ring Sadie, please?"
"Now looky here, Clem, you shore been talking to her plenty lately. What are you two up to?"
"You oughta know, Norma, you been listenin' in. Now ring the damn phone . . ."
So the operator takes Clem's plug and puts it into Sadie's jack and turns her crank to alert Sadie that she has a call. One ringy-dingy . . .

Later, a battery-operated ringing system was installed so that the operators rotated a little lever switch, which kept the operators from getting so cranky. The manual switchboard system was in use for many years. In some small towns, as late as the early 1960s, there was no formal telephone

company office, so it was often located in the operator's living room or parlor.

Phreaking in the 50s

Many a free long-distance call was made through these small-town switchboards. While I was traveling around the country, I could always stay in touch with people by calling a friendly operator in a small town near the city where I lived. Back then, the long-distance operators used manual routing codes; when someone wanted to make a call, the local operator would call the long-distance operator to get the codes. I had them memorized.

"Uh, operator, the LD code is 142 plus 114 plus 34D plus. WH on the line."
Two ringy-dingies.

So I would go to a pay phone, dial zero, and ask the operator to connect me with directory assistance and give her the code. The "WH on the line" would inform the local operator that I "will hold." So when the Roanoke operator answered, I would speak directly to her.

Elaine hears a ring, disengages herself from her boyfriend, and hurries to the switchboard. She looks at the panel for the blinking light and quickly plugs a cord in. The local operator in (wherever I was calling from) asks for directory assistance, and Elaine says she can help. So the local operator disconnects, and I am speaking, toll free, to Elaine.

"Hi, Elaine. It's me . . . your (old) boyfriend."

She asks who I want to call, I give her the number, she dials it and unceremoniously plugs me in. Then she goes back to her (new) boyfriend.

An early example of phone phreaking.

This new switchboard system was a great improvement, and it pleased just about everyone. No

Strowger's stepping switches.

more counting longs and shorts; a person's phone didn't ring unless the call was for him. This was, of course, before wrong numbers were invented.

ENTER MR. STROWGER

But there was one person who didn't like it, and unlike most people who don't like something, he did something about it. This was an undertaker named Strowger. One of his competitors had a wife who was an operator, and he believed that when someone tried to call his funeral parlor this operator told the bereaved that his line was busy and offered to refer the caller to another undertaker—presumably, her husband. So the inventive embalmer created the automatic stepping switch. No operator assistance required, just dial the number.

The process was simple: when the phone was hung up on a hook, it was turned off. So no current flowed through the "loop." (The loop is the complete circuit made up of the phone and the wires that connect it to the central office, or CO.) When someone picked up the receiver, this closed the circuit. Current flowed, which triggered a relay in the CO and told the CO that it wanted some attention. This sent a dial tone down the line to the phone, indicating that the CO was ready to place the call.

The phones used with these Strowger switches had rotary dials that opened the loop and then closed it again. If you dialed a three, the line opened and closed three times. The stepping switches were in banks, one for each digit of the number, such as BR-549. The first was the "line finder," then came the "selectors," followed by the "connector." When the receiver was picked up, the line finder selected an unused line from the trunk and waited for the first number. It then rotated one step (hence the name stepping switches) for each time the line opened and closed. The selectors would "ka-chunk" down so many steps and rotate as the next digits were dialed, and as the last digit was received, the connector rotated and physically connected the two lines together.

At this point, the CO sent out a signal of about 90 volts at 20 or so cycles per second, on the loop. This activated the ringer of the called phone—*three ringy-dingies*—and was heard in the earphone of the calling phone as a "brrrrr" sound to let the caller know that the called phone was ringing. This continued until the called party picked up the receiver, since there were no answering machines back then. When the call was completed and the calling party had hung up, the switches would reset with another loud ka-chunk. It may well have been in the rooms where these Strowger switches were installed, thousands of them, that earplugs were first conceived.

Stepping switches, and an improved version called *crossbars*,

One of the flaws of this early system was that the two lines stayed connected together until the calling party hung up. So if Strowger wanted to, he could have gone to another phone, called one of the other funeral parlors, and left the connection open. The only way to free the line was to go to another phone and call the phone company. There, a technician would note the last two digits of the captive line, refer to a chart and find the switch that made the connection, and lift the cover and push a button that reset it. Ka-chunk. The line was freed.

were in use for about a hundred years, and though there may be a few small independent phone companies that still have them, the new electronic switching system (ESS) has otherwise replaced them. With either system each telephone is connected by two wires called *ring* and *tip*. Ring has nothing to do with the ringer or bell inside the phone, as one might guess. It refers to the outer part of the plugs used in the old manual switchboards (tip is, of course, the tip end of the plug). They go to a CO where the switching and signaling equipment is located.

YOU CAN TALK, BUT DON'T TOUCH

Up until a few years ago, Ma Bell owned everything. The phones, the wires, it all belonged to the telco. And no one outside the telephone company was allowed to touch anything. You could not own a phone or change the wiring or connect anything to the line. To do so and get caught was to invoke the terrible wrath of Ma Bell. Indeed, kids who fooled with the lines could be, and sometimes were, arrested and taken to juvenile detention centers where they were lectured to and fed terrible food. Now we can own our own phones, mess with the inside wiring to our hearts' content, and attach once-forbidden devices to the sacred pair of wires: answering machines, fax machines, modems, and other interesting things you will read about later.

ALONG THOSE LINES 2

Have you ever wondered where those two little wires go after they disappear into the wall of your living room? I mean, we already know that they go to the CO, but how do they get there? And what is inside this CO? A few months ago, I decided that I should have a look at the inside of a telco office. I called Pac Bell and talked to several people who told me that they no longer give tours.

This might have been because I told them I was writing a book about wiretapping. Bad move. So I kept trying (using a bit more discretion) and was finally connected to a guy, who I will call Joe, in the maintenance department. "Sure thing," Joe says. "No problem. When you wanna go?"

I suggested the following Monday, which was fine with him, and bright and early I showed up at one of the telco offices in San Francisco. Joe loved his job and liked to talk about it, and because we both have always had an interest in things that ring, we hit it off right away. For several hours he led me around through the different offices and rooms, explaining almost everything, and he even let me take a few pictures. So the following is an explanation of where your little beige-colored wire goes once it disappears inside the wall of your living room or office.

THE SPSP

First of all, it depends on the type of building you are in. In a private home, it will go first to either a single-pair station protector (SPSP), which is a metal device about the size of a large soup can or a plastic box, such as the Telephone Network Interface (TNI) made by Siecor and other companies. Usually such devices are mounted on the back of a house or in the basement of an apartment building. From there a heavy rubber-covered "drop wire" cable leads up the wall and then out to a telephone pole in the alley.

The old SPSPs have two small screws holding the metal top in place. The TNI has a plastic latch that can have a wire seal or small padlock inserted. Instead of standard sheet-metal screws, they use the Torx brand screw that requires a special wrench to open. They are available at some electronics supply houses and provide a little security—keeps honest people honest, as the saying goes.

Inside is a plastic cover over the top held down by a second Torx screw. It is labeled "WARNING Telephone Company access only," and inside are the small fuses that protect the line. Inside the old-type SPSP is a pair of similar fuses. These protect the telco line from overloads, such as someone (somehow) plugging the phone wires into a 120-volt wall outlet and such. The older type of SPSPs were made of a ceramic base and a sheet-metal cover, but the TNI is made of genuine poly-something.

In a large apartment or office building, the lines disappear through the wall and may lead to, and become part of, a larger cable. Depending on the size of the building (i.e., the number of phones),

13

this cable may lead to a small room called a *floor closet*. This room provides access to maintenance and installation personnel (and spies) and may be on every floor or only on some floors. In some buildings, there won't be any floor closets, so the line will go straight down inside the space between the walls, or perhaps an elevator shaft, to the distribution closet.

THE 66 BLOCK

In the distribution closet will be a connection panel usually called a *66 block*, because it has terminals for 66 lines. There are, of course, larger connection blocks, but they are still usually called 66 blocks. There will be wires from all the other offices or apartments coming together here, each connected to a pair of these terminals. They may be little curved brass things, called *punch-down connectors*, or ordinary brass nuts and bolts. The outside wires enter through the back of the block and may be first connected to another panel containing overload protection fuses, called *heat coils*.

THE POINT OF DEMARCATION

The 66 block or SPSP is the point of demarcation, usually called *demarc*. From there to the offices or apartments, the wiring is maintained (or neglected) by whoever owns the building. Beyond this point, the wiring is the property and responsibility of the telco. The pairs of wires go into a tube, usually plastic that is filled with a jellylike substance that keeps moisture out, and into an underground conduit where it eventually becomes part of a larger cable. This may be any of a number of sizes, and eventually it becomes part of an even larger cable called a *feeder cable* or *feeder trunk*, which usually holds 1,200 pairs of wires for 1,200 phones. This large cable goes to the CO.

THE JUNCTION POINT

At certain strategic locations the telco maintenance and repair people have to be able to access the lines. One such place is the junction point, located underground and accessed through manhole covers. Here, cables can be spliced together and repairs made. When you see several of Ma Bell's trucks blocking an intersection, causing a traffic jam, and a large yellow accordion tube disappearing into the manhole, they are at a junction point. The tube is used to circulate air.

THE B-BOX

The bridging box, sometimes called a *pedestal box*, can be found on street corners in urban areas and along highways, sometimes hidden behind a sign or billboard, in rural areas. They are about 3 x 4 feet, usually painted silver or green, and often are locked with a standard cap screw that can be opened with a can wrench or standard socket wrench. They serve the same purpose as junction points: a place to access the lines.

Some of these lines are rumored to be REMOBS (REMote OBServation as described in my earlier book *Don't Bug Me* and later on in this chapter), which give the technicians direct-listen-only (so you can't hear them) access to any line they want—except for certain leased lines used by federal and local law enforcement. Others are "loops," a pair of numbers one digit apart, such as 292-0087 and 292-0088. If two people call these numbers, they will be connected together.

THE CABLE VAULT

Finally your line, your two wires inside a large cable, enters the telco through openings in the walls and into the "cable vault," usually in the basement. At the CO I visited the feeder trunks enter through plastic tubes mounted in the wall. The ones that are not used have tight-fitting caps to keep water out—most of the time. Joe told me about a time when someone had removed several of the caps from unused tubes on a day when it had rained and all the fun they had removing a foot of water from the floor.

There were about a dozen of them, from small, what looked like 50 pairs, to 1,200 pairs (which is usually the largest) and several in between. A few of the cables were sheathed in red translucent plastic and were fiber-optic cables that can carry many conversations on a thin plastic strand.

Also in the cable vault are several large control panels that operate and monitor the compressors that blow air into the underground conduits. This air forces out moisture that may otherwise get in and is measured by sensing devices that will detect loss in pressure from, for example, someone opening one of them to install a tap. Also nearby in the basement is the battery room where voltage from the incoming power line is rectified into direct current (DC). This is to charge the massive banks of batteries that provide the 48 volts that is on the telco lines. Instead of wires, they use a *bus*, a copper bar about 6 inches wide and 1/2-inch thick. From the vault, the cables go up through the ceiling into the frame room.

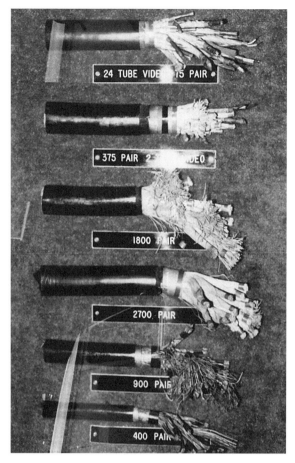

Some different kinds of telephone cables.

THE FRAME ROOM

The frames are large metal racks with a series of panels containing terminals (connections) for all the incoming lines. The ones shown here were about 15 feet high and perhaps 100 feet long, and there are two of them. The first is called the *vertical distribution frame*, which the incoming lines, from the cable vault, are connected to. On the other side of the room is the *horizontal distribution frame*. Wires connect directly from this frame to the telco computer. The two frames are connected together by thousands of pairs of wires in an overhead walkway.

INSIDE A SWITCH

Upstairs on the second floor is the "switch," the telco computer that connects the lines together. You have to go through five doors to get to it from outside the building, and some of the doors have two locks. Some of the doors have two locks. One is the higher security type (Medeco) and the other an electronic combination type. There is little chance of a master locksmith getting into it without the codes and keys. And even if a person could open the locks, someone would see him. Now one might reasonably assume, as did I, that there would be dozens of people in the CO, all of them running around busy as ants, so one more body might not be noticed. Not so. In the whole area I saw only six people, and naturally all of them knew each other. Anyone not supposed to be there would be noticed instantly.

Joe unlocked the door, and we entered. It was a fascinating place but a little different from what I expected. I had imagined dozens of whirring tape drives and security guards following me around with scowling, suspicious expressions. Joe and I were the only two people in the room. There were two computers, and Joe explained that one did the actual switching and the other handled intercept messages, such as a number that "is no longer in service and there is no new number." Each system has an open-reel data recorder that makes a backup of the information for billing purposes.

COSMOS

Your pair is identified from all the others by a code that includes the name of the switching office and the cable and pair number. I asked Joe how this worked, and he led me to one of the smaller computer terminals. He asked for my office number, which I gave him, and he punched it in. A second later, the printer zapped out a few lines of type. Interesting, I told him, and asked if I could keep it. "No," said Joe. He explained that it wasn't the actual information but rather the "format" of the information that was proprietary.

The system that does this is called COSMOS, and on the computer printout was (in part) the following information: Larkin 6003-221. The switching office is called Larkin (for Larkin Street, even though it is on a different street several blocks from Larkin, 6003 is the cable number, and 221 is my pair number. A telco maintenance or security person could find my line with just that information. Also on the printout was the long-distance carrier I used (AT&T), the fact that I had unlimited local call billing but no call forwarding, and some other things that I can't remember.

REMOBS

REMote OBServation, mentioned previously, is a way of "tapping" into one line from another, whether the line is being used or not. I asked Joe about tapping into people's lines from the switch and was told that in the restricted switch room, a telco employee could indeed tap into any line he wanted. When I asked if that included law enforcement and federal lines, he changed the subject. Joe likes to talk about his work, but he won't tell you everything he knows . . .

There's an old story that makes its way around among telco people. It seems that one night some maintenance people were in the switch room, tapping phones just for the helluvit, and listening on a speaker phone. They had tied into the line of one of the other telco people. That person just happened to walk into the room at the same time that his wife was making a date with some other guy . . .

So, from your home or office to the CO, that's where the wires go. Next, a look at how a line may be tapped.

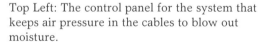

Top Left: The control panel for the system that keeps air pressure in the cables to blow out moisture.

Above: The frame room where the lines enter from the cable vault.

Above Right: The ESS computer.

Middle: One of the control panels for the ESS computer.

Right: The other control panel. The phone on the right is REMOBS.

HOW TO TAP
A PHONE
3

People tap phones for different reasons: some because they want specific information from or about a particular person or business; some just because they have access to a line or lines and are nosy; and some out of nothing more than innocent curiosity. The last was what motivated me when I was a kid, and over a period of several months I had successfully tapped every home on our block and then some. Guess I'm just a natural-born spy.

There is another reason to tap a phone: self-defense. Someone is doing something to someone else to make his life less than pleasant, and this someone else wants it to end. If you have read *Don't Bug Me*, you may recall the story of Sylvia. A neighbor had tapped her phone and used the information he obtained to interfere in her life. The person who did it was caught and put in jail, but he didn't stay there very long. And when he was released he continued to make problems for this sweet little girl, who was so naive that she just couldn't understand that someone would do such a thing. Finally, she decided that she would have to do something to stop him.

The man who was bothering her apparently never thought that she would turn the tables on him and tap *his* phone. But she did. Or, rather, I did. I was the "electronic kook" that a friend of Sylvia's knew in high school.

One day when this creep was away, Sylvia and I went down to the basement, made a cleverly concealed bridging tap, and ran a direct wire to her apartment. There we set up an old Akai open-reel recorder and a listen-down amplifier. If there were dropout relays back then, I didn't know about them, so Sylvia had to manually turn the recorder on whenever she heard the phone being used. After a few weeks we were able to get some damning information on this guy, and then we confronted him with it. I kind of felt sorry for the guy—for reasons I won't go into—but this harassment had to stop. He agreed to find another apartment, and that was the end of the problem. Sylvia was "eternally grateful," and I was, she said, "a sweet guy that any girl would fall in love with," but she already had a boyfriend. Oh well . . .

There is a point to this story. People have asked me if I think I have the right to publish the information that is in my books. I have always replied that it is not a right, it is a responsibility. Electronic surveillance may sometimes be illegal, but that does not mean it is immoral. Sometimes the use of eavesdropping devices is the only way that people have to fight back.

So let us suppose that you have decided, for whatever reason, to tap someone's phone. This chapter is about how you may or may not be able to accomplish your objective. Tapping a phone may be very easy, or it may be virtually impossible, depending on what you have available to you and who you are. There is no way in hell I could ever bug the U.S. attorney general, but President Nixon did.

In tapping a phone, there are a few things to consider:

- You need to know a little about your subject: where he lives and works, for example.
- You have to be able to get access to the phone lines to his home or office.
- You need to set up a listening post where you can intercept and record the conversations.
- You need to have the equipment to do the job right—the first time.

KNOW YOUR SUBJECT

Finding the address and phone number of someone you want to bug is beyond the scope of this book, but there are many others available on obtaining information about people from Paladin and other publishers. Once you have this information, you have to find a way to access the lines and then find the right one.

ACCESS

To tap the line, obviously you have to get to it. But once you get into the area where the lines enter the building, how do you find the right one? There might be hundreds of them.

- The pairs connected to the 66 block are rarely marked with the phone number (I have never seen this) but may be identified with the apartment or suite number. This will not tell you which line goes to a specific phone within that suite, but it may be all you have to work with.
- The lines coming in may be grouped and tagged by floor, particularly if they go to a floor closet. This is even more difficult to work with. If you can stay in the area for a long time, then use automatic number identification (ANI) to check as many lines as possible. Connect a lineman's test set to the pairs one at a time that you have reason to believe go to the right suite or the right floor and call ANI. A computerized voice will announce the number of the line you are using. But be aware that if someone picks up a phone on that line, he will hear the ANI voice, which may tip him off. An alternative, if Caller ID is available, is to call a friend from the various lines, who will read the numbers back to you.

  If there are too many lines to check in the time you have, here is another way that is faster, if you can get it to work. It is a variation of an old trick used in the days of Strowger switches called *raking*. Using the test set, you connect to a pair picked at random and call the number to be tapped. As soon as the connection is made, you run a metal object, such as a screwdriver, across all of the terminals. This momentarily shorts them out, causing a loud clicking sound in the test set when the terminals for the called number are shorted. With the ESS used today the lines are not connected until the called person answers. But there may be a way around this. First, you may get an answering machine. Rake during the outgoing message but not after the proverbial beep; if the owner has the monitor on he will hear the clicking noises. The second way is to get the person who answers to put you on hold and then you rake the terminals.
- If you don't know which is the right pair or the number, then you have your work cut out for you. Should you have unlimited access to the 66 block or you can access the lines from another location (such as an adjoining apartment), you can connect a listen-down amplifier. This is usually a small inexpensive amp that is battery operated and connected to the line through two small capacitors. Add a recorder and dropout relay to activate it, and the system is automatic. Just check the tape now and then. This assumes that you will recognize the person's voice.

  To avoid waiting for long periods, you might find a way to get the person to use his phone. Suppose you are trying to tap the line of the old biddy across the street who is constantly complaining to the police about everything real or imagined. Toss a few cherry bombs on her porch and there is a better than even chance she will be on the horn reporting a terrorist attack.

- If you are trying to eavesdrop on a particular person in an office that uses a PBX system, such as Centrex, you may be out of luck because there is no way to know which of the lines that person will be using at any given time. The only way to intercept a particular person is to tap all of the incoming lines or to install the tap on the phone inside his office. If it is necessary to place the tap on the line inside the office, obviously you have to get in. Let's take a hypothetical example.

The target is a lawyer in a large office building where there is tight security: guards who roam around and a distribution closet locked with a Medeco and protected with the magnetic switches of an alarm system and a closed-circuit television (CCTV) system. Mission impossible.

Pretending to be a telco maintenance person might get you in, but do you have an ID card that is convincing? A work order with the right date and address on it? Sample forms can sometimes be found in telco Dumpsters, but suppose someone in the building calls the telco to verify the work order? You are caught and in deep shit. So how are you going to get in?

If I were being paid a great deal of money to wiretap this person, here is one way I might go about it. This is an old trick, known to everyone who has been in "the biz" very long. It is a classic because it *sometimes* still works.

First, I would find out who does the janitorial work in the offices. If I pretend to be a new company interested in the contract, the building manager will probably tell me. Failing that, I would hang around the building and observe, looking for vans with the company name as well as private vehicles the workers arrive in. If I didn't see any, I would follow the van back to its shop, watch for the employees to get into their cars to go home, and write down some license numbers.

A little investigating would get me names and addresses as well as credit information, such as who is behind on their car payments. Then one evening I would go visit this person, perhaps finding a way to not make it seem too obvious. I'd see where he hangs out and hang out there too; I'd get a conversation going and listen to his problems.

After getting to know this person, I would give him an envelope with a few hundred dollars in it. No explanation other than I just want to help. A few days later, I am back with another

envelope. This time I ask questions and tell him a little about myself. I work for a new janitorial service that wants to bid on the contract at the lawyer's office building, implying that if my company gets the contract, wages would go up. Nothing sinister about that. I ask the guy how many people spend how many hours on a "typical" suite, typical being the one I want to bug.

I give him another

The proceeds of a black-bag job? Payoff for a sweep? I'll let you guess.

21

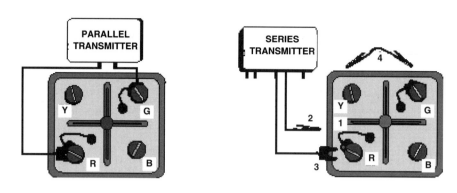

This drawing shows how parallel and series taps are connected to the phone line.

THE PRICE OF A TAP

I am asked, once in a while, to tap a phone. My answer is as follows:

1. Three virgin passports in names I choose
2. $250,000 in small, unmarked, used bills
3. A chartered Lear jet with a pilot who asks no questions and files no flight plans
4. Advance notice of 30 days

And then I do the tap, right?

Wrong. Then you get a postcard from South America advising that "I am having a wonderful time and am glad you're not here."

In other words, no. So please don't ask. I've never been in prison, and I don't particularly like the idea. I hear they aren't very nice places, the food is of questionable origin, and they probably wouldn't let me keep my radios.

envelope and leave, explaining that I will be back. This time there is a check in it. And if he cashes it, then I have a lot of leverage against him. He is mine.

Next time, I ask him to get me inside the suite. I promise not to steal anything—I just want to look around. If he gets me in, he gets a bonus; and if the company I represent gets the contract, he gets a fat bonus. He agrees to try it the next night, so I show up looking like one of the workers. If anyone asks, and this isn't likely, I am a replacement for someone who is ill. Once inside, I install the devices.

The next week I visit the worker again, give him another check as the bonus, explain that we failed to get the contract, and thank him. He never sees me again. And he doesn't say anything to anyone because I explain that it would not be a good idea if he did. A copy of the canceled check is convincing evidence. There are other ways to accomplish the same objective, some of which are in The Bug Book, but every situation is unique, so consider all possibilities and use your imagination. You'll probably be able to figure something out.

THE LISTENING POST

Getting the tap installed isn't much good if you don't have a way to monitor and record the conversations, so you need a listening post, usually just called the *LP*. It conjures up the image of a small room, lit only by glowing pilot lights, flashing multicolored light-emitting displays (LEDs), and flickering computer terminals. Spies in trench coats and fedoras and headphones are hunched over the equipment, whispering among themselves: "Ah! I got Groblovitch on installation three, and he's talking to Yamagucci." At least that's what it's like in the movies.

An LP can be that elaborate if you happen to be with the National Security Agency (NSA), but it will more likely be an empty room with nothing more than the tape recorder connected to a wire leading somewhere or to a communications receiver and one person who comes in every few hours to replace the tape. No fedora, no London Fog.

It can also be something as simple as a recorder placed inside an official looking box, mounted to the wall beside the 66 block. Make up a professional looking label such as Environmental Protection Agency Air Quality Sensing Unit, PLEASE DO NOT REMOVE, or Consolidated Computer Communications Company Interface Unit. It might be there for months without anyone noticing it; when was the last time you paid any attention to the equipment in the basement of your office building?

Is it possible to lease an office in this building? Maybe you can set up there and use a bridging tap. This is where you connect the two wires that go to the leased office to the pair to be tapped at the 66 block.

Can you use a phone line transmitter? Is there a place to conceal it? What kind do you have available? Does it have enough range to reach a nearby building where you have set up the LP? Is there a lot within range where a van can be parked and used as the LP?

THE EQUIPMENT

Once you have determined where the LP will be, you can decide on which method to use: direct wire or radio frequency (RF) transmitter. You will also need some basic hand tools, solderless connector kit, lineman's test set, electrician's tape, and a test receiver. Some other useful materials are a small hammer and chisel; some plaster, such as spackling compound; a container of water; a putty knife; and several cans of different-colored spray paint. The idea is to be able to disguise the tap, if possible.

Making the actual connection requires some kind of wire. Using the same kind the telco uses is best because it is less likely to be noticed. You should have some of the four-conductor cable that has the standard red, green, black, and yellow insulated wires, as well as the multicolored type. A short length of 25-pair cable can be found in virtually any electronics surplus store, or an old computer printer cable can be used because it has similar wires inside.

If the connection is to be made directly to the wires, use a mechanical device such as the Scotch-Loc. They may not be less noticeable than a splice (twisting the wires together) with tape on it, but are less likely to attract attention because telco installation workers never make splices. Finally, try to make the connection in a place that is as hidden as possible: within a bunch of other wires or in a place where there is enough slack in the line to move the wires behind something, e.g., a hot-air duct or water pipe. Sometimes you can loosen the staples to get some more slack.

THE DIRECT WIRE TAP

The direct wire is just what it sounds like; you connect a pair of wires to the line and lead them to the place where you will listen to the intercepted conversations. Obviously, the LP has to be very close to the target or in a place where the wires aren't likely to be discovered. For example, stringing wires out an office window and across a street to a parked van might attract attention. In a big office building you may have a bit of a problem hard-wiring the tap.

Leading from an SPSP box on the back of a house and pushed under the edge of the grass along a fence, the wires may never be discovered. This is how we bugged a neighborhood bully cop back in the 1950s and got the goods on him.

There are several advantages to a hard-wired tap. You don't need to be concerned whether or not the signal from an RF transmitter will reach the LP, which you may not have time to test, there are no batteries to run down and replace, and direct taps may be difficult to find with electronic equipment unless the person using it knows his stuff.

I remember a tap I installed some years ago that, if I say so myself, is an example of clever. The connection was made in the splicing boot on a telephone pole in an alley of a residential neighborhood. This particular pole was selected because the house where the LP was set up was on a lot adjoining the alley. Finding the right pair was easy, but how could I possibly get the wires to the house without it looking suspicious? I disguised them as an antenna. In this case, it was a folded dipole. One end of the antenna was tied to a vent on the roof, and the other was hooked to the pole with a short steel cable and ceramic "egg" insulator. The cable was covered with plastic insulation from a piece of heavy coax, which concealed two fine wires. They were wedged inside the cracks in the wooden pole leading to the boot. It was removed when the project was complete and so was never discovered. (Later, something was discovered. That's another story . . .)

And how was I able to get it in place without anyone noticing? I looked like I belonged there—except for the first time I used climbers and learned about the speed of falling objects, splinters, bruises . . .

THE PHONE TRANSMITTER

Although RF transmitters are starting to become harder to get, thanks to the feds raiding all of the "spy" shops, some of them are still available. Most are in kit form. This may be anything from a printed circuit board, parts, and a manual, which require complete assembly, to the Deco models that require only a few solder connections.

By first connecting the transmitter to the line and then cutting the phone line wire, you will avoid interrupting service. If someone is using the line at the time, he might become suspicious and go look for what has caused the interruption, and you are caught. Bad move. Also, there are devices that will set off an alarm if a line is tampered with.

It is also a good idea to have a test receiver already tuned to the transmitter frequency to verify that it is transmitting. Remember, you may get only one chance, and you probably won't have a lot of time to do the installation. On the VT75 there are two adjustments: the center, which sets the frequency (anywhere from 70 to 130 MHz), and an antenna tuner. Proper adjustment results in maximum power transfer to the antenna, therefore greater range. It is reviewed in *The Bug Book*.

One of the better phone transmitters is the one from SWS Security in Street, Maryland.

#5790 High-Power Phone Line Transmitter

Sometimes called the "turd" because of its appearance, the #5790 is a parallel phone line transmitter. It allows telephone surveillance by intercepting and transmitting both sides of a telephone conversation via radio to a remote LP. The #5790 attaches in parallel to a copper wire pair to any standard dial-up telephone line anywhere between the telephone instrument and the central office. The unit is in standby mode until the line goes off hook, at which time it transmits both sides of the conversation to the LP. Data (computer or fax) and voice are intercepted. The unit includes automatic gain control, noise and hum filtering, and audio shaping to provide the highest quality intercept even on poor-quality phone lines.

A unique feature of the #5790 is its power supply. Because of their design and high power, all parallel transmitters require substantial batteries. Most competitive units are short-range devices requiring frequent battery replacement. The #5790 uses a high-capacity rechargeable battery for high-power (long-range) transmission. When the phone line is not in use, the battery is recharged by small amounts of power drawn from the phone line. This allows high-power operation for an indefinite period without the need to change batteries. The unit can be installed and left in place for months without service. The #5790 can be used on any telephone system in the world.

Additional features of the #5790 include completely waterproof sealed construction, making a very rugged package ideal for installation outside buildings or on telephone poles. The unit is fairly small and inconspicuous, to blend in with ordinary telephone wiring. Simple two-wire parallel installation requires a minimum of tools or technical knowledge. High-power and long-range operation may allow monitoring from central locations ideal for dangerous operations where it may not be practical to set up an LP nearby.

The #5790 is a top-quality, top-performing telephone transmitter suitable for the most demanding, difficult, or dangerous surveillances.

Specifications

Operating frequency	148–174 MHz, one channel crystal controlled
Operating mode	Narrow-band FM, 16F3, 5 kHz for 100 percent deviation @ 1 kHz
Transmit power	100 mw
Transmit range	Depends on path and height, typically 1,500 ft. (450 m); however, if installed on top of a pole, range can exceed 1 mi. (1.6 km)
Operating time	Indefinite with 90 percent–10 percent duty cycle, typically 8 hours continuous
Battery life	3 years minimum, depends on environment, 5 years typical
Spurious and harmonics	Less than -40 dB
Audio shaping	12dB per octave pre-emphasis
Audio distortion	Less than 10 percent @ 1 kHz with 2 kHz deviation
Audio bandwidth	300 Hz to 5 kHz, suitable for voice or high-speed data
Frequency stability	0.0015 percent from -32° to +60°C
Weight	1.3 oz. (35g)
Dimensions	2.5 x .8 x 0.5 in. (63 x 20 x 13mm), not including leads and antenna
Antenna	Dribble wire, 18 in. (450mm), black insulated
Connection to phone line	Via two 8-in. (200mm) wire leads, can use alligator clips
Input impedance	20K ohms
Finish	Flat-black rubberized
Construction	Completely sealed, waterproofed, and encapsulated
Warranty	2 years against defects in materials or workmanship

Compatible accessories: SWS #RPT-1 or RPT-20 portable intelligence repeaters (used to extend range of this or other surveillance transmitters to 3 mi. (5 km)

This item is a Title III-restricted electronic surveillance device and is offered for sale to government or law enforcement agencies or for export only.

Electronic Rainbow

The Electronic Rainbow has an inexpensive phone transmitter that goes for about $15 in kit form. Complete assembly is required, meaning that one needs some experience in soldering and assembly. It is, or at least used to be, available assembled for around $30.

Ramsey Electronics and Elenco

Ramsey Electronics and Elenco also have inexpensive transmitters. Most of these are what is called *modulated oscillator*: a one-transistor unit. They work but aren't really stable. The frequency will shift enough that the eavesdropper will need to touch up the receiver tuning now and then. Range may be from across the room to a few hundred feet, depending on many things (see *The Bug Book* for details).

Sheffield Electronics

Sheffield Electronics makes several phone transmitters, including one that picks up and sends room audio when the phone is not being used. These are not modulated oscillators; they have several stages, which makes them more stable and increases the power output. I have not tested any of the Sheffield transmitters, but have heard only good things about them. I recently talked to Mr. Arrington of Sheffield Electronics, who told me that due to the new laws and raids by the feds on spy shops. He has relocated his operation to Dublin, Ireland.

AMC Sales

AMC Sales sells an "encased matchbox-sized wireless test mic, assembled and pretested. It can transmit up to 1/4 mile to any FM radio." It is tunable between 86 MHz and 108 MHz, is approximately 1 1/2 x 3/4 x 1/4 inches, is powered by a 9-volt battery, and sells for around $99. I have not tested this transmitter, and specs were not available when this was written.

TRANSMITTER RANGE

In the back pages of a *Scientific* magazine is an ad that says you can connect this particular company's Little Jiffie transmitter to any phone line and hear the conversations on an "ordinary FM radio" several miles away. Bullshit. The particulars of radio frequency transmitters would fill a book—*The Bug Book*. This is useful detailed information for anyone who wants to use a surveillance transmitter, but believe it, "miles" is possible only under perfect conditions and with a considerable amount of power.

The range of a surveillance transmitter, of the type available to the general public, varies from a few feet to a few blocks. This is something you need to consider. If the target is a house in an upper-class suburban area, where homes are built on large lots, where people may even know their neighbors, and where an unfamiliar vehicle would be noticed quickly, then you probably can't use a vehicle for the LP. So the transmitter will need a great deal of range, perhaps a mile or more, and, again, this can be very difficult to attain. Knowing the effective range of phone transmitters, antennas, and listening posts is a very complicated subject.

Installation

When you install the tap, work the line hot; don't unplug or otherwise disconnect the phone. Remember that it might be corrected. It might be connected to a device that would inform the owner that someone is tampering with his lines. If you received any documentation with the tap, you should have already read it; otherwise do so before you do the installation. You need to know exactly what you are going to do beforehand and not have to make decisions or figure things out when you are making the tap. Remember that the idea is to get in and out as quickly a possible.

The number of wires on a transmitter vary from two to five. Two wires indicate either a series or parallel that uses the phone line as both a source of power and an antenna. Three will be either series or parallel with the third as the antenna. Four usually mean a parallel battery-powered type using the lines as the antenna, and five a parallel battery-powered type with its own antenna.

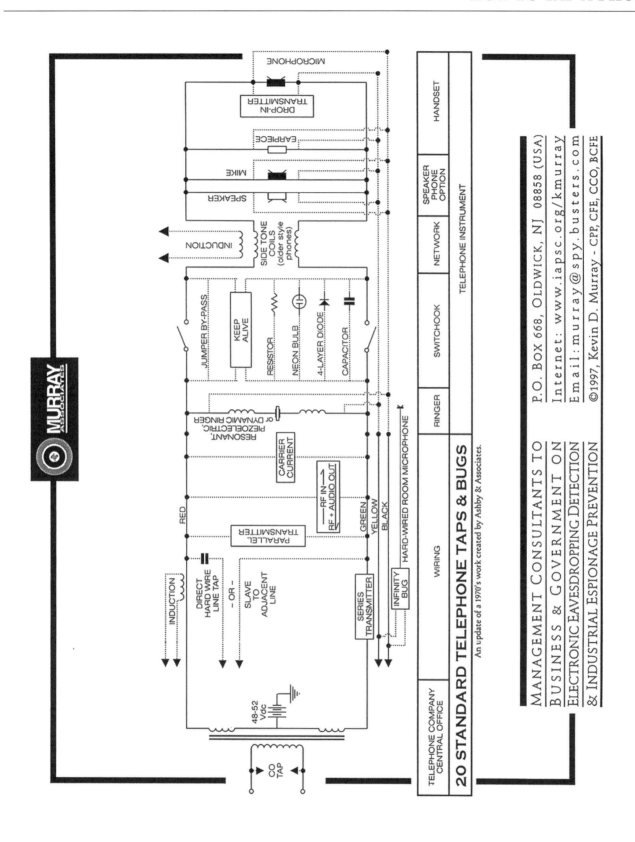

Twenty standard telephone taps and bugs.

A parallel type is installed by connecting the two transmitter wires to the two phone wires. A series transmitter requires that you cut one of the two phone wires and attach the two transmitters to the two open ends. Use the green one first. Once the connections are made, turn on the test receiver (which should already be tuned to the transmitter frequency), take the phone off hook by lifting the receiver, or use your lineman's test set, and listen for the dial tone. If you do not hear the dial tone, reverse the two wires or either the series or parallel type. If you still don't hear it, repeat the process with the red phone wire. Some phone bugs, such as the Sheffield models, have an LED to tell you when the polarity is right. This saves time, of which you may have little.

An old-time phone bug was the "drop-in." This was a small, short-range transmitter that was built inside the carbon microphone element. To install it, one unscrewed the cap, dropped the replacement in, and replaced the cap—an operation that took all of 10 seconds. Since all phones were essentially the same, made by Western Electric, the drop-in would fit. Today, because of all the different types of phones, the drop-in is seldom used. It won't fit. But there are still a lot of Western Electric phones in use, and the drop-in is still available. PK Elektronik, I believe, still makes them. A few drops of superglue on the cap will keep anyone from using the drop-in. It will also keep you from finding it. If you find that the caps can't be removed, be suspicious and replace the phone. Maybe the spy also had some superglue . . .

Antennas

Length and placement make a very big difference in range, as is explained in detail in *The Bug Book*. The antenna should be cut to a length that matches the frequency being used, which is determined by this formula:

L = 300,000,000 divided by F
Where L = length in meters, and F = frequency in cycles

If the transmitter operates at 100 megacycles (100 million cycles), divide 100 million into 300 million and you get three. So the right length of a full wave antenna is 3 meters, or about 9.8 feet. A 10-foot antenna may be a tad hard to hide, so you can cut it to one-half, one-fourth, or one-eighth. It should be positioned either vertically or horizontally, and the receiver antenna the same. Again, this makes a very big difference.

PLACEMENT OF TAPS

Now let's take a closer look at where the tap might be placed, depending on access and the type of tap used.

Inside the Phone

This can be an excellent place to hide a phone line transmitter because it can be installed in a few minutes and there is usually plenty of space. There are hundreds of different types of phones, but most have two to four screws on the bottom that, when removed, let you separate the plastic case from the insides. Where the wall cord connects there will be an RJ-11 "modular" jack. On the inside, there will be two to four wires that lead from the jack to a plastic or Bakelite block of some kind or a printed circuit board. Only two are used, usually standard telco red and green, but if you encounter more than two, touch the clips of the test set to the different combinations and listen for the dial tone. Then trace them to where they connect to the circuit board, usually with a spade clip under a machine screw.

Should they be soldered to the board, you will need to splice the leads from the transmitter by

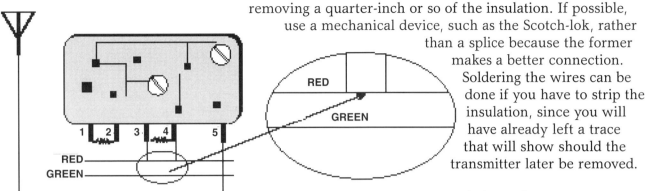

removing a quarter-inch or so of the insulation. If possible, use a mechanical device, such as the Scotch-lok, rather than a splice because the former makes a better connection. Soldering the wires can be done if you have to strip the insulation, since you will have already left a trace that will show should the transmitter later be removed.

This diagram shows how th VT75 transmitter is connected to the phone line. This is a series type. Remember to attach the two wives from terminals three and four to the line and then cut the line in between those two wires to avoid interrupting service.

Multiline Phones

Whether you are dealing with the old push-button type or the new electronic models, there is no way of knowing which line a given person will be using at any given time. So you have two choices: install a transmitter on all of the lines or connect one to the wires that go to the handset. Connecting the transmitter to the handset is iffy; sometimes it works, sometimes not. All you can do is try.

Tapping all the lines means figuring out which wires are for which line, and since there are so many different types of multiline phones, there is no way to explain it here, except the older push-button desk type, where the buttons light up when pushed. With this phone, use the color codes in appendix 3.

Wiring to a Closet or 66 Block

This can be anywhere from the connection block on the wall to the larger block. Sometimes the wires are strung along the baseboard and up and over door frames. Since they are visible, this is an unlikely place, but it is possible. One phone transmitter, made by PK Eletronik and described below, could be used. Often, in older buildings, the wires have been painted over. This makes installation of a tap very difficult because it is hard to conceal, unless the tapper has sufficient time and a can of spray paint in the right color. Also, he has to have time to vacuum up the chips that may fall on the floor.

The advantage here is that there is little doubt about which is the right pair. If there is more than one line it is easy to see which one goes to which phone or to the computer or fax machine. Once the wires disappear behind the wall, getting to them may be very difficult, as may knowing which is which. In apartment or office buildings the opening in the wall where the connection block is located may also open into the adjacent office or apartment, in which case getting to the wires is quite easy, if the tapper has access to that office.

In a Floor or Distribution Closet

A distribution closet is an area that is usually, but not always, locked and with restricted access, where the phone lines from the apartments or offices come together in one place. It is here that the lines exit the building. They go into a tube that leads to an underground conduit or a series of drop lines that are strung between the building and telephone poles. In large buildings, with many offices on the same floor, the lines may go to a floor closet. These are similar to the distribution closet but are located on some or all of the floors of the building. Each will have a large cable that goes to the distribution closet.

On the 66 Block

In smaller buildings there may be only a connection block, any of many types, which may be neat and orderly with the apartment numbers written next to each line. Or there may be a jumble of multicolored wires with little information about which goes where. Look around for a sheet of paper stuck behind the panel, lying on top of it, or elsewhere in the area. Also look for little plastic tags on the wires that may list the apartment numbers. If you are able to identify your line(s), make a note of the color codes.

If you have an LP in the same building, making the tap may be very simple. Connect the unused yellow and black wires from your line to the terminals of the line to be tapped. Very easy, but should someone discover the connection, he will be able to trace it back to you. If you can get to the wiring before it reaches the 66 block, in a place where the lines are less accessible, then make the tap there.

Downline Taps

As you read previously, the 66 block is the point of demarcation. Any tap beyond it is called *downline* and can be anywhere from the phone to the CO. Downline taps are usually not easy to install.

On the Telephone Pole

This is an excellent place for an RF transmitter, because it can be line powered and there are no batteries to replace. Also its height and its location out in the open increase the range. A direct wire tap, though, can be difficult. The above example, using an antenna wire, was a unique situation; the right lines were accessible in such a way that it was easy to connect it to the listening post. Some poles have large metal bolts that are used as steps. But most don't, which means you need to have climbers and know how to use them. More than one amateur has fallen from a pole while learning to climb. And you have to be able to get the transmitter installed without drawing any attention. One possibility would be using a van painted to look like it belongs to the telco. But then you have to open the splicing boot (some are metal, bolted together) and find the right pair. This is not a job for a beginner.

In a B-Box or Junction Point

Rotsa ruck. Although a B-box is usually easy to open (use a socket wrench), how will you find the right line? Do you know the cable and pair number? And even if you find the right pair, remember about the LP. Maybe you can install a long-play recorder with a drop-out relay and go back to switch tapes every other day, and if you look like you belong there, you might get away with it for some time. But if a real telco installer finds the recorder, he will report it, and the feds might set up a surveillance team, just waiting to take you to jail.

Accessing a junction point is even more difficult. First of all, you have to get in without attracting attention, and this is rather difficult to do in the middle of an intersection. Is there an alarm system setup? Sometimes the cables are inside Plexiglas tubes that if opened activate the alarm. Remember the equipment in the cable vault that monitors the air pressure? And, once again, what are you going to use for an LP? An RF transmitter isn't going to send very far from underground, and the middle of an intersection is not a good place for an antenna, what with cars and trucks running over it . . .

Now, if you had inside information, could find the line, get to it, and make a bridging tap to another line that led to your listening post, you would have the perfect setup.

Again, rotsa ruck.

In the Telco Office

Forget it. Oh, it is remotely possible that a telco employee could be bribed or blackmailed into installing it, but improbable. It would be noticed within hours, and someone would have a lot of explaining to do. Remember that there aren't that many people in a CO switch.

Inside the CO taps are for the feds. The way they actually do it, or rather supposedly do it, is something like this: The agent goes to his supervisor and informs him that he wants to bug

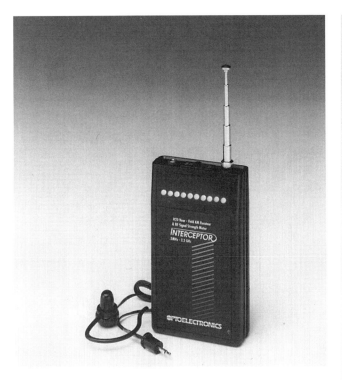

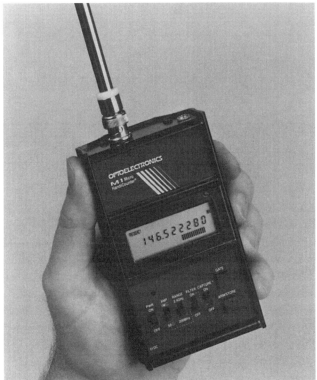

Four products from Optoelectronics. Top left is an FM Interceptor. Top right is the AM Interceptor. Bottom left is the Frequency Counter. Bottom right is the Scout.

someone. The supervisor passes the request on to the agency person responsible for making the authorization. Then the agents go looking for a friendly judge, who rubber-stamps it. (In 1995, literally every application was approved; not a single one was denied.) Then the agent takes the warrant to the telco security people, who do the actual installation. The bridging tap is done by a device inside a small plastic box, often blue, sometimes called a *slave*. It has an impedance balancing circuit to prevent it from affecting the target line. The other end of the box is connected to a special leased line that usually terminates in the agents' offices. Then the agents connect three recorders to the leased line inside an area set up for that purpose. This may be at the CO but will probably be at the feds' offices.

The reason for three recorders is that apparently a copy of the original tape is not considered the "best evidence" in court, so three originals are made. One for the prosecution, one for the defense (under the rules of discovery), and one for the court file.

I suspect, though, that there is a fourth recorder. It seems that the Omnibus law states that the agents can listen only to conversations in which a crime is being discussed. Otherwise, the law enforcement agents have to turn the recorders off, wait a certain amount of time, and try again. If the recorders are left on when they are not supposed to be, the tapes have to be edited and spliced, which would probably be discovered by the defense attorneys. The fourth could be used to capture everything said on the line.

So, as you can see, the number of places a phone can be tapped are limited, and access to them can be from very easy to virtually impossible.

This is an Optoelectronics Frequency Counter connected to the Opto Pre-Selector, which increases the range at which a signal can be intercepted.

DEFENSE AGAINST WIRETAPPING

You have seen the different places that a tap can be installed and how accessible they might be. So to connect the tap requires access to only a single place along the line that is suitable. But finding a tap requires that you physically inspect every inch of the line that you can get to. This means from inside the phones to the demarc and possibly beyond. So now we will go back over it again, this time in greater detail. As before, there are a few considerations; there always are in surveillance because every situation is unique and there are always variables and alternatives. The more you know about them, the better you become at either installing or finding wiretaps.

THE PROBABILITY OF BEING TAPPED

Why would anyone want to bug you? What is it that you know and would be talking about on the phone that anyone is interested in? Consider your life-style, your job, your friends, your enemies, all of the people with whom you are acquainted. Who would be interested? Are you privy to confidential or classified information? Are you or your spouse having an affair? Are you facing a divorce? Is custody or a property settlement in the making? These considerations should not affect how you make the search, but they are things to keep in the back of your mind.

If it is an unlawful tap by the feds, it could be anywhere, but probably not in the CO and probably not inside your home or office, depending on the security you have; more likely it will be in a B-box or junction point or maybe on a telephone pole. If the tap was installed by a PI type or amateur, it will more likely be in the SPSP or 66 block, or in your home or office if the tapper has access (e.g., husband versus wife) and probably not in a B-box. An amateur would most likely use something easily available, possibly a Xandi or Deco. An experienced industrial espionage specialist wouldn't use a Xandi transmitter; he might use a Deco and could get most of the other brands.

The feds make some of their own stuff or buy it from PK Eletronik or Audio Intelligence Devices, and this equipment is very expensive. Federal agencies might use spread spectrum or an X-Band type that operates at 10 GHz or even a microwave unit designed for television crews that operates at about 15 GHz.

Now on with the search.

USING ELECTRONIC EQUIPMENT

Some types of equipment used in searching are connected directly to the phone lines, e.g., telephone analyzers and the time domain reflectometer. Others, such as the many kinds of RF detectors, are not.

Caveat Emptor

A few years before I started writing books I happened across an ad in a nationally distributed magazine. It was placed by a company that offered to sell countermeasures equipment and teach the buyer how to use it. So I called to find out more, not volunteering that I knew anything about such things. The very first thing the firm's representative did was qualify me. Did I have the fee? Could I come to New York and attend the training sessions? I answered yes to both questions and was told what I would get for my five grand. When the person was telling me about telephone analyzers, I unexpectedly hit him with a question: "Will it detect an inductive down-line tap?" I was assured that the equipment would detect literally any kind of wiretap. This company is still in business and still telling prospective customers the same lies. A device that will find literally any kind of tap does not exist, and it ain't likely that it ever will.

The Telephone Analyzer

A good phone analyzer is expensive and takes time to learn to use effectively. Different types do different things, such as measure line resistance and voltage and detect RF and subcarrier transmissions. Most have a number of connectors that the phones to be checked are plugged into. Then each phone is activated (e.g., by making a call) and various tests are run. You need to know not only how to use it but also just what exactly it is that you are using—and whether it is any good or not.

Tech Stuff

Whenever an electric current flows through a conductor (in this case a phone wire) it generates an electromagnetic field. If that conductor, that wire, is wound into a coil, the field will be many times stronger. This is the basis of the telegraph you read about earlier—an electromagnet—and as the current changes in intensity that field radiates into space. Now if you were to place a second coil physically close to the first one, some of this electromagnetic field would be induced into the second coil even though there is no electrical connection.

In other words, part of the field picked up by the first coil would come out of the second one. This is how transformers work, such as the one that supplies power to your home.

An inductive tap is a kind of transformer that picks up the very weak field (i.e., a conversation taking place) from the phone line it is near and feeds it into an amplifier to make it loud enough to hear. But since the inductor is not electrically

After five years of varied experience with the telco, including wiretapping, I devoted the rest of my life to the science of wiretapping for local, state, and federal authorities . . . in the long course of my career, I have tapped in excess of 60,000 pairs of wires.

—William Mellin, 1954
The "dean of wiretappers," who worked for the IRS

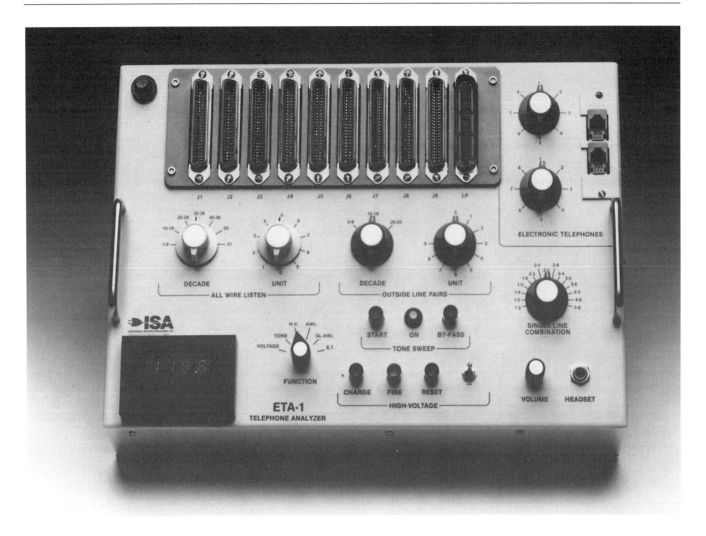

One of the telephone analyzers from Information Security Associates.

connected to the line, it has virtually no effect on that line. Any such effect would be extremely difficult to measure. Some technicians say that a time domain reflectometer (TDR) can detect the inductive tap if enough of the conversation on the line is induced into the second coil, but inductive taps are so inefficient that this may not be the case.

It isn't like two coils placed near each other; the inductive tap is trying to pick up the very weak field from a straight wire that doesn't generate the strong field that a coil does. As far as measuring the impedance difference made by the inductive tap, I am skeptical. Impedance is a combination of resistance and reactance. Copper wire has a certain amount of resistance, which changes with temperature. So when the temperature changes a few degrees, so does the impedance. And even this tiny change is, I believe, greater than what would result from placing an inductive tap near the line. But, again, others do not agree.

The Time Domain Reflectometer

The name somewhat describes this device: to measure (meter) a reflection in terms (the domain) of time. The TDR is used to locate "irregularities" in cables or pairs of wires. This may be a break or splice or possibly even a place where the wire has become weakened from being flexed too often or

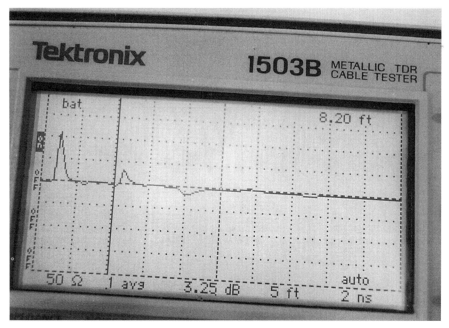

This is the screen of a Tektronix TDR. Note the reading of 8.20 feet: this was a test demonstration using an ordinary 110-volt extension cord. I checked it with a tape measure: it was dead right.

gnawed on by animals. An example is the underground transmission cable from a transmitter to the antenna that has been chomped on by a gopher. The cable may be several hundred yards long, so to avoid having to dig up all of it the repair person uses a TDR, which tells precisely how far down the line the little critter was having lunch.

The TDR sends a signal down the cable that will react to splices and breaks and cause part of the signal to be reflected back to the instrument. The amount of time it takes for the signal to return, based on the speed of the signal, is translated into the distance. This figure may be displayed as numbers on a digital display or printed out as a graph, like an EKG. The result is analyzed to determine what is being reflected—such as a possible tap.

A good TDR costs thousands of dollars and is very difficult to master; it takes experience to be able to detect the things that a beginner would miss. The same is true of telephone analyzers. Both are best left to technicians with experience. And it would cost much less to hire a good countersurveillance team than to buy these instruments.

Transmitter Detectors

Devices that detect RF transmitters are much easier to learn to use, with the exception of the high-end models that are sophisticated and very expensive. They are called *countermeasures receivers* and the low-end types are usually called *bug detectors*, though there is no real point at which one becomes the other. It depends on whom you ask. So let's look at some of them and how they work.

Suppose you had a radio that did not have a speaker; it had only a panel meter or an LED to indicate when you were tuned to a station. You wouldn't know what station it was, and you wouldn't be able to listen to the commercials. If all you want to know is when it is receiving a signal, fine, but if you want to know which station you are not listening to you need something a little more sophisticated. It is the same with transmitter detectors. There are many of them that will sound an alarm or turn on an LED when they detect a signal, but this doesn't tell you what the signal is.

Radio waves, especially at higher frequencies, do strange, unpredictable things. If there is a TV station in the area (and where isn't there?), the signal they broadcast will "condense," for lack of a better word, on any large metal object in the signal path. That object will "rebroadcast" the signal, and it will register on the RF detector (e.g., venetian blinds, a radiator, a filing cabinet, a metal desk, steel beams in the building frame, sheet-metal heating ducts inside the walls). So as you follow the phone line and you see that a signal is being registered, it may well be one of these things and not a bug.

This can cause a lot of unnecessary work and expense; you may end up taking things apart, loosening paneling on walls, only to find the signal is coming from a metal stud. Or you may

All you need know about...
TELEPHONE TAP DETECTORS

C O U N T E R E S P I O N A G E   C O N S U L T A N T S   T O   B U S I N E S S   A N D   G O V E R N M E N T

Theory of Operation:
A majority of telephone tap detectors sense the voltage level on the telephone line when the phone is in use. If the voltage falls below the *normal* level the detector alarms; usually a visual indication. The detector's *normal* level threshold is set, **by the user**, at a point in time when it is *believed* the line is not under surveillance.

Voltage drops can be caused by someone picking up an extension phone, improper use of a telephone lineperson's handset, or by attaching a very crude listening device to the line. Drops can also be caused by minor variations in voltage which occur normally throughout the day.

Some models include an additional defensive measure; they defeat tape recorders hooked to the phone line. This is done by raising the line voltage just to a point where the tape recorder thinks the phone is not in use, even when it is. Of course, not all tape recorders with telephone auto-start units are fooled so easily, and many operate on a voice-activation principle instead. Even if this technique does work, a surveillance operator will quickly notice that the recorder is not working and will switch to an alternate piece of equipment.

Do-it-yourself telephone tap detectors come in a variety of packages: mouth-piece screw-ons, line cord plug-ins, under-the-phone computerized models with key locks... The list goes on and on.

Pros:
• Inexpensive.
• Simple to operate.
• Useful on residential phone systems to detect eavesdropping from an extension.

Cons:
• Calibrated by the user under uncertain conditions.
• Cannot be used on business / electronic phone systems.
• Cannot detect all types of bugs and taps as claimed in the advertising.
• False positive readings from normal voltage fluctuations.

Cost: $30 - $800
Recommendation:
Use these devices to combat only the most amateur of eavesdropping attempts, eg. children picking up an extension telephone at home. Remember, not every alarm indication will mean eavesdropping is taking place. Better approach: Add-on electronic modules are available to make regular telephones inoperative when the line is in use by another extension.

In a business environment, these devices are worthless. Your conversations are important enough to warrant professional periodic inspections of your offices and communications systems.

For information on professional electronic eavesdropping detection services please contact us directly. Do not call from, or discuss your concerns in, suspected areas.

www.iapsc.org/kmurray
murray@spy.busters.com
Box 668, Oldwick, NJ 08858 (USA)

© 1997, Kevin D. Murray, CPP, CFE, CCO, BCFE

All you need to know about telephone tap detectors.

completely empty a desk and search through every item it contains, only to realize that it was the desk itself that was rebroadcasting the signal. This is not to say that these types of detectors will not find a hidden transmitter; they probably will. Just be aware of their limitations.

The next step up is a bug detector that has a demodulator. This means it will let you listen to the commercials. When it picks up a transmitter, you will hear it through the headphones and know whether it is a bug.

Optoelectronics Interceptor

Optoelectronics makes nice equipment, and the Interceptor is no exception. It is a one-piece device small enough to fit in a pocket and a demodulator. You can hear the signals you pick up. It also has different bandwidth settings and several other controls. The Interceptor works fine, but you have to keep hitting the reset switch because it will stop on commercial radio broadcasting stations. Or you can use a filter that connects between the unit and the antenna. It sells for around $300.

Capri Electronics TD-53

The TD-53 has a demodulator that you can switch in and out as desired. When searching, turn it off so that you don't have to listen to background noise or commercial broadcasting stations that can interfere with your concentration. If a signal is received it will be indicated by a series of red LEDs on the panel, so you can zero in on it. Then flip the switch to "listen" and hear what you have found.

The TD-53 uses an external probe connected to the unit with a cable, so you can easily poke it around into corners and hard-to-get-to places when following the line. It also works with several optional probes that detect carrier current and infrared transmitters. I have used the TD-53. It's a good product and well worth the price at about $500.

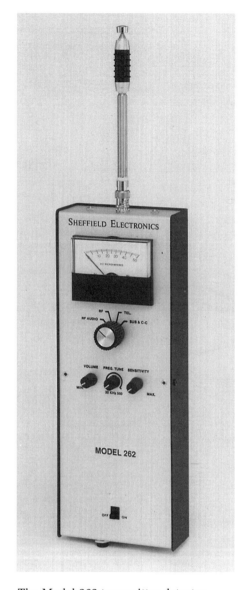

The Model 262 transmitter detector from Sheffield Electronics.

Lorraine Electronics

Lorraine makes a variety of products, three of which are the RFD-X, RFD-2, and RFD-3. The RFD-X and RFD-2 are similar except that the former has a demodulator. Both cover 10 to 500 MHz, FM narrow and wide band, and have an LED bar graph that indicates signal strength. The RFD-3 covers 10 to 1,000 MHz and uses an analog meter. (See Appendix 2 for the address to write for current prices.)

Sheffield Electronics Model 262

The 262 sells for around $685 and has some nice features. It covers 4 MHz to 2.1 GHz and somewhere beyond. The inventor, Winston Arrington, explains that the Hewlett Packard RF generator he uses tops out here, so the high end is not known at the time of this writing. The 262 is unique in that it detects not only RF signals but also carrier current devices in the 30 to 500 kHz area just below the AM broadcast band. It also has the following features:

One of the countermeasures receivers from Martin Kaiser. Although it doesn't have the bells and whistles of some of the more expensive receivers (for example, the Eagle Plus), the 2057A is a very high quality countermeasures receiver.

- A meter for monitoring the phone line voltage
- A tape recorder output
- A demodulator to eliminate false signals

Its size is 11 6/16 x 4 x 1 3/4 inches, and it weighs 2 pounds, 9 ounces. The antenna and batteries are included, and it has a one-year warranty.

Research Electronics, Inc. CPM-700

I have not used this one, but based on the manual that REI sent me and what those who own one have told me, it is a very good product. It is also versatile. It covers 50 kHz to 3 GHz, detects carrier current transmitters, and has a tape recorder output, a 60-cycle hum filter, and LED bar graph signal strength display. A number of options are now being designed and may be available soon. The manual is well done, easy to follow, and has some good information on searching for transmitters. This device costs about $1,300.

Kaiser Electronics 2075A

Quoting from Kaiser Electronics' catalog: "The 2075A is an ultra-sensitive 10 to 2000+ MHz. RF locator with audio and visual readout. It demodulates AM, FM wideband, FM narrowband,

and subcarrier signals, is battery powered, and is only 2 1/2 x 8 x 6 inches in size. Weight is 4 pounds."

CSE Associates' Bushwacker

The Bushwacker is a 25 to 1,000 MHz signal intercept system that is small, lightweight, portable, easy to use, and highly automated. It can capture short-duration push-to-talk signals that would be missed with scanner-type receivers. Bushwacker features include the following:

- Intercepted signals being automatically logged
- Signals being recorded on notebook computer hard-disk drive
- Being shipped complete and ready to operate from either 115/230 volts AC or 12 volts DC

Other options are remote operation over a single dial-up telephone line, including all displays and received audio transmissions; radio direction finding as a stand-alone unit or netted with other Bushwhackers; and extended frequency range.

The Bushwacker is easy to use by even untrained operators. Using computer-assisted signal-capturing techniques and automatic logging of intercepts and received audio, the system is highly effective. An operator's

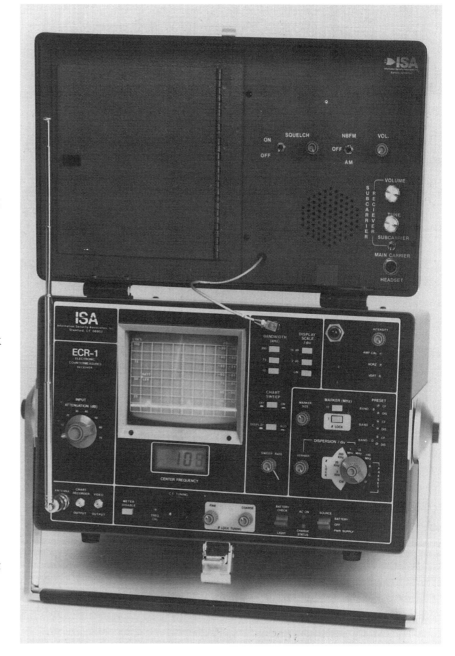

This is the ECR-1 professional electronic countermeasures receiver from Information Security Associates.

manual and tutorial are provided on the hard disk, which can be accessed by a click of the mouse. Relatively weak and short-duration signals can be intercepted and monitored, which can be very useful in such tactical operations as hostage situations.

The Bushwacker is reasonably priced.

The above products present a fairly good cross-section of transmitter detectors, but there are many other makes and models available. Some, such as the Eagle Plus from Technical Services Agency, Inc. and several models from Information Security Associates, are expensive (in the $10,000 range) and take some time to learn to use effectively. Others, such as the Informer II (sold by Sharper Image for around $129), are bottom end, and although they will detect RF signals, you will never see a professional using one of them.

No matter what kind of transmitter detector or countermeasures receiver you have, it isn't going to do you any good unless you use it right. Actually, it can do more harm than good by giving you a false sense of security if there is a transmitter on your line and you miss it. Read the manual. Read it again. Then practice. Have someone hide an operating transmitter somewhere and then try to find it. If you don't have a transmitter you can get a small one in kit form from The Electronic Rainbow for a little more than $10.

Finally, remember that all electronic countermeasures equipment has its limitations, no matter how expensive or sophisticated it is. Remember that the transmitter does not have to be in the same place as the tap. A pair of fine wires connected to the line may lead to a transmitter in another part of the building or on the roof, where its range will be considerably increased. The remote-controlled transmitter might be used. An experienced eavesdropper will recognize the sounds of someone searching and turn it off. An exotic type, such as the burst transmitter, might be used. These exotic types are very rare, but they do exist. Then again, consider the X-band transmitter, which is beyond the range of all but a few countermeasures receivers or some spectrum analyzers.

All this will be more clearly understood after you read Part 6, "On an Actual Sweep." The silent electronic search is done first, using the finest equipment money can buy, including telephone analyzers and receivers with sophisticated and carefully matched antennas. In other words, virtually any operating transmitter will be located before the physical search begins. The obvious reason for this is to not make noises that would tip off a listening eavesdropper. Also in such a sweep, all types of transmitters are being searched for, room audio as well as telephone transmitters. This book is about phone surveillance devices. Nevertheless, it is a good idea to make the search as quietly as possible.

THE PHYSICAL SEARCH

When you are ready to start the physical search, begin at one end of the line and work to the other, holding the antenna (or probe) at different angles and touching the line. Follow every inch of it if possible. If the unit you are using has other antennas available, repeat the search using them or move back and forth periodically, switching back and forth. If a telescoping antenna or probe is supplied, try it at different lengths. Any place where anything is attached to the line being searched should be checked out very carefully. What looks like an ordinary splice covered with tape could conceal a bug. A bug could be hidden behind the SPSP or 66 block . . .

The search itself may be very easy. You may need only to follow a 1/4- inch, beige, four-conductor cable 50 feet from your desk to the SPSP on the back of your house. Or it may be very difficult. You may end up spending all day crawling through the mud under the front porch, bruising your knees on the rafters in an attic filled with itchy fiberglass insulation, and fighting your way through a maze of wires in a basement filled with spider webs and wasp nests.

Partners

If possible, work with a partner. This will enable you to do the search in less time, especially if you have a pair of two-way radios with which to communicate. Also, you may be able to convince your partner that he should crawl around in the mud, rather than you. After all, you are the one who has this book.

Recon

If possible, walk through the area and make some notes. Do you have complete access to the area to be searched? W... ... ... Where is the 66 block? Is it in a locked area? Is there so... ... ... *know how to use*—lock picks? Are there times when othe... ... ...e not present for a long enough period for you to conduct t... ... ll need? Is a ladder necessary to reach the lines? Might you... ... t, and are you willing and able to do this? Does your buildi... ... n, or prevent you from, making your search? If at all p... ... can identify your line or lines. The lines may be marked ... ... they may not.

Equipment You May Need

- Battery-powered ultraviolet light
- Camera, preferably a 35mm with close-up lens and flash
- Dentist's mirror
- Diagonal cutters and long-nose pliers
- Electrician's tape
- Large and small flat-blade and Phillips screwdrivers
- Line tracer
- Lineman's test set
- Magnifying glass
- Mini-Maglite and extra batteries
- Set of lock picks
- Set of Torx wrenches
- Small crescent wrench
- Transmitter detector
- Volt ohmmeter

If at all possible, have everything on the list before you start. Otherwise you may have to interrupt your work to go get something you forgot or figured you wouldn't actually need. Bad move. You will more than likely be making the search on a weekend—when the stores are closed.

Lineman's Test Set

The lineman's test set is available at some electronics supply stores and through some mail-order catalogs. You don't need the bells and whistles some of them have; the low-end models that sell for under $100 will work fine. If you want to spend $300 you can get a TS-22 made by Harris-Dracon in Camarillo, California. The company doesn't sell direct, but it will provide the name of a dealer if you call it (see Appendix 2 in the back of the book for addresses and phone numbers.)

You can also improvise. Start with a cheapo one-piece Touch-Tone phone available for about $15. Remove the RJ-11 plug from one end of the cord and splice two wires about 6 inches long—one black, one another color—to the wires inside the cord. Connect the other ends to alligator clips.

The cord may have four wires, so to ensure that you use the right ones, connect them all to a flashlight battery until you hear a clicking sound in the receiver. Some cords use a thin foil strip wound around a string and are hard to work with, so take several inches of bare copper wire and wrap it tightly around the foil. Then connect the copper wire to the clip and tape the connection securely.

Another useful item is the Test Adapter, part number 10113, also from Harris-Dracon for about $10. It has a modular RJ-11 plug on one end of a short cable and a flat plate on the other, which is made for connecting the alligator clips from either the meter or test set.

Ohmmeter

There are two types of meters: analog and digital. The digital type shows the readings on a small liquid crystal display (LCD) similar to that of a clock, and the analog type uses a meter with a needle, or pointer. The analog type is recommended because it is easier to use for the line-resistance test. It should be of good quality, but need not be expensive. The excellent Simpson model 260 is recommended; it has been an industry standard for many years. Not recommended is the cigarette-pack-sized Handi-Tester sold in chain stores for about $7.95. The TENMA model 72-385, which retails for about $26, will work and is available from MCM Electronics or stores that sell electronics parts and equipment.

At the same time you buy the meter, purchase a few resistors. Start by reading the manual and learn about zeroing the needle and the ohms adjustment (ohms adj) control. Then use the resistors to practice. Note that the numbers start at the infinity mark (looks like the digit 8 lying on its side) on the left and go to zero on the right. This is the opposite of the other scales. It is a good idea to buy a resistor from an electronics supply store rather than a certain chain store, because the latter may sell parts that failed quality control at the factory. If so, the meter will not measure what it is supposed to, and this may seem confusing.

Lock Picks

If you don't know how to use picks, then there isn't much point in having them. If you do know how, then you are probably aware that they are, in many states, considered burglary tools. Possession of them can get you into a place that has locks you wouldn't be able to open even if your keepers let you keep your picks—which they probably would not.

Line Tracer

Suppose that the line or lines you are following disappear into a place where you lose sight of them, such as in an air or elevator shaft. Or what if they become part of a jumble of other wires, bundled together and painted over, and branching out here and there, such as in a large apartment building with old wiring? How do you continue the trace? A line tracer, available from Information Security Associates, is the answer.

You can get everything you need for about $150, and by improvising and using things you probably already have, you can reduce this to maybe $50.

When to Make the Search

Based on your recon, make a decision. Will you be able to get to the 66 block area twice? If working alone, you will have to. When are the most people around, and when are you most likely to be alone? Weekends are often best in office buildings because fewer people are around, whereas weekdays are better in apartment buildings because people are more likely to be at work, but your own unique situation will decide this. Have you assembled the tools, done the recon, decided on the best time, and advised your partner to wear some old clothes? OK, after all that, you are almost ready to begin the search.

What Are You Looking For?

Think about this for a minute. Telephone bugs come in all shapes and sizes and may be cleverly disguised so that you will not even realize they are there. They may or may not use a battery, and they may or may not be built on a circuit board. They may very well be built into a small metal or plastic box or hidden behind the connection block on the wall of your office. They may be located close to the line, and they might be 100 feet away. But phone transmitters all have one thing in common: they are connected to the phone line. It is a good idea to be thinking about little boxes and printed circuit boards and batteries, but don't let this break your concentration. Look for anything that is connected to the phone line.

The Inside Wiring

Now to begin the search, look at each possible place where a tap might be located, just as we did in the part on installing them, but in greater detail. If you have a transmitter detector, turn it on and if necessary adjust the sensitivity control. You learned how to do that in the manual—which you did read, didn't you? Take the phone off hook and make a call and then hold the probe close to the phone at different angles, watching the indicator and listening with headphones. If a bug is present and you are using the speaker, it will cause feedback that could alert the eavesdropper that you are searching. At least for now, you don't want that. Use headphones and listen for the sounds you are making or have a radio playing nearby.

Next, check the connection block where the phone is connected and then follow the line until it leaves the premises. It may go directly into the wall from the block or along the baseboards and over door frames and then into the wall. Do the same with extension phones on the same line and then repeat this for phones on a second line or however many lines you have.

Inside the Phone

As you will see in the Part 6, "On a Sweep," an expert will take a phone apart. Not just remove the cover, *take it apart*. Every bit of it will be inspected very carefully. But the expert has years of experience and knows what to look for. You may not.

PK Elektronik in Germany makes an RF phone bug that is about the size of a pea and resembles an ordinary electronic component, the tantalum capacitor. As sold, the bug will probably be green with the letters PK inside a white circle, but whoever installs it will likely paint it another color, just in case the intended victim has read books like this one. It may be very difficult for an inexperienced person to find; if it has been soldered to the phone's printed circuit board, it will look as if it belongs there. If one of these insidious little bugs is in one of your phones, you just might miss it. The best thing you can do is replace the phone.

But if this is not possible, then remove the cover and look inside. Everything should look professionally made. There should not be any loose wires; all should be connected with spade clips or soldered to the circuit board or Bakelite block. There should never be two wires spliced together, soldered or otherwise. If it is necessary to connect the ends of two wires, a mechanical device such as the Scotch-lok should be used.

Look at the printed circuit board and observe the material it is made of. Look at the metallic traces on the underside of the board. Then look for a second very small circuit board that is different, not made of the same material or with wires that are of colors different from the rest of those connected to the main board. Look for small scraps of plastic or fiberglass from removing screws, tiny drops of solder or a flaky brownish substance that looks like dried glue. This will be the flux residue from soldering, and it should not be there.

Take the handset apart if possible and look for the same things. Remember the drop in? If you have a standard Western Electric phone, you might replace the microphone element. They are available in surplus stores for a few cents, or just buy a similar phone at the same place for about $5.

After you have completed the search, or if you replace the phone, seal it in such a way that it cannot be opened without your knowing about it. Clear fluids that glow under ultraviolet (UV) light are available at spy shops and through mail-order dealers for $10 or less. Paint the fluid over the screws that hold the phone together, or use nail polish or spray paint or whatever is handy.

Now check where the phone cord is connected. There will be a small square metal or plastic block or plastic plate where the phone is connected. Remove the cover and look inside. Remove the connection block from the wall and examine the back. Use the mirror and flashlight to look inside the wall to see whether there is a plate covering a metal connection box. There should not be anything there except wires—no circuit boards or electronic components, nothing. If you find something that looks suspicious, leave it alone for the time being. More on this coming up.

Series and Parallel Taps

Remember from the previous chapter that a phone tap is connected to the line in one of two ways, whether it is a direct wire or an RF transmitter. The parallel type will have two wires that are connected to the two phone wires, usually red and green, and can be direct wire or transmitter. A series type is connected by cutting one of the two phone wires and connecting those two open ends to the two wires from the transmitter. Series is not used for direct-wired taps.

Follow That Wire!

Next, start tracing the wire. If you are using a transmitter detector, you need to put some kind of signal on the line for it to detect. Call someone who will agree to leave the connection open as long as is necessary and place a cassette or CD player near the phone. Put on something you will recognize and that will last as long as the search. Mahler's Fourth Symphony will do.

Now back to the wire. Does it disappear through a wall, or is it strung along baseboards and over door frames? If the latter, follow it and examine it carefully—especially in places where it isn't out in the open: over a door frame, in a closet, or behind furniture that is seldom moved. The wires may have been painted over, so look for places where the paint is a slightly different color. Turn the lights off and use the UV light, which will show such changes more clearly. Look along the edges of carpeting for small paint chips, which would indicate that someone has done something to the wires. Anywhere you see such signs, pull the wires away from the wall and examine them carefully. Remember the PK bug? It operates from the power on the phone line, so it does not need a battery. It could be hidden under a layer of tape that has been painted over, so remove it and see. Whereas the PK transmitter is line powered, others are not. So also look for batteries that are more often than not larger than the transmitter.

Another clever way to tap a pair of wires is to use two tiny spikes, such as the tip ends of needles. They are hidden in a small crack in the wall, and the wires are pushed against them. The sharp tips pierce the insulation and make contact; then the wires are held in place with a staple. Keep things like this in your head while searching.

At some point, the wires will leave the room and go into a hall (e.g., in an apartment building) or to another room where an extension is located. Once you have searched all of the exposed wires inside your home, office, or whatever, it is time to follow them to the 66 block. The wiring from the connection block to the point of demarcation will be one of three types:

1. *A 1/4-inch cable that may be beige or another color.* Inside are four small (usually AWG #22) wires. The insulation will be red (RED), green (GRN), yellow (YEL), and black (BLK). This is typical of newer small apartment/office buildings and private homes.
2. *A 25-pair cable, also with beige insulation, about 1/2-inch thick.* This cable is used mainly in office buildings, where there are a number of phones, or in apartment buildings. Look at the wires connected to the little block your phone plugs into; they should be red and green. If they are any other color, they probably go to the larger cable. Look inside the wall again and see whether there is a large cable with these different colored wires coming from it. Make a note of the colors; you will need this information later.
3. *Two, possibly three, larger wires with heavy black insulation.* These haven't been used since the 1950s and are found only in buildings at least that old that have not been rewired. They may also

still exist where rewiring has been done, but they are disconnected. Because they may still enter the target area, they can be used for audio surveillance. (Although this book is about phone devices, you can also be looking for microphones of the type that goes in a phone; they can be any size from that of a pencil eraser to 3 or 4 inches across. They all have one thing in common: there has to be one, or more, opening for the sound to get in, but this opening may be the size of pencil lead.)

Follow it as far as you can. If it disappears into a wall or floo, try to find out what is on the other side. If you are on the ground floor, then there will probably be a basement or crawl space; or the wires might be stapled along the outside of the building, in which case someone is going to have to go there and look. Did you remember to ask your partner to wear some old clothes?

If you come to a dead end, take a short break and give it some thought. Is there anything you have not considered, such as being able to get into any vacant rooms or picking the locks on a basement door? If you cannot get to where the lines have gone, then can someone else? A pro would probably find a way to get in. If you intend to make this search 100 percent effective, then you are going to have to do the same thing—or hire someone who can. Can you obtain the building plans from the city or county office that maintains such information? Will someone in maintenance help you?

Sometimes the wire you are following will become part of a large bunch of similar wires that are bound together and maybe painted over. Look closely, as you did in the beginning, for any signs of tampering. You may lose the pair you are following, and farther on the many wires may separate. How will you determine which is yours? Read on.

The Line Tracer

If you left the line open, listen for the music you have playing. Otherwise, you can use a line tracer, available from Information Security Associates. This device comes in two parts: the transmitter, which you attach to the line at your end to send a signal down the line that can be detected with the other part, the receiver. Hold it close to the lines in question until your hear the unique signal.

Once you reach the 66 block, SPSP, or whatever else is used to connect the wires together, you need to determine which wires are yours. If you were able to follow them all the way without losing sight of them, fine. If not, are they the same colors as they were at your end? If not, somewhere they were changed. This indicates that there is a floor closet somewhere in the building. You need to find it because this is a very good place for a tap.

Now you have to identify the wires. They may be labeled, but don't count on their being tagged correctly. If I were tapping your phone, I would switch some of the tags around just to fool you.

Connect your test set across the line you believe is yours and call the ANI number. There are many of these numbers, different ones for different areas, that can be found on some computer bulletin board services (BBSs). Check it from your own phone to make sure it works. There is also the universal ANI number 107-321-404-988-9664. It works, as far as I know, anywhere in the United States. However, there may be a $4 long-distance charge for using it. Then there is Caller ID, mentioned previously. If you don't get the right number, then start checking the other ones. No one said it was going to be easy.

Now make the same kind of check you did inside the phone, paying particular attention to your lines. Loosen the block and look behind it. Use the flashlight and mirror. Look for tiny wires that may be very hard to see and may be disguised or painted over. There should not be anything on the block except wires and connectors, and only two wires per connector. One is the incoming line from the CO, and the other is the one that goes to your phone. If there is a third, it is either an old unused one or a bridging tap. If you find a third wire, leave it alone for the time being; we'll get back to it. Remember, there should not be any circuit boards, electronic components, or anything else.

The Resistance Test

Making this test is easier if you have a partner to work with. If you don't, you will have to make two trips from one end of the lines to the other. Can you access the 66 block twice? If you have two-way radios or cellular phones (remember that someone may be listening), you can instruct your partner to open the wires to make the parallel test, then short them for the series test. First, make a note of where your line or lines connect to the 66 block. Make a mark on it with a pencil or write down the terminal numbers. Then disconnect both wires and position them so that they will not touch anything. Go back to the other end and disconnect the wires from the connection block.

The Parallel Test

With the wires not connected to anything, there should be an infinite resistance. Set the meter on one of the higher scales, touch the test leads together and set the ohms adj control so the pointer is on zero. Then clip them to the two phone wires. The needle may swing to the right and then drop back to the infinity mark. This is normal; the wires are acting like a capacitor being charged. Select the next lower scale and repeat the process, remembering to set the ohms adj first. On either scale, the needle should be on the infinity mark. If the reading is less than infinity, such as 10 megohms or less, then there may be a parallel device on the line that you missed.

The Series Test

The next step is to short the two line wires together. Use a screwdriver to connect them to one of the screw terminals on the little connection block or twist them tightly together. Now go back to the other end, where the wires were left unconnected, and repeat the measurement. This time set the meter on the lowest scale, usually R x 1 ohm. Set the ohms adj and connect the test leads to the line. The pointer should swing to the right, stopping just short of the zero mark. Make a note of the actual number.

The copper wire used in inside phone cables has a resistance of about 16 ohms per 1,000 feet. If the distance from one end of the line to the other is 500 feet, then the meter should read about 16. Remember that you are measuring the wire down and back. Two wires 500 feet long equals one wire 1,000 feet in length.

If the reading is more than 25 ohms, then something is wrong. It may be a bad connection somewhere, such as in a floor closet, or there may be a series-type transmitter on the line. Search the line again more carefully. If there was any area of the line you could not get to, see if you can find a way—or call in a professional. You might try to get the building owner or manager to check it by claiming that your phone isn't working right. However, you'll have to give him some reason—but saying that you think your line is tapped is not the right one. There are devices that use high voltage to burn up phone transmitters, but if it is a series type, then this will cause an open line or break in the line, and the phone will no longer work.

Downline Searching

If your line coming in from the CO is through an underground conduit, there is little you can do to search any farther. If it goes to a telephone pole and you want to make sure nothing is there, you really should call in a pro or, if possible, get the telco to look for you. If you are determined to see for yourself, decide how you are going to get up there. Remember about using climbers? Not for beginners. Do you have a ladder that will reach the splicing boot? Can you open it? Can you do all this without someone wanting to know what you are up to? If you have *and know how to use* a TDR, it is possible to get the telco maintenance people to physically disconnect your line at the CO so you can make measurements. Some TDRs have a built-in printer that makes a permanent record of the readings. If the one you are using does not, make a record of the readings. Also check and record the line resistance.

At this point, you have done all you can. Connect the wires back to the 66 block and make sure everything is as it was. Then take a few minutes and write a report to yourself. Make notes on areas of your line that are the most vulnerable or that you were not able to physically inspect. Were you satisfied with the equipment you used, or could you improve on it? Was there anything you needed but didn't have? Does this justify making another search?

DEFENSE AGAINST WIRETAPPING

You have completed your search, and there were no taps on your line. You did a thorough job and are convinced of this. Now what can you do to make it difficult for anyone to install a tap at some later date? You might remove any label or tag that identifies your line, just to make it harder on anyone who should try to tap you in the future.

Restrict Access

How easy was it for you to physically access and trace your line? That's probably how hard it would be for someone else. So to start, look at some ways to make this more difficult. Would it be possible to replace weak locks with high-security types? Paladin has a number of books on locksmithing from which you can learn which brands offer the highest security. Medeco and Abloy are two, but if the hinges are on the outside of the door, locks aren't much good. Paladin also has books on burglary, from which you can learn the tricks of the trade—and use them to your advantage to stop someone from wiretapping you.

Second Billed Number

Remember that installing a tap requires that the tapper either know your number, and can use ANI to find it, or can physically determine which lines go to your apartment or office. If the latter situation exists, installing a second line for billing purposes won't help, but if the former is true, you can have a second line installed that is billed to your old, first, number. Use it for confidential calls and don't give it to anyone. Second billed numbers are more difficult to get, even for someone who can usually get unlisted numbers. Details are available from the telco.

The Yellow and Black Alarm

Since the yellow and black wires of a four-wire cable are not connected, they can be used as a simple alarm system. Connected to a magnetic switch on the cover of the 66 block, an alarm will sound in your office if someone opens it. Then you can go and investigate. Any company that sells burglar alarms has these switches, and a hobbyist or technician can easily hook it up for you. Viking International, among others, has telephone security devices that will set off an alarm if the line is tampered with.

Secure Phones

In spite of these precautions, it is still possible for an experienced eavesdropper to find your numbers and get in to install a tap. Secure phones, of which there are many, will defeat them. More on this coming up.

ABOUT BUGS 5

WELL, IT LOOKED LIKE A BUG

Once again, I remind you that in searching for phone bugs, or any other type for that matter, you need to know what you are looking for. This chapter is about learning what is and what isn't a listening device by applying what you know about bugs so far, and also other things that you might not have thought about. Here are two examples of things that looked like phone transmitters but were not.

The Nervous Neighbor

One day, several years ago, I was sitting on top of my motor home resealing the roof in the July sun. The guy next door comes running over waving his arms. "Hey, Shannon, someone tapped my phone. I found a bug on my line! Can you come and have a look?"

Well, it was really hot sitting on that aluminum roof, and I needed a break, so I went over to see what he had found. It was a 1-inch-square circuit board with a number of electronic components (resistors and capacitors) covered in black lacquer. Two wires, red and green, connected it to the SPSP in the basement.

To someone not familiar with bugs, it looked like one. But there was one thing that tended to rule this out. It had a 1/4-inch square plastic block with three small slide switches, the kind used on some computer boards. There is no reason I know of for such a switch on a phone transmitter.

This did not by itself mean it was not a bug, only that it was unlikely. But I knew what it really was. So what was it already? It was an RF filter used to prevent nearby AM radio stations from interfering with the phone line. But since there are super-tiny series phone bugs, it was possible that a company like PK Elektronik could have modified some of these filters by replacing one of the components. So to be sure, I connected it to my phone line and ran some tests. It was not a transmitter.

Like a lot of people, my neighbor was very relieved, but still a little disappointed. Funny how that works. I asked him to think about it, and for a minute he did. Anyway, he was so happy that he went over to the store and bought me a case of Heineken. What the hell, I had already worked hard enough on the Tioga, so I decided to start working on the beer. After I twisted his arm a little, he decided to help. Then a few neighbors drifted over . . .

Betty's Bug

The first edition of *Don't Bug Me* was photocopied and spiral-bound at a copy shop. Because I made hundreds of them (before selling the rights to Paladin Press) the people at the copy shop got to know me. Well, one day this lady came in with a Polaroid photograph that she wanted to make enlarged color copies of. She was upset and told Kevin, who was working the counter, that she thought the object in the photo was a bug. He told her that he knew this guy that writes about that stuff and asked if she would mind if he made a copy to give to him. She was a little hesitant, but agreed. So a few days later, when I went in to do more copying, he handed the photocopy of the suspected bug to me and explained about the lady I will call Betty.

There is a reason for this long-winded explanation of what it wasn't before I tell you what it was. In learning about electronic surveillance, one needs to apply all of the other things he has learned, and not just what he picked up from books and videos and seminars.

It was a little hard to see the details from the photograph, but I will relate what I saw when I looked at it closely. First of all, the suspicious object was mounted in a little plastic holder that had a hinged cover with a little window. This told me that it was injection molded and that a set of dies had been handmade in a tool and die shop to produce it. Dies cost thousands of dollars, and no one would spend that kind of money unless he was mass-producing the things. It wouldn't be cost-effective, and remember that economics is taught in spy school, too.

Was it possible that the circuit board was placed inside it just because whoever made the bug happened to have one? No, for two reasons. First, it fit too well. Whatever it was, the case and the board were made together. Second, why bother to place the little circuit board inside anything? Especially something that would attract attention? You couldn't tell in the photo, but the plastic was bright pink.

This is a photograph of the phone that Betty thought was bugged.

So far, I had deduced a couple of things. First, it was mass-produced, so only someone with a lot of money made it—a big corporation or the government. This meant that it was not made by an amateur, technician, detective agency, etc. The next observation was the types of electronic components on the circuit board. A transmitter has to have one or more transistors or certain type of diodes to oscillate, i.e., generate a radio frequency signal. There were no transistors. It did have a diode, but it was a bridge rectifier and not the type that can transmit.

It was not a room audio bug, because it did not have a microphone, and even if it were, why place it inside a phone where the audio sensitivity would be reduced?

So what the hell was it already? A voltage regulator. Some older fax machines could not be used on the same line as a telephone because they had too much effect on the line voltage, so a regulator was used. Because of improvements in technology, voltage regulators are no longer needed.

SECURITY ALERT
WIRELESS MICROPHONES

C O U N T E R E S P I O N A G E   C O N S U L T A N T S   T O   B U S I N E S S   A N D   G O V E R N M E N T

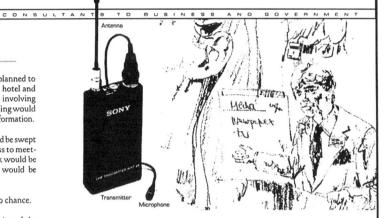

A CASE HISTORY

Our client, an international corporation, planned to hold their annual sales meeting at a resort, hotel and conference center. A year's worth of effort involving new products, marketing strategies and pricing would be discussed that week. Very confidential information.

Security was going to be tight. Rooms would be swept for electronic eavesdropping devices. Access to meeting rooms would be controlled. Paperwork would be collected after each session. Participants would be briefed on industrial espionage awareness.

Their security manager had left nothing to chance.

In the early morning hours before the opening of the meeting, our electronic countermeasures team detected a strong radio transmission emanating from the main conference room. The signal permeated half the hotel room wing and reached out into the parking lot.

A wireless stage microphone, belonging to the audio-visual contractor, was found near the podium.

HOW IT WORKS

Basically a miniature FM radio station, a wireless microphone is worn by a public speaker. The sound of the person's voice is transmitted to a nearby radio receiver, amplified and played through loudspeakers so the audience can hear more easily. In some cases it is also used to establish a link to a video camera, or tape recorder.

Unfortunately, these radio transmissions do not stop at the receiver. Wireless microphones can transmit for distances of 1000 feet to a mile. *Any* receiver tuned to the same frequency can listen in.

Wireless microphones are among the latest gadgets to catch the fancy of public speakers. Along with laser pointers, and large screen computer displays, wireless microphones allow the presenter more freedom of movement. In many meeting situations they are a welcome addition. But, not when the discussions are confidential.

WIRELESS MICROPHONE
Range: .25 miles.*

* From the manufacturer's specification sheet.

DON'T BUG YOURSELF

Commercial wireless microphones are *designed* to broadcast crystal clear audio, and their signals travel much further than most people realize. Anyone can exploit this. Competitors, the press, even employees who are not invited to senior level meetings, for example.

When targeting your meetings, the opposition will set up radio receivers and tape recorders in one of the hotel's rooms, or in an unoccupied car parked nearby. They are betting you will use wireless microphones, cellular telephones, and make a variety of other simple security mistakes. You will never see them.

In our *case history*, the audio/visual aids contractor *was* told not to use wireless microphones. They didn't. The microphone we found was packed in their excess gear, left near the podium. Was it left operating inadvertently, or was someone paid to leave it on? There is no way of knowing for sure, and it doesn't really matter. The entire meeting would have been broadcast in either case.

ESPIONAGE *IS* PREVENTABLE

Ban wireless microphones from your meetings. Be explicit and be firm. Do not allow this equipment in the room, even if it will not be used. (Since guest speakers often bring their own equipment, be sure to advise them of your rule too.)

When securing meeting rooms, and during the meetings themselves, be sure to check the radio frequency spectrum for all types of emissions which could carry room audio from your location. Common wireless microphone frequencies fall in the range of: 150-200 MHz, 450-452 MHz and 947-952 MHz.

Bugs, wireless mikes designed specifically for surveillance use, do not have assigned frequencies and can be found anywhere from 25 MHz on up.

Also...
• Avoid using a public address system of any kind if possible. If not...
• Use a podium system at low volume. If necessary...
• Use the hotel's direct wired microphone and room speakers, at low volume.
• Don't use cell, cordless, rail or air phones for confidential calls. All are radios.
• Call us to secure your next meeting. There is much more to do.

Eavesdropping on wireless microphones at conference centers is only one spy trick. There are hundreds more. Remember – Espionage is Preventable. For further information about pro-active programs to combat espionage, electronic eavesdropping and wiretapping please contact us.   Box 668, Oldwick, NJ 08858

Security Alert wireless microphones.

BEWARE OF GEEKS GIVING GIFTS

Oh, lucky you. The UPS driver just delivered a package: a snazzy new telephone from a Mr. Dave Wilson. There is a card explaining that once, long ago, you befriended Mr. Wilson, so he is sending you this appropriate gift. It might go something like, "My car broke down in front of your house, and I asked to use your phone. Thanks to you, I was able to let a customer know that I would be late, and I was able to make the sale after all." Or some other such story.

So you plug in your new phone in the kitchen, and a little while later it rings. Someone asks for Joe Boomfotz. You tell the caller that he has the wrong number, there is no one by that name there. The caller asks if you are sure. You assure him that if there were a Mr. Boomfotz living in your house you probably would know about it, and hang up.

Or you think you hung up. But you didn't.

Inside the phone is a gimmick that keeps the line open, and the microphone in the handset is still hot. And Mr. Wilson (Boomfotz) can hear every word being spoken while you are fixing dinner.

The infinity transmitter. It worked with the ESS system because you answered the incoming call.

WELL, IT IS A BUG!

OK, so what looks like a bug isn't necessarily a bug. But it might be. This part is about some that are. *The Bug Book* covers this in greater detail, so you might refer to that work, but here are some things to consider. Keep in mind that this book is about telephone transmitters, rather than other types of bugs. The basics of what to look for were in the part on searching your phone lines, but here is some additional information.

The Infinity Transmitter
The original infinity transmitter is actually a room audio surveillance device, meaning that it sends the sounds made in the room where it is installed through the phone line and not telephone conversations. As you recall, the old stepping switch systems connected the two lines together when the last ka-chunk was dialed. Then the ring signal was sent down the line.

The infinity transmitter, which was usually installed inside the phone, used what is called a *hook switch bypass*. This shunted across the hook or cradle switch and turned the microphone on and also prevented the phone from ringing. To activate it, the user called the target number and, before it could ring, fed an audio tone into his phone. Since the ESS does not connect the two phones until the called party answers, the old infinity transmitter will not work.

Tele-Monitor
There are many similar devices that do work, in a slightly different way, including the Tele-Monitor. This is a plastic box about the size of a paperback book that has a switch on top. This is what a bug looks like. There is no way to get it inside a phone, so it is connected to the line somewhere out of sight. A physical search would turn it up in short order.

Listen Electronics
Another transmitter that works is made by Listen Electronics. It consists of a small circuit board that is made to fit inside a desk-type phone. Take the phone apart and even a beginner will spot it instantly. It just doesn't look like part of the phone. This is what a bug looks like. But maybe you wouldn't know that. An easy way to tell for sure is to obtain another phone of the same type and compare them. Standard Western Electric phones, should that be what you have, can be found in secondhand stores for $5 or less. If you see anything that is different, replace it. It's so inexpensive, why take the chance?

Viking International
Another type of infinity device is made by Viking International in San Francisco for use on a fax line. The phone

may still ring or beep, depending on the type of fax machine, and anyone in the vicinity of the machine will be alerted that "a fax is coming in." But when it doesn't hear the handshaking tones, the fax gives up. After about 50 seconds, it "times out." Normally, this would free the line, but the Viking keeps the line open and the microphone turned on. I installed one on my fax line and called it from the voice line to see. It worked fine after I remembered to adjust the gain control. It is sealed in a black plastic box about 2 x 2 x 1/2 inches, has two wires that go to the phone line and a small screw slot—the gain control—and a small toggle switch to set it for voice or fax line operation. This is what a bug looks like.

As a rule of thumb, anything that looks like it doesn't belong where it is probably doesn't. Any wires or any kind of electronic device, printed circuit board, or small cube or box with one or more wires attached that cannot be explained—this is what a bug looks like. And also remember that unless the bug gets power from the phone line, it will need a battery or to be connected to the power line. Something else to look for.

WHAT IF YOU FIND A TAP?

There was this little dog that liked to go out and chase cars. This continued until one day its mother asked a question for which the puppy had no answer, "Son, if you catch one, what are you going to do with it?" OK, it's true that comedy school dropouts write books, but it illustrates a point. What are you going to do if you find a wiretap? Well, you have a number of options, and the time to consider them is now rather than when you are lying in the mud underneath a porch or itching your way through the fiberglass insulation in an attic so hot it could cook a pizza.

Do Nothing

Probably the best thing you can do is nothing. Leave it alone. Don't touch it. At least for the moment. This gives you an advantage over whoever is listening because the guilty party doesn't know that you've discovered the tap. Make notes and take pictures from different angles, including close-ups. At this point you might consider consulting a pro. Have the pictures and notes with you. If the bug is still transmitting—and until you know otherwise assume that it is—you can feed information to the eavesdropper that may draw them out. Cause them to react a certain way that you will be looking for. *Don't Bug Me* has more on this.

You could also leave the tap there, set up a surveillance TV camera and VCR, and wait to see whether someone comes in to replace the batteries. Or you can disable it by placing something in front of the microphone so it can't pick up any sound and see whether someone comes in to repair or replace it.

You are the buyer for a medium-size company, negotiating the purchase of 10,000 widgets. The supplier's representative is trying to feel you out to see how desperate you are and how much you are willing to pay. Just when you are getting down to the price, the rep gets another call and asks if you could hold for a moment, which you do.

While waiting, you discuss the price with your boss, and he mentions the highest amount you are authorized to offer. A few minutes later the rep comes back on the phone and tells you the lowest he can go, which is exactly what your highest offer would have been. So you make the purchase.

What you don't know is that the supplier is overstocked because of the cancellation of a government contract and would have sold the widgets to you for 30 percent less than what you offered. But the rep heard your top offer while you were on hold.

How did he do that? He used the Hold Invader available from Shomer-Tec. This device sells for about $100 and connects to your line with the usual standard modular cable. Everything you need is included, including a little manual. Just plug the device in between the base of the phone and the handset, and when you put someone on hold, flip the switch. This kills the microphone on your phone so the person on the other end cannot hear you. It even has a little button you can push to simulate the

continued on next page

"beep" sound, indicating an incoming call for you. The other party has no way of knowing that you are still listening, so he talks to his boss or someone else. And you hear.

And what do you do to prevent someone from using this trick on you? Well, obviously you are careful what you say when you (think you) are on hold. Or anticipate that someone is using this trick—just before this party tells you that he has another call, he will ask a question or make an offer, hoping you will discuss it while you are on hold and he will hear something useful in his negotiations. In this case, you might feed the party some false information. You say to your boss, "Gee, I think they are going to want more than we can pay for the widgets. We can go $80 (actually you expected to pay $120) so I guess we may have to get them from Walter Whompus at Wexlers Widget Works in Winnehaha, Wisconsin."

And the game goes on . . .

Remove and Destroy It
Not a good idea. If you want to disable it, fine—disconnect the power source. But there is no reason to destroy it.

Remove and Keep It
Also keep the batteries. The bug and batteries can be analyzed, and possibly some useful information can be obtained. (For more details, see *The Bug Book*.)

Damage Assessment
This is a term used to describe what the consequences of having been placed under surveillance might be, what time period the device was operational, and what may have happened during that time. The first step is to consider what type of device was discovered. If it is a direct-wired microphone or phone tap, then you know that the wires have to lead to a listening post. They can be followed to see where they go and who has access to that place. It might be a utility closet where a long-play recorder and drop-out relay have been concealed. Who has access to this place? Is it normally kept locked? Who has a key? How secure is the lock—is it easy to pick? Sooner or later, someone will have to replace the tape, and you can be waiting for them.

Maybe it is an RF transmitter, and the batteries seem to be dead—that is, the device is not transmitting. It could be a remote-control type. The listener hears the sounds of a search and turns the transmitter off. He waits a while and switches it back on to see whether the search has ended. You want to be sure that the reason the device is not transmitting is that the batteries really are dead. Then you can have the device analyzed.

It isn't like on television where the PI glances at the device and says, "Oh, I recognize this by the blue and green wires. Only Rabinski uses those colors, so it is one of his devices." Just doesn't work that way. But the type of device may tell you something about the spy.

If it is an inexpensive modulated oscillator that sells in chain stores for $20 and has a range of across the room or so, then you know it wasn't federal agents who installed it. If it is a very sophisticated spread-spectrum phone transmitter, then you know that it probably was a government agency or an experienced industrial spy and not an amateur. These devices aren't easy to come by.

The next consideration is where the device was placed—on the 66 block or inside a phone? This is important because it tells you how long it probably took to install it and, therefore, at least some of the people who had the access to install it.

Next, consider the LP. Analyzing a transmitter and the antenna and batteries it uses will tell you much about the probable range. Where, within that range, might the LP have been set up? In an adjoining office? Or suppose the target was a small building that was out in the open and a mile from the nearest other building. Did the bug have enough power to transmit that far, or would the LP have been set up in a parked vehicle near the target? Is it possible for a strange vehicle to have been parked within receiving range without being noticed by security personnel?

If you keep the transmitter, you can activate it and use a portable scanner to check around the area. See from how far away you can hear the signal. Make notes. Then extend the distance by about 50 percent and see what is in that area. The reason for this is that the eavesdropper may be using a sensitive communications receiver with an outside antenna. He will be able to hear it at a greater distance than you will with the portable scanner.

The final step is to take whatever measures are possible to prevent this from happening again. Some ideas are in the different parts of this book and in *Don't Bug Me*.

PHONE PHREAKING
AND TOLL FRAUD

Every now and then the news media run a story about "hackers," which (like most media reports) is usually inaccurate. From reading these articles or listening to the TV reporters, one might conjure up an image of something like the NSA LP described earlier. Or you might imagine a small dimly lit room where a handful of teenagers and college students hover over flickering computer screens. Punctuating the whirring of disk drives and chatter of line printers are excited whispers, "Far out, man, I just got into the telco system and downloaded 10,000 calling card numbers. We can make millions!" and "Wow, I'm online at the Social Security Administration. Let's wipe it out."

IncludeTd in such reports there is generally a quote from some "expert" explaining that this was one of the largest "rings" of hackers ever brought to justice: "It was a very sophisticated operation using the latest technology . . ." Sometimes they throw in a blurb like this: "If they hadn't been stopped, they would have wiped out the Department of Defense computers, leaving America at the mercy of hostile forces." Big business, the security industry, and government call hackers "high-tech thugs who steal anything they can get and destroy whatever is left."

I don't know that there is an official definition of a *hacker* or a *cracker* or a *phreaker*. These terms refer mostly to people who have an intense interest in the workings of computers and communications equipment and only want to understand them, as well as those few who actually are dishonest and destructive. This chapter is about how some people, whatever they are called, use their skills to have their long-distance calls billed to someone else or to obtain information they are not supposed to have.

TOLL FRAUD

It is hard to say when phreaking actually began, but it was probably in the late 1950s, not long after someone at AT&T published a list of audio tones used to control the long-distance switching networks. One of these tones, 2,600 cycles per second, or Hertz, could be used to open up long-distance lines. First, the phreaker would call the toll-free number of a large company, such as a car rental agency. When it started to ring, he would feed the 2,600-cycle tone into the mouthpiece, which stopped the ringing and left the line open for the phreaker to place calls anywhere he wanted.

Back then, however, it wasn't so easy to generate these precise audio tones: transistors were fairly new on the market, and not everyone had the skills to build such a device. So other methods were developed. One was to play certain notes on an electronic organ and record them. And, of course, there was "Blind Joe" who could whistle the precise frequency.

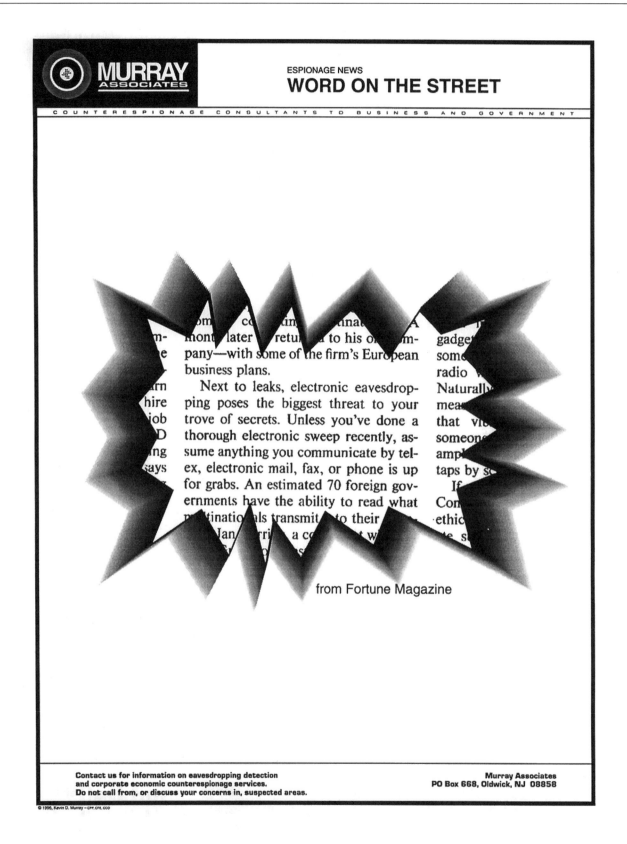

Espionage News Word on the Street.

Soon after, John Draper, the famous "Captain Crunch," discovered that the toy whistle included free in boxes of this cereal produced a perfect 2,600-Hz tone. This was documented very well in the October 1971 issue of *Esquire* magazine. (Incidentally, I spoke with John a few months ago. He is alive and well in the Bay Area.)

As time passed, Touch-Tone pads appeared on the surplus market, and inventive individuals converted them into the famous "blue box." This also was well detailed in the *Esquire* article.

The reason this technique worked was because the control tones went out over the same line as the voice conversations, known as signaling "in band." To defeat this, the Bell System developed "out band," in which the tones were transmitted over a different pair of wires. So today "blue boxing" no longer works. But there are other techniques that do. Some of the ways a hacker can make long-distance calls without paying for them are as follows:

- Through an extender
- Through a PBX system
- Through the "red box"
- With a calling card number (or a telephone company credit card)

Extenders

An extender is a dial-up number that, when called, opens up a second line from which long-distance calls can be made. The access (dial-up) numbers were given to subscribers of some long-distance companies. If you sign up with Sprint or MCI or whatever, you will be issued one or more of these dial-up numbers and an access code. When you call the number, you are required to enter your access code and then you can make your calls.

For those intent on getting free long-distance calls, the dial-up numbers initially weren't difficult to find, and the access codes sometimes were not that difficult to crack, although this is starting to change.

PBX Systems

For a business that has more than a few phone lines, the private branch exchange (PBX) is often installed. It usually has a control console located at the receptionist's desk. With some PBX systems, it is possible to call into it, from outside, and get connected to one of the outgoing lines. Once the caller has done this and gets a dial tone, he can make long-distance calls that will be billed to the company. As an extra precaution against getting caught, the hacker can use one PBX to call a second one and then a third, making the calls from the last one. This is called *stacking*.

One example of this kind of phone phreaking was reported in February 4, 1991, issue of *Business Week*. The article, written by Mark Lewyn, was entitled "Does Someone Have Your Company's Number?: Phone Hackers Are Tapping PBXs, Running Up Millions in Charges." It seems that one month the phone bill for Philadelphia Newspapers, Inc. was a little high. Something like 90 grand. More than 6,000 calls had been made to Pakistan, Egypt, and the Dominican Republic. A number of other businesses and agencies had also been hit, according to the article, including a social service office in New York City. According to Rami Abuhamdeh, executive director of the Communications Fraud Control Association, a group of phone companies and law enforcement officials, "This is one of the fastest-growing problems in the communications business." He estimates that the cost of this type of fraud could be as high as $500 million a year.

The Red Box

Whereas the blue box generated a 2,600-Hz tone and Touch-Tones, the red box produces the electronic tones that are generated inside a pay phone when coins are inserted. A red box is a simple device that can

FRAUD CONTROL

Ring . . . ring . . . 4:22 A.M.

"Hello, is this Mr. Thomas?"

"Uh, yeah. What's the matter?"

"Mr. Thomas, this is Randy Williams at the telecommunications fraud control center. Sorry to bother you, but we are seeing unusual activity with your calling card—more than $500 worth of calls to Honduras as of 20 minutes ago. I assume you have no knowledge of these calls?"

"No."

"Let's suspend your card immediately so you won't be charged for any of this. Just give me the last four digits of your calling card for verification. We will get a new card to you in about 10 days."

A month later . . . you still don't have a new calling card, your phone bill arrives in a shoe box, and the phone company is saying, "Randy who?"

What happened? "Randy" picked your name out of a phone book. He caught you sleepy and unaware with a good story. You, unfortunately, have one of the many calling card numbers that use your phone number plus four random digits—the exact thing Randy asked for.

be made from scratch with about $5 worth of parts. Another way is to modify a "pocket memory dialer," which is a battery-powered speed dialer. The user can program it with frequently called numbers, hold it close to the mouthpiece, press the right button, and get the number dialed automatically. If you replace one component that costs about $5 and make a few other simple modifications, the red box will produce the sound of a quarter being dropped in the coin slot. The device does not work with all pay phones or in all areas, and with some phones the user has to first insert a real quarter to turn the microphone on. But then the user just keeps beeping the device every time it asks for more money, and it will thank him in a sultry, synthesized voice.

Calling Cards

Another way to make long-distance calls that will be billed to someone else is to use a calling card, which just about everyone has these days. There are any number of ways of getting these numbers, such as the information on fraud control at the left from *Inside Information* by Murray Associates, Clinton, New Jersey.

This happens. It works because some people don't know better, and the fear that if the card is not canceled right away they might have to pay for $500 in calls makes them likely to cooperate with the "telco employee" and give out the rest of the number. But think about it for a minute. Why in hell would the telco need to ask you for your calling card number? The telco issued it. So if someone calls and asks for your calling card number, be a little suspicious.

Other ways to get calling card numbers are by snatching wallets and purses on the street, burglarizing homes, and overhearing people using their cards and copying the numbers down. This is especially easy to do at the banks of pay phones in hotel lobbies. Many a time I could have obtained these numbers from business persons who didn't bother to look and see whether anyone was close enough to overhear them before reading the number to the operator.

Preventing this from happening to you is simple enough. Memorize your number and don't carry the card with you. Don't leave the card lying around where a burglar might find it. If your card, or the number, is compromised, the obvious thing to do is call the phone company and report it. It will cancel the number—without asking for the last four digits.

Prevention

Telecommunications toll fraud is an increasingly popular crime that collectively costs its victims billions of dollars each year. Although carriers have responded with a wave of security products and services, the problem might be much bigger than was once thought. Some carriers claim that industry-wide toll fraud losses amount to between $2 billion and $5 billion a year, but the true figure is closer to $8 billion, according to Bernie Milligan, president of CTF Specialists Inc., a consulting group that studies toll fraud and markets security services to large corporate telecommunications users.

Despite the offensive against telecom fraud, the problem is becoming more frequent, and new technologies will only represent potential new adventures for hackers, CTF's Milligan asserts. Hacker activity is growing at an annual rate of 35 percent. Some 65 to 80 percent of toll fraud involves international calling, and fraud occurs on a much wider scale than just inbound 800 calls, Milligan says. So, while losses of this type of fraud drop, collective fraud losses are increasing by 25 percent each year. Customers are still liable financially in toll fraud cases, and the carriers continue to get paid.

The Communications Fraud Control Association has information you can use to prevent losses through your phone system. Write the association at 7921 Jones Branch Drive, Suite 300, McLean, VA 22102.

The AT&T Fraud Prevention Resource Center can be reached at 800-851-0439. This organization has a series of publications you can order, one of which is *Toll Fraud: A Tactical Guide for Telecommunications Managers*. This well-written 38-page booklet provides very useful information for businesses that have PBX systems and want to eliminate toll fraud. The info is for anyone, not just AT&T customers. Also available is *AT&T NetProtect Service*, a booklet, explaining how its system can help you prevent toll fraud, including establishing a liability limit, monitoring your long-distance calls (real time) to prevent unauthorized calls, and conducting seminars for corporate security personnel. Blocking of calls to areas that your company does not normally call, as well as those areas called most often (e.g., the Caribbean, Central and South America), is also available. These publications are free for the asking.

Toll fraud involving calls coming into AT&T's 800 network has dropped 75 percent since the introduction of NetProtect, while Sprint estimates a 95 percent decrease from last year (since the introduction of its fraud detection service). Average losses across the industry have plummeted from $120,000 per incident to $45,000. All of these products and services are available to reduce or prevent toll fraud and unauthorized access. But they won't do you much good if you don't use them.

INFORMATION FRAUD

Another kind of phreaking has nothing to do with toll fraud. Its purpose is to get information. About you.

Answering Machines

You get home after a long day at work, kick your shoes off, and look to see if you have any messages on your answering machine. The only thing there is some telephone solicitor trying to sell you a "free" subscription to the *Daily Blatt*. You were expecting at least one important message and wonder why it isn't there. So you call the person you expected to call, and he doesn't understand. "I called at 11:15 this morning and left the information on your answering machine," he tells you. Why isn't it there? Someone erased it.

Most answering machines have a remote control feature that allows messages to be retrieved and erased from another location. To access the remote mode, you have to enter a code at the phone you are calling from, usually two or three digits. This is not difficult for someone else to do if he knows how.

The first way this is done is a "brute force" attack. Just keep trying different combinations of numbers—either manually or with a computer (much faster)—until you hit the right one.

A more sophisticated and effective attack is with a device known as the Answering Machine Intruder, available from Shomer-Tec. This little device is the essence of simplicity. The user connects it to his phone with the included modular cable, calls your number, and the Intruder takes over. It's all automatic. Once he has access, the user can listen to your messages and, depending on the type of machine, may be able to erase them and even record a new greeting message. Some machines have a synthesized voice menu that explains all the options available for the user to follow.

What can you do to prevent this from happening to you? Shomer-Tec also has a product called the Answering Machine Protector. It sells for about $129 and connects to your line with a standard modular cord. Once installed, it "listens" for tone bursts from the Intruder or some computer program. If the right code isn't heard immediately, the device disconnects the caller. This means that someone would have to keep calling back over and over, trying all the different codes, an extremely difficult task. And you would know that the attempt had been made because the message counter would read 99 but the tape would contain only a series of beeps.

Voice Mailboxes

Voice mail has become a necessity in the business world, what with people "away from their desks" so much. So a caller leaves you a message, you in turn return his call and leave your message on his voice mail system, and so on. Phone tag. Some such messages are business, others are personal. Either way, if someone could get into your box and listen to the messages, he might learn a great deal about your affairs. The person might also be able to change your greeting: "Hi, this is Jim Dingle, and I can't take your call right now because I'm in the stock room with the receptionist." Some people might find that offensive—such as your boss . . . or the receptionist.

Breaking into a voice mailbox is much the same as breaking into an answering machine in principle, but in practice it is usually much more difficult. It depends on the type of voice mailbox you have.

A few years back this was very easy, because the passwords were only three or four characters. The Answering Machine Intruder would have worked against these.

One way that phreakers can gain easy access to voice mailboxes is for people not to bother to change the default password they were issued. They sign up and get the box, their dial-up and access numbers, and a page or two of instructions that they don't read. With some systems, the default password is the same for every user and is known to anyone familiar with the system. Another way is to intercept the password from a cordless or cellular telephone call.

To make your voice mailbox secure, just do these little things:

- Change the default password when you get the box and change it again every few months.
- Use a password with at least six digits that includes the # or *.
- Don't call your box from a cordless or cellular phone.
- Don't give the password to anyone else.
- Use a system that has a cutoff feature that disconnects the caller if a wrong password is used.

There are many different types of voice mail systems to choose from, two of which are Centagram and ASPEN.

Centagram

This is the system I use. It is reasonably secure. It has its own individual phone number (mine is 415-561-9709) but a different number for accessing stored messages and a five-character password that includes the use of the * and #. That comprises millions of possibilities. If I should happen to punch my password in wrong (which happens now and then) I have to reenter it correctly twice. Otherwise I get disconnected and have to call back. Centagram boxes are available from various private companies at a nominal fee of $10 or $15 per month, which even a starving writer can afford.

ASPEN

The ASPEN system, a product of the Octel Corporation, is sold as a complete unit to businesses and used in house. The individual boxes are issued to the employees. At one time, it was possible to hack ASPEN and get a box to use for free, and even get into boxes that had been assigned. There is an old program, called simply ASPEN, made for that purpose, but it no longer works. Octel has changed the security so that a new box can be assigned only by the system administrator and only directly at the system and not by remote control. Octel also increased the password length to a minimum of eight characters (which is a little difficult to hack since it makes for hundreds of millions of combinations) and incorporated an automatic disconnect feature for incorrect password entries. A new feature on some systems, which is being installed in selected areas, uses voice recognition. A sample of your speech is recorded and digitized, so when you call for messages, you speak a key word, and it is compared electronically with the stored sample. If it doesn't match, you don't get in.

WAR GAMES DIALERS

Whether his target is a long-distance extender, a PBX system, or a voice mailbox, there has to be a way for a hacker to get the access or dial-up numbers. This can be done by computer programs that automatically dial phone numbers and listen for different electronic signals that identify another computer, fax machine, long-distance carrier, or a voice mailbox. Some programs will then start trying different access codes. Others will simply make a record of the number and what it received, which is stored on the hard-disk drive. Then the hacker can try different ways to get in.

The automatic dialer, which was sensationalized in the movie *War Games*, started off as an expensive hardware device that mechanically dialed the numbers and sold for as much as $500. Today, there are at least a dozen different software dialers, the AIO (All In One) Hacker, ToneLoc, and others, available for free by downloading from BBSs and the Internet. Most of them maintain a record of the numbers called and the results.

Sequential Dialers

The sequential type is first assigned a prefix and then dials the numbers within the range the user specifies. This can be from 0000 to 9999, or any other range.

Nonsequential Dialers

The telco security system is rumored to have a monitoring function called Overlord. Whether it actually exists or not I don't

AND THE NUMBER IS

With most telcos, the first 100 numbers of most prefixes are reserved for internal use and testing purposes. XXX-00XX are all telco numbers. Try calling some of them, and you'll get various tones or recorded announcements. One of the interesting ones is a monitoring system for various telco installations. It answers, and a synthesized voice announces the temperature and humidity, and some other stuff and then turns on the microphone so the caller can listen to see whether anything is happening in the area.

know, but what it is supposed to do is detect more than two sequential numbers being called from a particular line. When this happens, Overlord is supposed to print out a record of the numbers called, the number called from, and the date and time.

Someone who should probably know, based on his considerable knowledge of the telco, tells me this is a myth. Other people report that in years of retrieving computer printouts from Dumpsters behind telco central offices, they have never seen a record of Overlord.

But because some people believe that Overlord exists, automatic dialers have been written that dial the numbers at random. After you enter the prefix and fire it up, the device will cross off the numbers called until it has tried all 10,000 in that prefix, keeping a record of what it has found.

HOW TO END PHONE HARASSEMEMT

There are a lot of weird people in this world, some of whom use the telephone to harass others. It all started back in the days of the party line.

"Now, Clem, yew an' Sadie stop yer fightin' over the tele-phone or I'll disconnect yew . . ."

Of course there was no way to be anonymous with this type of phone system, since everyone knew everyone else, but as manual switchboards were replaced with Strowger switches, and because tracing was a very difficult process (see below), anonymous calling became possible. And the creeps crawled out of the woodwork. This chapter is about what can be done to eliminate the problem of harassing, threatening, or otherwise unwanted telephone calls.

An expression of concern is on Perry's face as the pretty innocent client (who has only $1.63 in her purse) dabs the tears from her eyes with the handkerchief proffered by the always sympathetic Della. "We better get Paul," Perry says in his quiet dramatic way, and after the commercials, Mr. Drake taps on the door and makes his entrance. "Hi, Beautiful. Hi, Perry."

Perry explains the situation. Someone has been making threatening calls to his client (who will of course later be charged with murder), so he asks Paul, "Can your contact at the phone company get a record of the calls made to this number?" He hands a slip of paper to the glib PI, who glances at it and says, "I'll see what I can do."

And they all lived happily ever after. Except Hamilton Burger.

So much for TV. There were no records kept of local calls back when *Perry Mason* was being filmed because the technology didn't exist. Only records of long-distance calls were kept, for billing purposes.

OK, if a real person is using the phone to harass you, here are some ideas.

DON'T GET EXCITED

If someone is harassing you, the first, and possibly the most important, thing is to not let the harasser rattle you. Try not to get upset or show any sign of fear. This only encourages him. Just be cool and hang up. You might add some comment like, "Oh, drop dead, creep," or whatever. Almost always, the people who make these calls are harmless. If someone intends to harm you, he will probably do it, not talk about it. If the harasser persists, there are many things you can do to stop him.

LET SOMEONE ELSE ANSWER: VOICE MODIFIERS

Many harassing calls are sexually oriented, usually a man calling a woman. I suppose in the age of liberation this works both ways, but I don't really know—no one like that ever calls me. Anyway, if the caller hears another man answer he will probably hang up. Something that will make it sound like a man answering is a voice changer. To some extent they can make both sexes sound androgynous. Voice changers are not perfect, and the caller may well know that such a device is being used, but they are usually effective. And they have the advantage of masking fear or nervousness. One source for voice-changing phones is Akzo Marketing, 111 East 14th St. Suite 311, New York, NY 10003, 800-379-2515. The present model sold by Azko is a simple, no-frills, one-piece phone made in China. It is a push-button type, but not Touch-Tone: it converts the number key to pulses. It doesn't have last-number-dialed memory or anything else. It's just a cheapo phone, but it works. The price is about $30.

Viking International has a voice modifier that is a little more sophisticated. It is a stand-alone unit, not built into a phone, and has a variable pitch control. There is a microphone built into the case and a speaker that is placed on the mouthpiece of the phone being used, so it will work with any phone. It goes for about $195. It also has a built-in recording of a large dog barking, which may discourage the caller. Now don't misunderstand—there is nothing wrong with talking to dogs. But over the phone?

". . . AND THERE IS NO NEW NUMBER . . ."

One of the easiest and cheapest things you can do is change your number and make it both unpublished and unlisted. This can be inconvenient, because you have to get your new number to those you want to have it, but it may solve the problem. Then, again, it may not. There are ways of getting unlisted numbers. If you know how to do it, you can get them from the phone company. They have a department of "nonpubs" that provides the numbers, based on a name or address, to telco employees who have a "need to know." Some people outside the telco know how to access this department and get the numbers, which is called "social engineering." So if after you have a new number, the calls continue, then one of two things is true:

- The caller can get unlisted numbers.
- The caller is someone you know and gave it to.

Using a second billed number (as described in Chapter 4) makes it a little more difficult for phreakers to get your number. Use the second line for calls and the first for a computer or fax machine.

WHO IS IT?

If you can get the number the harasser is calling from, you may be able to figure out who he is. Here are some ideas.

Caller ID

Some areas of the country have Caller ID, which works like this: When you receive an incoming call, the number of the line that is calling you is displayed on the screen of a calculator-like device plugged into your phone. If you do not recognize the number, or know it is someone you don't want to talk to, such as a mother-in-law or a collection agency, you can ignore it and not answer. Now the person calling you has the option of blocking Caller ID by entering a code on the keypad before he punches in your number. This way, his number will not appear on your screen. Then you have the option of blocking the block; you can enter a code that will prevent your phone from ringing unless the caller's number is sent first.

Call Return

In some areas there is available a telco feature known as Call Return. For a nominal fee you can have this installed, and when you receive a crank call you enter a code number that causes the phone of the last person who called you to ring. If that person is not expecting this to happen, he may answer and give himself away. Especially if you wait a little while. You may recognize his voice. It was your old boss after all! This may not do much good if the caller is using a pay phone, but there may be a way to handle that too. Read on . . .

Call Trace

The next step can be to call the telco "annoyance bureau" and arrange to have this option added to your line. It will make a record of any number that calls you more than once. Also recorded are the date, time, and length of call. The telco won't give you the caller's name, but, if you insist, it will pass it on to the police, who may or may not look into it—unless you push them, too. Meanwhile, since there was more than one call, you could give some thought to having a lawyer subpoena the records and reveal the identity of the caller or at least the number the calls originated from and the name it is listed under.

The Trap

If your telco does not have Call Trace, it will have the pen register, or "trap." This is similar to Call Trace and works like this: You call the phone company, complaining of harassing calls. It screens you, because it gets a lot of very strange requests, and may try to discourage you. You have to be firm with the telco and insist that it help you. Once this is out of the way, the telco will set up the trap, and a record of every call you receive will be made and placed in the telco computer's memory. You will be instructed to keep a log of all calls received, noting the exact time of the ones that are threats or harassment. Periodically, you are required to check in and report any calls received. Then the phone company security people will compare telco records with the times on your log, and if there are matches they will forward the information to the police—who may or may not do anything about it, but if you push, they may reveal the caller's number.

Tracing Calls

Anyone who watches TV knows that a call can be traced in three minutes, right? After all, "they" said so on TV, right? Well, *not exactly*.

As you will recall from the discussion on Mr. Strowger's switcher in Chapter 1, in the early days of stepping switches, seizing and releasing the line of another undertaker was easy, but tracing the line that made the call was another matter. Tracing was a very complex process. First of all, the person receiving the call had to get in touch with the phone company, but since few people had two lines (or a need for two lines) they had to go to another phone to make the report. When the complaint was received, the technicians would start as they would to free a line, but instead they would observe the position of the switches and work backward from the last digit to the prefix. A later improvement in tracing was the *called-party control*. The technicians would go to the switch of the called line and place something called a *shoe* on the line, which kept it open, even if the calling party tried to hang up.

Several technicians would find the pair for the line the report was about and from the trunk determine the prefix of the line the call originated from. Then they had to start checking each of the last four digits by connecting a lineman's test set across different terminals that narrowed down the search until they finally got the line they were searching for. In the earliest days of the stepping switches, this could take hours.

With the ESS, making a trace is even more difficult . . . not for the telco, for *you*. You can no longer just call the telco and ask to have it done. What you have to do is call a local law enforcement agency and convince an officer that there is sufficient cause for it to make the trace. If the agency is convinced, and this may not be easy to do, then one of its officers will contact the telco, which can make the trace in a matter of the few seconds it takes to punch a few numbers into the computer.

FINDING WHERE THE CALLS ARE COMING FROM

Once you have a number, there are ways you may be able to find the name of the subscriber and the physical location of the phone, the street address.

Central Names and Addresses

Central Names and Addresses (CNA) is a service of the telco that maintains the records of its subscribers' numbers. Depending on the telco, this service may or may not be accessible to the general public, because the same service may have records of both listed and unlisted numbers. To find out, call the business office and ask whether it will give you the street address for a particular phone number. Someone will refer you to the right department, and if it is a listed number, the person you speak with there will give you the name of the subscriber and maybe the address of the "termination": the street address. Some people list their number but not their street address in the white pages. The telco representative will tell you only what is published in the white pages. If the number is unlisted, you will be told that the information is not available.

USA Today 900 Number

There used to be a 900 number published in *USA Today* that one could call to get the physical location of a phone. You gave the operator the number, and you then received the address (this did not include unlisted numbers). The cost was two bucks, which you paid whether the company found the address or not. Other such services are available in different areas and may be advertised in other papers or magazines.

The Haines Directory

Sometimes called the *crisscross* or *cross directory*, the Haines Directory is essentially a phone directory listed by number and street address. Available in most public libraries, it is published by the Haines Company, 29410 Union City Boulevard, Union City, CA 94587.

Unlisted Numbers

Unpublished, or *nonpub*, means that the number is not published in the white pages, but it may be available from directory assistance. Unlisted means it is not available from directory assistance or publicly accessible CNA, but it might be in the white pages. It is possible that an unlisted number might be published, usually for a business. In other words, unlisted and unpublished are not necessarily the same.

The telco may have a separate department for unlisted numbers. You need to know the number to call and how to ask for what you want. The procedure varies from one telco to another, so this is something you will have to find out for yourself. *Hint:* Look around on certain computer bulletin boards.

Ask Paul Drake

Some PIs can get unlisted numbers and addresses, some can't. Some will, some won't. Some are reasonable, some are expensive. All you can do is try. But have a believable story ready and shop around. This will cost you from $50 to whatever.

The Internet

If you have not experienced the Internet, you are in for a pleasant surprise. There are tons of Web sites where information is available on all phases of investigations. Get to know your way around and see for yourself.

Inside Help

One last possibility is knowing someone inside the telco who will get the records for you. This may not be easy: any employee caught digging into areas he or she isn't supposed to be in can get in a lot of trouble. But if you can convince some employee to help you, the higher up the inside person, the better.

Keep in mind that knowing the number of the line the caller is using or having the address where the phone is located doesn't necessarily tell you who the caller is. There may be any number of people who have access to that phone. But if you do know the identity of the caller, then there are several options available to you to stopping him.

STOP THEM!

Once you have determined who is harassing you, you want to stop it. Permanently. Once you know the identity of the phantom caller, you can handle it however you see fit. A good place to start is to find out everything you can about the person. *The Paper Trail* has information on how to investigate people and some ideas on how to deal with them.

Civil Action

This is your legal right, and a jury may well award you damages—if you have evidence. Convincing evidence might include witnesses who listened on an extension phone and made notes about date and time and content of conversation, tape recordings of the conversations, documentation to show that the caller was at the phone that was used at the times of the calls, and records from a telco trap.

Criminal Action

It is a criminal offense to use the telephone to harass people. So if you have evidence, take it to the police department. It may be able to help you end this harassment. Naturally, the police already have their hands full, what with all the street crime in the United States, but you have nothing to lose by trying. But, the same as in a civil action, without evidence, it is your word against the harasser's.

If you know who the caller is but neither civil nor criminal action is possible, then you may have to deal with the perpetrator directly.

Make a House Call

Once you know for sure who the caller is and where he lives, you can confront him in person, but give this some thought first. It would be to your advantage to be prepared. Find the caller when he is the most vulnerable. For example, a married person would rather not be confronted in front of his family, nor would a working person want you to show up at the workplace. So the following is what you might do.

Confront the caller and let him know why you are there. Advise him that unless he agrees to cease and desist, you will blow the whistle in front of everyone. You don't have to, it is not necessary for any innocent person to get hurt, but the guilty partner won't know that. At any rate, be ready to back up your threat. The objective here is to stop the harasser any way you can.

Invite the Cops and Your Friends

In some areas, the local police will accompany a person who is expecting trouble, to "keep the peace." This is not at all an unusual request, just part of the job. And it may save the officers a lot of time writing reports later if they don't go with you. You can also take a few friends and, if possible, a video camera. Record the entire incident, starting before the caller opens the door.

As I said, with all that you have going for you, you don't have to put up with someone using the phone to harass you. Give 'em hell.

RECORDING PHONE CONVERSATIONS

At least once in your life you have had a telephone conversation that you wish you could have recorded. C'mon, admit it. It may have been something intimate that you shared with a very special person or perhaps just a record of business information. Or it may be that someone was using the phone to harass and threaten you, and you wish you could have recorded the call to be used as evidence. If there is a next time, you want to be prepared, and that is what this chapter is about. Here you can learn everything you need to know so that next time you will indeed be ready.

IS IT LEGAL?

If you want to comply with the laws that be, you might consider consulting an attorney. But since getting a specific yes or no answer from a lawyer is not so easy, you might also consider what the phone company has to say. Presumably, this was written by the company's lawyers. The Pacific Bell Customer Guide Information line has a recorded message that says one of two conditions must exist before you can legally record a phone conversation:

1. All parties to the conversation must give their consent.
2. All parties to the conversation must hear a beep tone every 15 seconds.

This is known as an *all-party consent* law. Such a law is in effect in some states, including California. Other states and the federal government may have the single-party consent law, meaning that only one of the parties has to be aware of the recording. Here are two examples:

The All-Party Consent Law
Joe calls Sam and wants to record the call. So Joe turns on a recorder that has an automatic beep tone. Joe knows he turned it on, which is one party. Since Sam is talking to Joe, it is reasonable to assume that he is not deaf and can also hear the beep tone. This is the other party. Sam might later claim that he did not hear the tone, but it will be on the recording. Joe could also ask Sam for his permission before he starts the recorder.

Now suppose Joe or Sam decides that a third person, Molly, will be joining them in a conference call. The same thing applies since she is now a party to the conversation. *All parties.*

All you need know about...
TAPE RECORDER DETECTORS

COUNTERESPIONAGE CONSULTANTS TO BUSINESS AND GOVERNMENT

Theory of Operation:

Many tape recorders generate a very low power radio-frequency signal as part of their recording process (known as the bias oscillator signal). Small amounts of this signal radiate from the tape recorder's circuit boards and tape heads to the area surrounding the tape recorder. This signal can be detected with a radio receiver tuned to the signal's frequency; a pocket tape recorder detector.

Pocket tape recorder detectors are sometimes packaged with bug detectors (see our *All You Need To Know About Pocket Bug Detectors* fact sheet). They are pocket-sized, as the name implies, and include an antenna which is approximately 3" x 1" x .25" in size. The antenna is connected to the detector by a 3 to 4 foot cable. This allows covert placement of the detector in a breast-pocket, and attachment of the antenna to the forearm or wrist. Once the detector is turned on, the arm can be used to nonchalantly maneuver the antenna close to where a recorder might be hiding. This may be awkward if you suspect the recorder is being carried by another person.

Pros:
• Simple to operate.
• Inexpensive.
• Small.

Cons:
• **Not all tape recorders generate a bias oscillator signal.**
• Range of detection – 0 to 18 inches from the antenna, depending upon the recorder.
• The bias oscillator signal is generated *only* when the tape recorder is in the *record* position.
• Subject to false positive readings. Potentially embarrassing.

Cost: $700 - $1200

Recommendation:

At this point in time we are not recommending any tape recorder detectors to our clients. They are not effective enough to provide a reasonable degree of assurance.

This device can give the user a false sense of security. A healthy sense of caution is still the better choice.

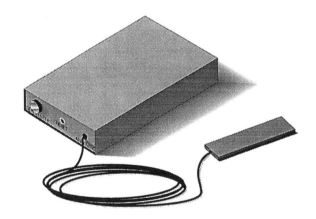

For information on professional electronic eavesdropping detection services please contact us directly. Do not call from, or discuss your concerns in, suspected areas.

www.iapsc.org/kmurray
murray@spy.busters.com
Box 668, Oldwick, NJ 08858 (USA)

© 1997, Kevin D. Murray, CPP, CFE, CCO, BCFE

All you need to know about . . . tape recorder detectors.

The Single-Party Consent Law

Joe calls Sam and wants to record the conversation. Since Joe knows he is recording it, and he is one of the parties to the conversation, then this is legal. Sam doesn't have to know.

METHODS OF RECORDING

There are many methods of recording telephone conversations. As you will see, each way has its advantages and disadvantages. Choose the one that best suits your needs.

1. Drop-out relay
2. Line-ready recorders
3. Direct connect
4. Inductive recording
5. Acoustic recording
6. Recording from a cellular phone
7. Recording from a pay phone

Drop-out Relay

This is the easiest and most dependable method. The typical relay is a little plastic box about the size of a pack of cigarettes that has three cables attached. One has a standard RJ-11 modular plug that goes to the phone line. The other two go to the recorder microphone and remote control jacks. They are different sizes, so that you won't be able to plug them in incorrectly. On the box is an on-off switch that is set to the on position when the cables have been plugged in.

Press the record button, make a call, and note that the recorder starts automatically. Then rewind the tape and listen. Adjust the record level until the audio is clear. Then rewind the tape, put it back in record mode, and it is ready. The most important feature of this device is that you do not have to remember to start the recorder. In a stress situation, many people will forget. The drop-out relay eliminates this problem.

Line-Ready Recorders

Some recorders have a modular jack built into them, so that all you have to do is plug it into the phone jack. The Marantz PMD-200 and PMD-201 are so equipped and are both excellent cassette recorders. Some recorders also have a drop-out relay built in, so recording is automatic. Others may not, so you have to remember to push the record button.

Direct Connect

The direct-connect method is the least expensive, requiring only a few parts and a cable that has a 3.5mm microphone plug on one end. You have to remember to push the record button, though.

Inductive Recording

This method uses a coil of wire placed on or near the phone to be recorded from. It may be inside a flat plate placed under the phone or a suction cup mounted on the receiver. Neither one works very well, but if nothing else is available at the time, one uses what one has.

Acoustic Recording

Should you get a call you want to record but are unprepared with any of the preceding methods, you may be able to get some of it on tape by holding the recorder as close as possible to the receiver earpiece. This is a little awkward, and the sound quality won't be too good, but it is better than nothing. There are ways to clean up the recording by removing some of the background noise. Check the yellow pages under Recording Services. This may be expensive, but how important is the recorded information?

Recording from a Cellular Phone

One way to do this is the acoustic method, with which you have the same problems as with landline phones. Another is to use one of the commercial cellular monitoring systems you can read about in Part 2, which are rather expensive—and rather illegal. Also, there is a new device, recently released, that will detect the signal from a cellular phone and has a cable to attach the recorder. Some of them may be available from private parties, but in July 1997 a federal district court judge ruled that the producer, Tech Support Systems, could no longer make them.

A third method requires taking the phone apart and tapping onto the speaker terminals. A thin cable (shielded) is soldered to the speaker, and the other end, through two capacitors, is plugged into the microphone jack of the recorder. This will probably void the phone's warranty and, because of the way these phones are put together, is better left to an experienced technician.

A fourth way is with the test mode cable, the type used by technicians for testing and changing the mobile identification number (MIN) and number assignment module (NAM) indicator. The cables are available from the phone manufacturer, as are the service manual, which you will need. This, too, is better left to a technician.

Last, there is the suction cup inductive method, but, again, don't expect too much.

Recording from a Pay Phone

This has to be done a different way since you will probably not be able to get to the line to make an electrical connection. In addition, since it is not your phone, this is illegal wiretapping, so you use an acoustic modem, a gizmo used to send computer data. This type of modem, which can be found in surplus electronics stores for a few bucks, has two foam rubber cups into which the receiver fits snugly. Modifying it is a simple job that any hobbyist or technician can do in half an hour. There are several ways the modification can be done, one of which is to add an ordinary telephone receiver with a switch on the microphone. When the call is placed, insert the pay phone receiver into the foam cups and listen through the second receiver. Having the microphone switch turned off prevents background noise from getting in, but when you want to talk you can switch it in.

EXTENDED-PLAY RECORDERS

The type of tape recorder to be used may depend on the anticipated length of the recordings to be made. The recorder may be in a place where you can access it only at certain times. Since ordinary recorders are limited to whatever time the tape can store, you may want to consider an alternative.

The Marantz PMD 201 is a dual-speed model. Setting it on the slow (15/16 IPS) speed doubles the recording time, up to 90 minutes per side. Some recorders have the auto-reverse feature that electronically "turns the tape over." This also doubles the recording time, which may be more than the battery life. Use an adapter if you can find a place to plug it in. Better yet is a modified recorder that is capable of five or more hours on each side of the cassette.

There are some cheapo types that have had minor electronic changes to slow them down and are often sold through mail-order ads, but the right way to extend the recording time is by making internal modifications and including circuits that compensate for the slow speed.

One source of very good extended-play recorders is Viking International in San Francisco. Its catalog, which is free, lists a number of other products, many of which Viking manufactures. The company specializes in audio equipment, and its products are of very good quality.

PLAY BACK INTO THE LINE

At some point there may arise the need to play a recorded conversation back into the phone line. For example, someone is harassing you and you want the person to know you have recorded him. This may be enough to get the harasser to back off, but are you sure that you want him to know? Would it be better to hold off until you have made more recordings?

If you plan to play a recording back from a pay phone, the modified acoustic modem can be used. If you use your phone, the direct connect should be used. All you need to do is remove the plug that was in the microphone jack and put it in the external speaker jack. Experiment with this by calling a friend and playing a recording back at different levels until the sound is easily understood. You can also mount a small switch, a DPDT CPO, in a plastic box and Velcro it to the phone. In one position it is set to record from the line, in the other to play back into the line, and in the center it is turned off.

WHAT CAN I DO WITH THE TAPES?

The tapes may be admissible as evidence in either a civil suit or a criminal action, depending on whether you were in compliance with the law when you made them. If the content of the tapes is denied, but the defendant denies that he ever made the calls, the actual tape may be used to show perjury on his part and that the calls were in fact made. If you plan to file a complaint with the police, the officers may be sympathetic to your plight and overlook the fact that the recordings were not exactly legal. Even though the tapes can't be used as evidence in court, the cops may at least investigate and perhaps interview the caller and suggest that he cease and desist.

HOW CAN I ID THE CALLER?

You have a recording of someone who has threatened you, and you think you know who it is. So you need to record the suspected person and use that tape to make a comparison. If you can get physically close to the suspect, you can use one of the many pocket-sized recorders available. The Olympus PearlCorder is excellent, as is the Nagra, but anything small enough to conceal will do. Some such recorders sell for less than $30 in secondhand stores and pawnshops.

Once you have the person on tape, this recording can be compared with those made from phone calls. There is an investigative agency in Kentucky, owned by a retired FBI agent, that specializes in audio and video recordings and can do the job. However, the company does not want its name

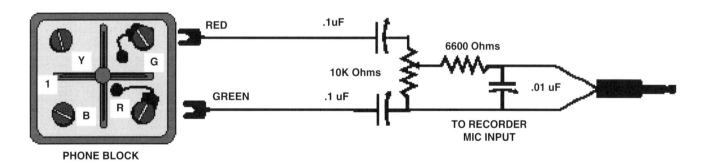

A simple device for playing recorded conversations back into the phone line. To use it for recording, switch the plug from external speaker to microphone jack.

published. So if you are interested in the services of this firm, send a name and mailing address to me in care of the publisher, and I will forward it. Include a note saying that you are interested in having two recordings compared. Use whatever name you like; I don't need to know who you are.

PREVENTION

Is someone recording you? If the recorder is on your end of the line, you will be able to find it by tracing the wires. But on the other end, there is no way to tell and nothing you can do to prevent it. If you are at all suspicious, watch what you say.

PART 2

CORDLESS AND CELLULAR/PCS PHONES

THE GOLDEN
AGE OF RADIO

Radio. The stereo in your living room, in your car, the one clipped to your belt as you jog along the pathways of life—something that was just always there and taken for granted. Was there really a time when there was no radio? Indeed, and a wonderful part of Americana was the development of the "wireless," without which the society of today could not function. The people who made radio communications possible were visionaries, geniuses, dedicated scientists who created the magic medium in spite of the many who said it couldn't be done.

THE INVENTORS

Remember from Part 1 that it was Michael Faraday who first conceived and later proved that a magnetic field was generated when an electric current flowed through a wire coil. In 1864 James Maxwell reasoned that if this current were to change in intensity, the magnetism would radiate into space. Heinrich Hertz demonstrated this in about 1885, but it was Marconi who is credited with first applying this principle to long-distance communication. He demonstrated it just before the turn of the century, and in 1901 the first transatlantic communication was sent from England to Newfoundland. This was the wireless telegraph, not the wireless telephone, which was to take a few more years.

Marconi's mechanism was the spark gap transmitter that zapped Morse's dots and dashes through space. Transmission of the human voice or of music was not yet possible. Soon, improvements in the spark system were made, and Reginald Fessenden used something called an *alternator* to broadcast a musical concert to the wireless operators aboard ships. The signal wasn't quite high fidelity, nor was the receiver, but it worked.

What was to make possible radio broadcasts of high-quality sound was the vacuum tube. The true inventor of the tube was Thomas Alva Edison; the filament of his light bulb emitted not just photons, or particles of light, but also electrons. But Thomas Alva, in spite of his genius, apparently did not realize this. John Fleming understood the flow of electrons and theorized that they (the electrons) could be captured if a metal "catcher" could be placed inside Edison's glowing invention. And so he did. He called this the *plate*, or *anode*, and the first vacuum tube, called the *diode*, was created. Another of the great minds that helped invent the radio was Lee De Forest. Working in his garage in Palo Alto, California, De Forest conceived the idea that a shield could be placed inside the diode tube to control the flow of electrons. This was the *triode*, which he called the *Audion*, and it enabled the tube to amplify.

TECH STUFF

The term *amplify* suggests that a small signal is made larger. Although this is the result, it is a little more complicated. What an amplifier actually does is use a small signal to vary a higher DC voltage in time with, in proportion to, that signal. An example of a signal could be the variations in current made by a carbon microphone, the telephone. Alone, it can be heard only by placing the receiver close to the ear. So to make a telephone conversation loud enough for everyone to hear through a speaker, we feed it into the grid of De Forest's Audion. The signal variations at the grid change, or vary, the amount of current that flows through the Audion tube. These variations are then taken from the plate of the tube at a higher intensity, through a capacitor and a transformer, and fed into the speaker. The speaker is then placed on the front porch so everyone in the neighborhood can hear Sadie tell Clem what a dirty dog he is.

In 1916, Charles David Herrold, the father of broadcasting, wrote a memo in which he stated: "I have in mind a plan of development which would make radio a 'household utility' in the same sense as the piano or phonograph."

THE FIRST STATION

In 1916, Frank Conrad used a vacuum tube transmitter to entertain his neighbors on experimental station 8XK, and in November 1920 it was licensed as the first commercial station, KDKA in Pittsburgh. The golden age of radio had begun. The narrator, standing behind his microphone, paused . . . while the sound effects men created the thundering hooves of a great white stallion galloping across the plains. The Masked Man, looking for wrongs to right, uttered a mighty "Hi-Ho, Silverrrrr, awaaay!" from the dynamic speaker of the Philco Cathedral radio.

I remember it so well . . .

COMMERCIAL BROADCASTING

The motivation to develop radio may originally have been to improve communications between individuals, but it didn't take long for business types to realize that the new technology was something to be exploited. On 28 August 1922, less than two years after KDKA signed on for the first time, the first commercial was broadcast over AT&T experimental station WEAF in New York City. Queensland Realty advertised a new apartment building, and the ad cost $100 for one minute. That's not very much compared with the millions of dollars or so for an ad running during the Super Bowl.

LARGER AND SMALLER AND . . .

The first commercial radio receivers were about the size of a bread box. One of the earliest Atwater-Kent models was built on a slab of polished walnut with the tubes in ceramic sockets and had three tuning knobs. Like all products (except commercials) the radio improved with time. Radios became more sensitive, so that listeners could hear AM stations as far away as 150 miles. The audio was improved, larger speakers were designed, and the works were placed inside wooden cases. Some of them, the old consoles of the 1940s, were 4 feet tall and had magic-eye tuning indicators and short-wave bands.

But even the smaller models were a little too big to tote around, and people wished they could take this wonderful new invention to parks, the beach, and other places where there were no electrical outlets. For it to happen, they had to get smaller and be made to run on batteries. Briefcase-sized AM radios using tiny tubes appeared on the market, and there was music to go . . .

at least for a few hours until the batteries went dead. Although this was long enough for an afternoon picnic, it wasn't quite good enough. In 1948 three physicists from Bell Labs invented the transistor, and radios started getting much smaller and able to run on batteries for much longer. Pocket-sized models appeared in the late 1950s. And then radios started getting bigger again when someone thought of the portable stereo, the "boombox"—ear pollution to go.

If radio receivers could be portable, then why couldn't transmitters? Police departments were quick to realize how useful it would be to communicate directly with officers driving around in their patrol cars, and engineers started working on it. At first, only receivers were used because transmitters were much larger and required greater amounts of power. In the 1920s, the first mobile transmitters went into service. They were the size of the early AM console radios—the rear seat of the patrol car had to be removed to install it, which left no space for hauling the bad boys to jail. The early mobile transmitters were powered by a battery-driven generator, called a *dynamotor*, and being AM, the system was prone to static and ignition noise. Reception left a great deal to be desired, but it was a beginning.

Improvements in the transistor, being able to work at higher frequencies and power levels, reduced the size of mobile transmitters to the proverbial breadbox. The "works" were installed in the vehicle's trunk, and a heavy cable connected it to a control head mounted underneath the dashboard. The microphone plugged into the control head and had a push-to-talk button. A red light indicated that the radio was turned on, and a green one came on when the operator pushed the button. These pilot lights were so bright that they could be seen across the street, which for a while made unmarked police cars easy to spot.

10 PHONES ON WHEELS

Soon, these newfangled radios became available to the general public in the form of the mobile telephone service (MTS). As with the radios the police used, the equipment was in the trunk and the controls under the dash or between the bucket seats. To make a call, the user would pick up the handset and push a button. After a little while the operator would come on and ask whether the person wanted to make a call. The user would politely tell the operator that, yes indeed he wanted to make a call, which is why he pushed the button. The operator asked for the caller's account number, which was written on a billing ticket, and once the paperwork was done, she would dial the number.

Five ringy-dingies . . . or was it six? After a few clicks and beeps, the connection was made. Lo and behold, mobile telephone conversation was possible! Paul Drake was able to contact his contact and get the information that Perry would present to the judge and save his client with seconds to spare before the final commercials.

With the first mobile telephone service came eavesdropping and fraud. Anyone who had a mobile phone could listen to the other users, hear their account numbers, and then use them to make calls. The users would be billed for the calls, much like the cloning process 40 years later. And should anyone have a radio that tuned the very high frequencies (VHF) that were used, they could listen in. This was slightly improved on with squelched MTS, which used a technique later to be called Private Line by Motorola. Each mobile phone was equipped with an electronic switch that would "lock out" other conversations. A special audio tone was assigned to each mobile phone that would activate only that phone, and it would not hear other calls. But all the owner had to do was open the squelch control or push the monitor button, and he could hear any other conversation on the channel.

IMTS

So the improved mobile telephone service (IMTS, sometimes called IMPS) came to be. Instead of callers giving their mobile account number over the air, for others to hear, it was transmitted using audio frequency shift keying. This prevented other users from hearing the account number and then making calls billed to others' phones, but did nothing to stop experienced technicians. The ID number was set by placing a number of wire jumpers inside the phone, and it was a simple matter to change them. The IMTS system is still in use in some areas of the United States, on the 155 and 450 MHz radio common carrier bands.

ESPIONAGE ALERT
WIRELESS TELEPHONES

C O U N T E R E S P I O N A G E   C O N S U L T A N T S   T O   B U S I N E S S   A N D   G O V E R N M E N T

KNOWN OFFENDERS

- Cellular Phones
- Home Cordless Phones
- In-flight Airline Phones
- Railway Phones
- Ocean Liner Phones
- Remote Area Phones

FUTURE WATCH
- Personal Microcell Phones
- Wireless Business Phones
- Satellite Cellular Phones
- Wireless LANS

SUGGESTIONS
- Avoidance
- Discretion
- Codewords
- Encryption

ACTION
- Notify employees who use wireless phones.

YOUR WIRELESS TELEPHONE CALLS ARE INTERCEPTED

Guaranteed. No ifs, ands, or buts. Believe it. Get used to it. Develop a protective strategy. Monitoring phone calls has become a national pastime. Everyone from electronic hobbyists, to shut-ins, to law enforcement, to career industrial spies is involved.

Is it easy to do? Yes. Can specific telephones be targeted? Yes.
Is it legal? No.
The point is academic however.

How is it done?
All wireless telephones are basically radio transceivers. Your voice is transmitted through the air on radio waves. You receive the person you are talking with the same way.

Radio waves are not directional. They disperse in all directions. Anyone with the proper radio receiver can listen in.

Radios which can receive wireless telephones are readily available. So are books showing phone frequencies and tips on *how to listen*. Eavesdropping can be accomplished for as little as $250.

How can you regain some privacy?
- *Assume someone is always listening.*
- Try not to use wireless phones. But, if you must...
- Be as vague and uninteresting as possible. Don't attract attention.
- Use only first names. Invent codewords for sensitive topics.
- Do not use company names or other identifiers.
- Set up a call-in number to be answered with a simple hello.
- Remind the other person that you are using a wireless phone.
- Educate others about wireless phone eavesdropping.
- Consider adding speech encryption. Expensive, but very effective.

Wireless telephone monitoring is only one spy trick. There are hundreds more. Remember – Espionage is preventable. For further information about pro-active programs to combat espionage, electronic eavesdropping and wiretapping please contact us.

www.iapsc.org/kmurray
murray@spy.busters.com
Box 668, Oldwick, NJ 08858 (USA)

© 1997, Kevin D. Murray – CPP, CFE, CCO, BCFE

MONITORING

With the synthesized radios of today, one just punches the desired frequency into the keyboard, but in the days of IMTS, radios required crystals, a small slab of quartz mounted in a holder, for both the transmit and the receive frequency. These crystals, called *rocks*, had to be ordered from the manufacturer; this took several weeks, and sometimes the manufacturer asked why the customer wanted them. If the manufacturer didn't like the answer, it might refuse to sell the crystals; that happened to me several times at International Crystal Co.

In addition to being controlled, crystals were expensive, beyond the means of many ham operators and hobbyists, who were limited to finding used ones at swap meets or through auctions at taxicab companies and the like. In addition, crystals would receive only one channel; a different crystal was needed for each station one wanted to monitor.

Some years before I had built an AM radio from a National Radio Institute kit, and I remembered how the frequency could be adjusted by turning the trimmer screws on the tuning capacitor. Why, I wondered, wouldn't this work on an FM radio? So I obtained a big, old tube type and started experimenting. I adjusted the screws, added and removed turns to and from the oscillator coil, and then readjusted the screws until one happy day the voice of the local police dispatcher came blasting from the 12-inch dynamic speaker. Word got around, and soon kids from all over the neighborhood were pouring into my basement workshop to see if I really could tune in police calls. The frequency was about 151 MHz, where many interesting stations transmitted. Among them were federal government agencies, whose employees, not knowing that anyone could listen to them, were very blunt in what they said over their "secure" radio system. Ah, the stories I could tell . . .

In the 1960s scanners appeared on the market, but they, too, required crystals. And while they were becoming easier to get, they were still expensive and took several weeks to be delivered. There had to be a better way. In the mid-1970s, the programmable scanner made its debut. One of the first was the Regency Touch Series—just touch a few buttons on the front panel and the frequency was changed to whatever was within its rather limited range. The name Touch was appropriate—these early models were indeed touchy. Sometimes the frequency would be accepted by the microprocessor, sometimes not. Sometimes they received, sometimes they did not. A year or so later, Bearcat, then a division of the Electra Corporation, introduced its line of programmable models. At the time, these were the finest scanners available. Pioneers in the field, Bearcat included features in its early models that few scanners have today, such as search and store and lockout in search mode. The number of different frequencies that a scanner could store went from 10 to 50 to 100 to 200 and 400, and 1,000. Some models (the PRO-2006) could be modified to increase this to more than 4,000. And now, in the 1990s, this number is virtually unlimited, thanks to the RS-232 C interface that allows the scanner to be controlled by a computer.

The IMTS may have helped reduce fraud, but it did not eliminate it, and did nothing to prevent eavesdropping. Also, the number of channels was limited. There were only 13 VHF and 21 ultrahigh frequency (UHF) radio common carrier frequencies, and as more people began using mobile phones, the bands became crowded and sometimes a caller had to wait for an unused channel. So, in the early 1980s, the phone companies and independent businesses started designing a better system.

A CELL IS BORN

With millions of people wanting to use mobile phones, it seemed at first that there would have to be hundreds of thousands of frequencies. But the VHF area was taken up entirely. Mobile phones moved to the UHF bands, but soon the same thing happened. Today, all of the VHF and most of the

UHF frequencies have been assigned, and though they are not all used in all areas, they are still assigned to someone. There was no place for the new system, except in the higher UHF area, above television channel 69. The band from 806 to 890 MHz was assigned to land mobile use, and this is what was used. It was, at the time, relatively safe against eavesdroppers, since the few radios that tuned that high were (and still are) expensive. But this still did not solve the problem of having more users than there were channels. So the frequencies would have to be used over and over again—at the same time, without interfering with each other. And that is how the idea of cells came to be.

YES, VIRGINIA, IT'S A RADIO!

For some reason, it never seems to occur to people that a cellular telephone is a two-way radio station. A small one, but nevertheless it's a radio station—that others can listen to. I remember a lawyer who was about to give a talk to some other lawyers about the security of their telephone conversations and their responsibility for confidentiality of client information. He called me for suggestions, and I explained the system to him. Like so many others, he had never thought about it. I did a street corner interview on this issue, and while a few people realized that cellular monitoring was possible, no one seemed too concerned. It might seem that the designers of the cellular system weren't too concerned, either; 30 years after IMTS, they made the same mistakes: easy-to-monitor, easy-to-commit fraud. Fortunately the designers of the new personal communication system (PCS) did learn from the original phone system and made their transmissions digital with anticloning features built in.

Some people who did care were the cellular service providers. They cared a lot, not enough to spend the money to fix the system, but enough to influence Congress into passing the Electronic Communications Privacy Act (ECPA). That way they could "guarantee" that their customers could have private, secure conversations. Just ask them.

MYTHS ABOUT CELLULAR
TELEPHONE TRANSMISSIONS

If you go to a store to buy a cellular phone and ask whether your conversations will be private, the odds are that the salespeople will say yes. What would you expect them to say? Some will even elaborate, saying that it is impossible for anyone to monitor your calls for any of a number of different reasons. The following are the most common myths that are perpetuated about the privacy of cellular telephone transmissions:

- *The frequency changes every few seconds.*
  Not true. Cellular telephones do not automatically change frequencies (channels) "every few seconds." If the phone remains in one cell, the frequency probably will not change at all. There is one interesting incident where a call made from a guy in a Jaguar who was driving around within a particular cell lasted for six hours without changing frequencies even once. The driver had called a 900 sex line. If the call cost him two bucks a minute, his bill would be something like $720! I guess if you can afford a Jag . . .

- *It is against the law to listen.*
  True. According to the ECPA, monitoring cellular conversations is a misdemeanor, the first offense punishable by a $500 fine. The only person I know of to be prosecuted under this law was in the infamous Newt Gingrich incident. One person was arrested for violation of the same law, in this case a cordless phone, but his conviction was reversed by an appellate court. It was appealed to the U.S. Supreme Court, but the justices let the reversal stand by refusing to hear the

case. Sooner or later such a conviction will be upheld, but with hundreds of thousands of scanners and communications receivers already sold, enforcing this law is impossible.

- *It is against the law to own a "scanner" capable of receiving cellular frequencies.*

  Not true. The law that went into effect in April 1994 says that it is unlawful to manufacture radios (originally it was just scanners and not communications receivers) that could tune cellular or could be "readily modified" to restore these frequencies. Radios that were made before April 1994 could still be sold. This does not apply to "authorized" purchasers such as government and law enforcement agencies. Also, the law did not prohibit anyone from modifying radios to restore cellular after they were sold. In many cases, all the manufacturers have done, apparently, is to design the scanner's microprocessor to lock out the cellular band. Before the law even went into effect, at least one engineer had defeated this. He just removed the microprocessor and replaced it with a different one. More on this coming up. Meanwhile, be careful abut ordering a cellular-capable scanner (such as the AR-8000) from outside the United States. U.S. Customs will seize it, your name will go in a file, and you will lose your money.

- *The frequencies are "confidential" and not available to the public.*

  Not true. Cellular frequencies are a matter of public record and available from the Federal Communications Commission (FCC) as well as many other sources. In Appendix 1 are listed the entire band of 832 channels.

- *The police have ways of knowing whether you are listening.*

  Not true. Radios use something called a local oscillator (LO) that generates a signal used to tune the radio to the desired frequency. With the old tube-type radios, the signal was strong enough to be detected some distance away. Countersurveillance experts who found a hidden transmitter could measure its frequency and from that determine the LO frequency of the radio being used to listen to the bug. Then they could use sensitive radios with directional antennas to find the listening post, often to the great surprise of the spy, who would instantly be shot with a Walther PPK (spies always use Walther PPKs). But the solid-state radios of today generate such a weak LO signal that it barely transmits across the average living room, so this doesn't work very well.

  Should someone have an outside scanner antenna, it is possible that it might be noticed, and someone might wonder who is being listened to, but this is not probable cause to kick the person's door in in the middle of the night and confiscate the radios. At least not yet.

A little later, I will get into some ways that cellular can be monitored, but first an explanation of how cellular works, which I'll discuss in the next chapter.

HOW THE CELLULAR SYSTEM WORKS

When a cellular telephone system is installed in a given geographical area, that area is divided into a number of sections called cells, hence the term *cellular*. These cells average about 5 miles in diameter, but depending on use and terrain they may be as little as 1 and as many as 25. San Francisco, for example, is only 49 square miles in area, but GTE Mobilnet has about 20 cells. This is because there are a very large number of cellular phones in use there. In the financial district, half a dozen cells are only a few blocks apart. The cell sites are connected to a central location called the mobile telephone switching office (MTSO), where the computers that control the system are located. This is usually by fiber-optic cables or an 18 GHz microwave link. The MTSO is then connected to the telco CO, where cellular and landline phones are connected together.

VENDORS

Within each area, the FCC licenses two providers of cellular telephone service, a wireline (W/L) and a nonwireline (N-W/L) company. These are the cellular mobile carriers (CMCs), called vendors in this book. The wireline vendor is an established "wire" telephone company, such as General Telephone (GTE Mobilnet), and the nonwire is an independent company such as CellularONE.

FREQUENCIES

Each of these two vendors is assigned a group of frequencies in the band 869.040 to 893.970 MHz. These frequencies are for the cell transmitters. Cellular radio is a "full-duplex" system, meaning that both parties can talk and listen at the same time. The mobile units (cellular telephones) transmit at exactly 45 MHz lower in frequency than the cell transmitters, which is called a "minus offset." So if the channel being used has been assigned the frequency of 877.680 MHz, the signal from the cell transmitter will be on that frequency, and the cellular phone will transmit on 832.680 MHz.

SETS

The first cellular system was called *advanced mobile phone service* (AMPS), which is still used in most of the country. There were originally 666 channels, 333 for each vendor, but because of the dramatic increase in the number of users, a few years later this was increased to the present 832 channels. Each vendor has 416 channels spaced 30 KHz apart. They are arranged in 21 sets, and each set has from 17 to 21 channels. One cell uses, usually, three sets. The sets are arranged in seven groups of three, tagged A through G. So one cell uses one of the seven groups. Other systems have been developed that increase the number of channels, such as N-AMPS (more on this later).

Voice and Data Channels

Each set uses one channel for transmitting data back and forth from the cellular phones to the cell site equipment. This is called the *control* or *data channel*. The remaining channels are for voice transmission. The signal from the cell to the phone is the forward channel, and from the phone back to the cell the reverse channel. So there are forward and reverse data channels and forward and reverse voice channels.

Odd and Even Streams

The forward voice channels contain two separate streams, odd and even. The even stream carries the transmissions to cellular phones that have an even last digit and the odd stream to those with an odd last digit. If the cellular phone number is 249-1774, the last digit being a 4, it is an even number. If the number is 249-1775, it is an odd number. The reverse voice channel, from cellular phone has only one stream. This is transparent to the user, but is of interest to the users of some commercial test/monitoring systems.

Page Channel

In some cellular systems one channel per vendor is assigned as the incoming page channel (IPCH), through which the cell equipment informs a cellular phone that it has an incoming call. They are channels 333 and 334. If the phone is known to be in roam mode the page call may go out on all 21 control channels.

Sites

Each cell area generally has one "site," the physical location of the computer-controlled transmitter/receiver. In some high-use areas, there may be more than one transceiver per cell. There is also, on occasion, a portable radio system located in a given cell, called a "cell on wheels," or COW. Each CMC uses its own equipment and frequencies and is distinct from the other.

Control and Registration

When a cellular phone is turned on, it sends out a data transmission called *registration*. This signal will probably be received by several cell sites, the strength of the signal measured at all of them, and the phone assigned to the cell that receives it at the highest signal level. This is normally the cell in which the phone is physically located.

The registration and calling information (when a call is placed) that is passed back and forth between the mobile telephone and the cell site transceiver is called *capture voice channel assignment* and is in a frequency shift format called "Manchester." The number called, the electronic serial number (ESN), the MIN (the phone number of the phone making the call), system ID for the home system (SIDH), etc., are transmitted four or five times in a 260-millisecond burst. The technical specifications for this are in a publication called *Recommended Minimum Standards* (publication EIA/15-3-B), which is available from the Electronic Industries Association (EIA) at 2000 Eye Street NW, Washington, D.C. 20006. The price is $21.

Handing Off

When the phone moves into another cell, or sometimes when it is located at the edge of the cell (called a fringe area), the signal may be received at a higher signal strength level by the adjacent cell equipment, at which time it will switch to a channel assigned to that new cell. This is called *handing off*.

Outgoing Calls

When the target phone places a call, a series of numbers are transmitted from the phone to the cell site computer over the reverse data or "control" channel assigned to that cell. This data includes the ESN, MIN, the number being called, the power output of the phone, the name of its manufacturer, and various other data. This information is processed by the cell site computer, which compares the ESN and the MIN to make sure they match, and verifies that the account is valid and that the phone has not been reported stolen or turned off by remote control. When this has been done, the computer searches for a vacant channel, assigns it, and then places the call.

Incoming Calls

When a call is placed to a cellular phone, the computer sends out a "page call" that includes various information, including the number of the phone being called. This page call is transmitted either over the IPCH or over the data channel, depending on how the particular vendor has its system set up. If the called phone is turned on, it hears its MIN, and the ringer is activated. Otherwise the system intercept recording is activated, advising the caller that the called phone is either out of range or not turned on, or imparting a similar message.

Borrowing Channels

Normally, the channels used by, or assigned to, a given cell do not change, but at times of unusually heavy use, one cell may "borrow" one or more channels from an adjoining cell. Now it would seem that this could cause the co-channel interference that the layout and assignment were designed to prevent, but that problem is eliminated by shutting down these borrowed frequencies that are normally used in other nearby cells. This is called *blocking*. So a blocked channel cannot be borrowed by yet another cell until it is released.

Reallocating Channels

As near as I have been able to determine, this is a sort of automatic borrowing system. Rather than wait until one cell has all its channels used, the MTSO computer assigns unused cells where they are most likely to be needed. This is done through the channel status table, which is a constant record kept of which channels are being used and which are vacant. Apparently when the borrowing process stops, each cell reverts to the channels permanently assigned to it. This becomes significant when using monitoring systems capable of "specific monitoring" mode (more on this later).

CELLULAR MONITORING

THE LAW

The ECPA does make it unlawful to monitor cellular communications, but some people do not agree with this federal law. They believe that if radio waves cross their property and pass through their bodies, then they should have the right to listen to them. This gets into the enigmatic argument about the right to privacy versus the right to know. People should have the right to privacy in their communications, but privacy should be made available by the providers of the communications equipment, rather than laws telling people that they are not allowed to listen to a radio in the privacy of their own homes.

When Congress was deciding on how much money to give to the FCC in 1992, Rep. Matthew J. Rinaldo (R-NJ) introduced H.R. 1674, which contains the following provision:

> SEC. 8 (d)(1) INTERCEPTION OF CELLULAR TELECOMMUNICATIONS—Within 180 days after the date of enactment of the Federal Communications Commission Authorization Act of 1991, the Commission shall prescribe and make effective regulations denying equipment authorization . . . for any scanning receiver that is capable of
> (A) receiving transmissions in the frequencies allocated to the domestic cellular radio telecommunications service, (B) readily being altered by the user to receive transmissions in such frequencies, or (C) being equipped with decoders that convert digital cellular transmissions to analog voice audio.
> (2) MANUFACTURE OF NONCOMPLYING EQUIPMENT—Beginning one year after the effective date of the regulations adopted . . . no receiver having the capabilities described in subparagraph (A), (B), or (C) of paragraph (1) shall be manufactured that does not comply with the requirements set forth in paragraph (1).

When the law took effect, cellular capable scanners that had been made previously were still readily available. There didn't seem to be any shortage anywhere, but then they slowly started to disappear. This had little effect on people's ability to listen because most of the scanners that were thought not capable of readily being altered actually were—depending on the definition of readily. The Realistic PRO-2006, for example, could have cellular reception restored in 15 seconds using nothing more than a fingernail clipper.

So much for this discussion, now on to monitoring. There are two ways to monitor cellular

93

telephone calls. One is to use a radio, a scanner, or communications receiver. The other way is to use a commercial monitoring or testing system. Some ideas on using a radio, as well as information on the commercial systems, will be presented here, starting with finding the cell sites.

LOCATING THE CELL SITES

If you intend to track calls, it is necessary to know the locations of the cell sites, if possible, the street addresses or the nearest major intersection. There are various ways to find them, and it is suggested that you obtain as many as possible at once, rather than having to go back and do it over again. Remember that there are two vendors, and each has its own site and frequency, completely separate from the other. Keep this in mind as you read through the rest of this section.

Cellular System Maps

Maps showing the location of the cell sites are available from the two companies listed below. Contact them to get specific information, which was not available when this book was completed. Whether the maps have the street address rather than just the latitude and longitude is useful to know before you buy them because the maps are fairly expensive and some of the alternatives may be cheaper. This is particularly true of maps of a large metropolitan area.

Communications Sources
Mobile Services
1919 M St. NW Room 628
Washington, D.C. 20037

International Transcript Services
2100 M St. NW Room 148
Washington, D.C. 20037
202-857-3800

Use a Radio

This method will not get you the actual location, but using it with the field trip will narrow it down considerably. The easiest way to start is to program the 21 data channels for either of the vendors, A or B (but not both at the same time), into one bank, or two if necessary, of a scanner. Lock out the unused channels and start scanning. Make a note of which ones you hear the strongest. Having a radio with an "S" meter makes this much easier. Pick out the three strongest ones and then refer to the frequency tables in Appendix 1 to see if they are all in the same letter group. They probably will be because they are coming from the same location. Lock them out and repeat the process, again referring to the tables, to locate the next strongest cell transmissions, and, again, as far as you are able to go. If possible, change locations and repeat the process. Make notes.

A Field Trip

In a rural or suburban area the sites can be found by the antennas. They are usually mounted on a heavy steel pole 50 to 100 feet in height and are recognizable by the one of two types. The first is the earlier type. On top of the mast is an equilateral triangle made of steel beams, and at each corner is a vertical antenna element. The newer type, made by Decibel Products Corporation, has two to four small metal boxes mounted on each of the three sides. They slightly resemble floodlight fixtures. In an urban area, they are often located on top of tall

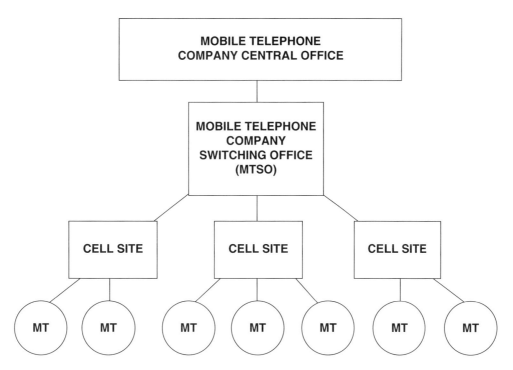

A simple sketch of the cellular system layout. MT = individual cellular telephone.

buildings and cannot be seen from the street. If you have a good vantage point and a telescope, you will see some of them, but making a complete list this way can be difficult.

Keep in mind that in a large city the cells are smaller, so there are more sites to try and find. Having a portable scanner is useful because you can wander around checking out data channels, which will help find some you might have otherwise missed. If you have a radio that has an "S" meter, make notes of the readings and reduce the sensitivity to help zero in on the signals. When it is time to start assigning scanner banks to certain cells, this information will be useful.

FCC Records

The easiest way may be to refer to FCC records. Maybe. Following are short reviews of several sources of these programs. One of them has some of the street addresses of the cellular transmitters, one shows the locations on a computer generated map, and the others have the latitude and longitude. From any of them, you can pinpoint the location or at least narrow it down enough for successful monitoring.

The FCC is the federal agency responsible for assigning licenses and frequency allocations to amateur and commercial radio stations. This includes all local and state (but not federal) government agencies; police and fire departments; and such private businesses as taxicab companies, trucking and construction companies, private investigators and security companies, and paging and mobile telephone vendors, including cellular radio. The information the FCC maintains for each transmitter license is in the following fields:

• Address
• Antenna polarization
• Call sign

- City
- Class of station
- County
- Effective radiated power (ERP)
- Latitude and longitude
- Name of licensee
- Number of mobiles, aircraft
- Number of mobiles, marine
- Number of mobiles, pager
- Number of mobiles, portable
- Number of mobiles, vehicle
- Power output
- State
- Street address of transmitter
- Transmitter elevation
- Transmitter height
- Transmitting frequency
- Type of emission
- Type of service
- ZIP code

These records are divided into the following groups, called subsets, for type of service:

- Broadcast Services
- Common Carrier
- Experimental
- Microwave
- Land Mobile 470–512 MHz
- Industrial Services (except itinerant band, IB)
- Public Safety and Land Transportation
- Industrial Services (IB)
- Special Mobile and 900 MHz
- Aviation and Marine

There are a number of ways to get this information.

Write the FCC

While you are waiting for a reply, you can get married and have kids or go back to college and get your degree. Seriously, this is a waste of time; you probably will never hear from the FCC office.

Visit an FCC Office

It would seem that the field offices don't like people coming in and asking them for information. The last time I visited the FCC was a few months after the Loma Prieta earthquake. The office had moved to the East Bay area equivalent of the boondocks, Hayward. To access FCC records, I was required to give it my driver's license to hold.

Then I was issued one microfiche (no computer terminals here). The reader was on a shelf near the receptionist's window, which was not large enough for a notebook or pad on which to write, and there was no chair, so I had to do the searching while standing up, and I had to lay my coat on the floor because there was no place to hang it. I have had other similar experiences at various FCC offices; the employees at FCC offices I've visited were most definitely not user friendly. Perhaps you may have better luck than did I, but thanks to the following sources, you don't have to find out. Check out the FCC Internet Web site at www.FCC.gov/.

PerCon FCC Database

PerCon is a privately owned corporation that purchases FCC records from the National Institute of Standards and Technology and makes them available to the public. These massive files are available on five CD-ROM disks, for five areas of the United States: northeast, southeast, north central, south central, and western.

Each of the disks contains all of the information fields listed above. They include a search program with which you can find the records you want in any of these categories. The program was written in Clipper, and the records are in .DBF format. It is a very good program, but somewhat tricky to use, and the manual leaves a little to be desired. Give it some time and you will be able to find what you are looking for. This is the only program I am aware of that has the transmitter (including some cell site) street addresses. Installation is easy and takes only a few minutes. Because it is on a CD, only the search program and a few other files are installed to the hard disk drive. This takes fewer than 2 megabytes (MB), but leave space for the custom searches you may decide to make.

The manual could be improved on. Although it does contain the information needed to make a search, it isn't laid out very well. You have to skip around some to follow it, and there is important information it does not include. For example, if you want to find the street address for the cellular sites, you need to know which field defines the type of service you are searching for (e.g., cellular). It is RADIO_SERV. But then which of the many designators is cellular? There are many of them, and nowhere in the manual are they listed.

I tried the browse command but gave up and used X-Tree Gold to search for the key word, *cellular*. Once I found the first occurrence, I scrolled through the fields until I found the designator for cellular. It is CL.

Start the program by changing to the subdirectory where the files are installed and type FCC. The opening menu presents you with a number of choices. One is System Setup, where you can set the screen colors you want (or use monochrome), turn compression off and on, etc. Then there is Import Data, Export Data, and Select Database. The remaining selections are for searching.

In the Browse Data mode, you view the entire listing, the file FCC.DBF, which is, for the western region, 400 MB, and more than 600,000 records. Here, you can search for data in any of the above fields. When you locate something that you want to see in detail, hit the V (for view) key, and the entire record is on the screen, with all fields shown.

Switch to Advanced Query and you can customize your search. Let's say you want to find only the street address for GTE Mobilnet transmitters in the city of San Francisco. This function will build you a database containing only that information. First, at the main menu, make sure that you have selected the main database on the CD: FCC.DBF. Then go to advanced query and enter the information.

The PerCon CD uses Boolean algebra for searching. On the screen is a vertical list of all the fields. Move the cursor to the first field you want to search. In this case it is RADIO_SERV. Hit the ENTER key and you are asked if you want to search a second field or quit. Enter as many fields as you want. To find the street addresses of cellular transmitters in San Francisco, select the city field and enter SAN FRANCISCO. For the next field select AND, then move the cursor down to RADIO_SERV and type in CL, then AND to select the next field, street address. Then select DONE, and it starts to build the database, which you can name whatever you want. In a few minutes it is done.

The Radius Search lets you find records within a specified distance from a given latitude and longitude. Enter the latitude and longitude and the radius (in nautical miles), and the program will find the record of all transmitters within that area, listing only the fields you specify or all fields.

The Box Search is similar to the Radius Search, except that you enter the coordinates (latitude and longitude) for the upper left and lower right corners of the area (box) to be searched. The information returned is the same as with the radius search; you can select what you want to have listed.

In any of these modes, you can build your own custom database, print it, export it to a word processor or database program, and save it under your own filename. Once the database is exported, you can rearrange the fields in dBASE in any order you like, which makes printing easier. If you don't know how to use dBASE, you can also import into the Microsoft Works database View mode, and rearrange them there. This program is very easy to use.

Before you start, read the manual carefully. Some parts seem incomplete in that they don't finish the subject, but you can refer to other sections that have the rest of the information. Although this program is a little tricky to learn, it does do everything it is advertised to do—and more. Although you may have many other uses for it, remember that it is the only program that has street addresses. Also, it has never crashed on me. Each CD costs about $100, and the set of all five is about $450.

The FCC records, in the subsets listed above, are also available from PerCon:

- 01) Broadcast Services
- (02) Common Carrier
- (03) Experimental
- (04) Microwave
- (05) Land Mobile 470–512 MHz
- (06) Industrial Services(except IB)
- (07) Public Safety and Land Transportation
- (08) Industrial Services (IB)
- (09) Special Mobile and 900 MHz
- (10) Aviation and Marine
- (A) Common Carrier and Microwave (2-CD set)
- (B) Industrial Set (2-CD set)

Each CD covers the entire United States. The complete set of 10 is about $1,200. Individual CDs (01 to 10) are about $150 each. The last two listings, (A) and (B), are sets of two CDs and are about $225 each. (A) consists of 02 and 04, and (B) is 06 and 08. PerCon also offers a Master Frequency database for the entire United States, in dBASE format. It has frequency, call sign, type of service, DBA (licensee name), city/county/state (but not street address), and latitude and longitude.

System requirements: A DOS computer 286 or above with DOS 3.1 or above. Recommended is a 386 or 486, with 4 MB of RAM. This program does not require Microsoft Windows, and although you can run it from desktop through a DOS window, this is not recommended unless you have Windows applications that you have to keep running. It will slow the search considerably.

Contact PerCon at the following address or phone number:

PerCon Corporation
4906 Maple Springs/Ellery Road
Bemus Point, NY 14712
Phone: 716-386-6015
Fax: 716-386-6013
www.perconcorp.com/

Scanware Associates

If you don't have a CD drive, consider Scanware Associates' FCC Frequency Retrieval System. This PC-based database, the latest version 2.11, is available on floppy disks. It includes a menu-driven program for finding and sorting the particulars you want, and you can build your own custom databases. They can be exported to dBASE or Works or to a word processor and, of course, can be printed.

The disks are available by state. California, for example, is a set of seven high-density 3-inch disks, compressed with the latest version of PK-Zip. This is a very large program. If all subsets are loaded, California requires a little more than 100 MB. But you don't have to install them all. If you just want cellular and land mobile information, then install only those subsets. You probably don't care what the call sign is, or need the class or service codes or even the DBA, so don't load them. Be sure to leave space for building your own custom files. Usually, 3 to 5 MB should be sufficient.

Installation is easy. Just place the first (program) disk in the drive and type INSTALL. You will be prompted when to change disks. On my 486 DX2 66, it took 17 minutes to load the entire listings. When the program is installed, you will be at the DOS prompt in the subdirectory where you placed the files. Type FCC, hit Enter, and the opening screen presents an ANSI graphics picture of a scanner. Hit any key to begin.

The main menu offers a utility selection where you can change the screen colors, choose any of several screen savers (alas, no flying toasters), turn the sound off and on, and remove/rename files. Once you have made the settings you want, you can use the Browse, or City/County Database search features and format them however you like using the Custom Report Generator.

In Browse, you can look through all the records, selecting which of the 26 fields you want to view. Perhaps the most useful feature is the City/County Database. Here you select the records for whichever city or county you want. In selecting the records to be displayed, you use Boolean algebra, the same as with the PerCon CD: this field AND that field, etc. The Custom Report Generator lets you determine exactly how you will store the information in a file, or how it will be printed.

As with PerCon, the software is a little tricky to use, but after an hour or so you should be able to find what you want and start building your own custom files. Some other interesting features are included: a calculator, notepad, and a pretty good 32-page spiral-bound manual. Read it. Carefully. It is better than a lot of software manuals I have tried to fight my way through. You can separate the listings into different files by city or county, with all other information included and work from there. You can combine two databases into one, use a mouse, and password-protect your files. This is indeed a large program, but remember that you don't have to install all of it.

System requirements: An IBM or PC clone computer 286 or better, a hard-disk drive, floppy 3.5-inch drive. The monitor can be either color or monochrome. This program does not require Microsoft Windows. It does include a PIF file and icons if you want to run it from Windows. This makes it possible to copy customized files to the clipboard to use with other applications such as Word or Works, but will slow it way down. These disks have been released into the public domain and are available, as far as I know, only on the Internet. For more information, contact:

Scanware Associates
7910 NE Double Hitch Court
Bremerton, WA 98310
Phone: 206-698-1383
Fax: 206-698-8207
BBS: 206-871-4228
www.oz.net/~gmcavoy/sw_scanr.html

Grove Enterprises

Grove is perhaps best known as the publishers of *Monitoring Times*, an excellent magazine dedicated to all phases of radios and listening. It has something for everyone. The Grove database is on a CD-ROM, and the map program, called Geo-Whiz (from Kositzky and Associates), is on three floppies.

Installation takes only a few minutes. Place the CD in the drive and type INSTALL. It takes all of one minute. Then put in the floppies (you are prompted when to change disks), which takes about three minutes.

This program is very easy to use. It is also powerful, and therefore a little complex (there is a lot you can do with it), so by all means read the manuals and then take enough time to learn the program.

A simple search goes something like this. You want a printed record of the police frequencies for Portland, Maine. From the main screen, select new search, then enter the city (Portland), the state (ME), and the service type (PP). Hit F10 to start the search and, when the search is done, F5 to print. It's that easy. Now, since there are too many fields for the width of the paper, you can select Custom Output and select only the fields you want (e.g., the frequencies). If the search is for a large area such as Los Angeles, this may take 10 or 15 minutes, but of course smaller areas are much faster.

You can search by any of the fields, such as frequency range, and also set how the files are sorted and displayed on the screen. One example I tried, from the manual, is to find all of the cellular towers in Michigan. When the main screen opens, just enter MI for state, CL for type of service, tab the cursor down to OUTPUT, select MAP, and then hit F10 to start. In a few minutes the search is complete, and you are back at the menu, from which you select OPEN MAP. This takes a minute or two to draw, and then you will see the outline of the state and tiny dots appearing, representing the cellular transmitter locations. On the left is a dialogue box with a list of the sites, with latitude and longitude, that you can scroll through.

From this screen you can do many things. Move the cursor to one of the dots or whatever else and click the left button, and the latitude and longitude are displayed at the bottom of the screen. You can define a geographical area by drawing a box on the screen, Zoom On Area, which can be a state, area code, or ZIP code. You can also zoom in to see the main highways and roads and, with the optional Geo-Whiz Streets program, can find addresses by street and number. This program is easy to use and has many other features and options. I believe you will be as satisfied with it as I have been. Contact Grove for the latest prices and options:

> Grove Enterprises
> P.O. Box 98
> 140 Dog Branch Rd.
> Brasstown, NC 28902
> Phone: 704-837-9200
> Fax: 704-837-2216
> BBS: 704-837-9200
> www.grove-ent.com

Communications Engineering Technologies

If you do not have a CD drive or enough free hard-disk space for the Scanware program, Communications Engineering Technologies (CET) will do a custom search for FCC records in a particular geographical area. You provide the latitude and longitude, and CET will return the data on floppy disk in ASCII or comma-delimited form, which can be imported into a word processor or database file. Records within a 30-mile radius used to be about $80 but may be higher if this area includes a major metropolitan area. A 70-mile radius search is about $175. CET also has an online system, where people can log on to their computers and search themselves. Cost is about $1.50 per minute, paid by credit card. Contact CET for more details:

100

Communications Engineering Technologies
1001 S. Ridgewood Ave.
Ridgewood, FL 32132
Phone: 800-445-0297
Fax: 904-426-0099

Which of these four sources you might want to use will depend on your needs and the type of computer you have, whether you have CD, and the amount of disk space available. I have tried three, PerCon, Scanware, and Grove, and recommend them; I have not tried CET, but a number of postings about them on the Internet have all been positive.

Finding the Latitude and Longitude

There are many ways to find the latitude and longitude of an area. If you have Internet access, you can Telnet the University of Michigan's geographic name server at 141.212.99.93000. When connected, enter your ZIP code, and the latitude and longitude will appear on the screen. Libraries have any number of reference books that will provide the information, including *Dernay's Latitudes and Longitudes in the United States*. Then there are those little brass markers located on sidewalks—the ones you always wondered about. They are called monuments, and if you look closely, you will see a number. Make a note of it and call the U.S. Geological Survey, and you can get the latitude and longitude for that monument.

Another possibility is to use a global positioning receiver (should you have one) or to visit the office of a business that uses two-way radio and look at its transmitter license, which just might be on the wall, where it is supposed to be.

MONITORING
TECHNIQUES
13

ow that you know about finding FCC records and cell sites, let's get back to cellular monitoring: about using a scanner or communications receiver to listen to cellular phone calls, and how it is possible to track a cellular conversation as it is handed off to another cell. I wish to clarify this. I posted a message about tracking on the Internet that several people misunderstood. They seemed to think I meant automatically track, as if the scanner could somehow know which channel the handoff would go to and tune itself to that channel before their wondering ears. It doesn't work like that, but it is sometimes possible for the radio's operator to track a call, if the operator has the know-how, a radio or radios with enough channels, and the location of the cell sites (obtained with the information from the previous chapter).

As part of my former job, I had to learn about the cellular system to demonstrate commercial monitoring equipment and to write the manuals for it, so I know that this works from having done it a number of times. It's tricky and takes concentration, but it does work. I'll get to that shortly, but first things first.

CHANNEL ASSIGNMENT

Because the 395 voice channels have to be used over and over again, they have to be assigned to the cells in such a way that they do not interfere with each other. If two adjoining cells used any of the same frequencies, such interference would happen, especially in the fringe areas. To avoid this problem a number of assignment strategies have been devised, such as fixed assignment, locally optimized dynamic assignment, hybrid assignment, and others. The details are not important here but are published in the Interim Standard IS-3-D by EIA, should you be interested. The price is approximately $35.

Since there is no universal method, different vendors in different areas can assign and tag, or name, the channels however they want to as long as two conditions are met: (a) interference must be eliminated or at least reduced to where it isn't "significant," and (b) the system must be compatible with an adjoining system. At the edge of the system operated by the Jones' Cellular Company in Eastville, Idaho, the channels have to be assigned so that they do not cause interference to the cells at the edge of Smith's Cellular Company in Westville, Idaho.

The cells are often represented as hexagons, making up a "honeycomb," but they are actually more or less round, depending on the terrain. You might make up a list of the cell locations you have and mark them on a map, with your monitoring station at the approximate center. A suggestion to make this easier is to use a separate map for each of the two vendors, W/L and N-W/L (more on this coming up).

Which Channels Go with Which Cells?

The next step is to determine which cells use which frequencies. If you are listening from a rural area, this will be easy enough to figure out (remember about fringe areas), but in an urban area where there are a lot of cells in a small area, it will be a little more difficult.

If you haven't already, program the control frequencies as described earlier. Make notes of the strongest channels you hear. Look them up in the tables (the control channels are in bold type) to see if they are in the same group, A to G. They should be, because most cells have three control channels. Now lock them out and repeat this to get the next strongest control channels. Having a directional antenna is most useful here. Repeat this process until you can no longer determine which signals are stronger than the others. The idea here is to try to map the cell sites based on the strength of the received signal. It will take some practice and patience because the control channel signals are different in intensity from a given location.

There are several computer programs, one of which is Cellular Manager, version 1.0, that shows which cells are adjacent to any other. Enter the strongest control channel that has been received, and the screen will display a honeycomb drawing with the cells designated by a number, 1 through 7, each of which corresponds to A through G. They are available on some BBSs and the Internet.

At this point, depending on how you went about finding the cell sites, you should have a map marked with the locations of one or more of them, the center being the cell whose control channels were received at the strongest signal strength, the cell in which your monitoring station is located. Tag this cell with the letter that corresponds to the group, as listed in the frequency tables. Clear as mud? OK, I'll go over this again.

1. Use the location you are monitoring from as a reference point and mark it on the map.
2. Mark the locations of as many cell sites as you have street addresses or locations for.
3. Lightly (so they can be erased) draw in circles around each site (the size is based on how close they are to each other), so they don't overlap.
4. Program the radio with the 21 control channels and determine which three you receive at the strongest level. Use Cellular Manager if available.
5. Look these three frequencies up in the tables and determine which of the seven groups they go with.
6. Mark the circle where you are located with the letter of that group, A to G.
7. Mark the adjacent circles with the other letters.
8. Continue this with the cells immediately outside the seven original ones, which you might tag A1 through G1. When a call is handed off, it won't necessarily be to one of the six cells surrounding your location. It might go from A1 to G1. This is why I suggested that you get the locations of as many cells as possible at one time.

    If so, then you may or may not still hear the call, depending on two things: (a) the new cell might be out of range, or (b) the new frequency is being used in one of the closer cells, which means that you will hear it rather than the original call because the signal of the frequency in the closer call is stronger.

You now have a map with your monitoring station at the center, the location (as close as you can get it) of the six surrounding cells, and as many outlying cells as you can. The boundaries are temporarily drawn in, and each is tagged with the group (A to G) of frequencies used by each. The boundaries can be changed as your search progresses.

PROGRAMMING THE RADIO

Supposing you programmed all of the 395 voice channels for either of the vendors (A or B) into a 400-channel scanner such as the PRO-2006. Scanner channel 1 would be cellular channel 1 and so on up to channel 395. This is the way some people program their radios, and they can hear only calls at random. When a call is handed off, it is lost, and there is very little chance of getting it back.

The PRO-2006 would have to scan through all 10 banks, which takes too much time. It would stop on every transmission it heard, and you would have to quickly decide whether any call is the one you were trying to recapture. By the time you checked all used channels, the original caller would probably have ended the call. One exception is the one made by the lonely gent in the Jaguar—if it lasts long enough, sooner or later you will find it again, but remember that most cellular calls don't last very long.

A better way would be to program each of the seven groups into their own individual banks, but this would require that the radio have seven banks of 63 channels: the cell your monitoring station is in plus the six that surround it. Another arrangement would be 21 banks of 20 channels, one for each set. Unfortunately, few scanners have such capability, so we do what we can with what we have.

Let's use the PRO-2006 as an example. It has 10 banks of 40 channels. If you want to monitor only one cell, then you can program each of the three sets of 21 into the first three banks, remembering to lock out those that are unused to speed up scanning. To monitor three cells, use banks 4, 5, and 6 for the second cell, and 7, 8, and 9 for the third. Simple enough, but to track a call you need to be able to monitor all seven.

You could program 40 of the channels in each group into banks 1 through 7 and be able to scan all seven, but there are up to 56 voice channels per set so you have, on average, a 71 percent chance of hearing a call originated or handed off. How you program the radio will depend on how many channels and banks there are. Again, work with what you have.

Modify the Radio

Some radios can be modified to increase the number of channels. The PRO-2006 modification increases its 400 channels to more than 1,000, and some of the Bearcat models can also be modified. For more on this, see the scanner modification handbooks available from Electronic Equipment Bank.

Use Two Radios

Using the PRO-2006 as an example, you could have 20 banks, each with one set of voice channels. This would leave one of the 21 sets, which could be added to the 20 banks, one channel per bank.

Listening to two radios at the same time? You cannot listen to two conversations at once and understand what is being said, but you can listen to part of each one, particularly the content of the conversation and the difference in voices. This takes some getting used to unless you have experience in monitoring. After a while, you get used to alternating back and forth by adjusting the two volume controls, or if you want to be tricky, use headphones with one radio going to the right side and the other to the left.

Computer-Aided Scanning

You can also use a computer-aided scanning (CAS) system. I don't want to get into this right now; it is discussed in detail later in the book.

TRACKING

When the phone is about to be handed off, you will hear a low-frequency buzz (the data burst) that lasts about one-fifth of a second. This will alert you to be ready to change banks. Note that this buzz is used for things other than handing off, such as a change in power, but when you hear it, be ready for the switch.

Here, again, is where monitoring experience pays off. Were you concentrating on the sound of the person's voice? When you switch banks, you will often find that one voice sounds much like another. Concentrate. If you are trying to write down what you are hearing, this will interfere with keeping your mind on the voice. Use a tape recorder, if possible, and note only what is necessary: the bank used and, if known, the direction of travel. Maybe you can make up a kind of shorthand using abbreviations and arrows to point directions.

When the handoff comes, deactivate the present bank and turn on the other banks—as many as necessary, depending on which cell you believe the phone is about to enter. Again, remember to consider such things as time of day, direction of travel, etc. Hit the scan button. As radios get smaller and smaller, the buttons get closer together, making it easy to hit the wrong one. Using the eraser end of a pencil or something smaller than your finger helps prevent hitting the wrong button.

As soon as you hear the next channel, it should take only half a second to make the decision. Do the voices sound different? Is the conversation between two women, when you were listening to two men?

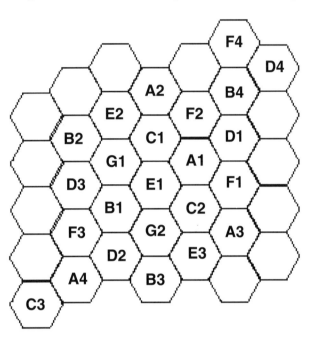

One way that the cells are arranged so that one causes less interference to another.

Watch the display, the bank indicator numbers, not the radio's channel numbers. When the radio switches to the next bank, and you did not recapture the lost conversation, hit the number key that controls that bank to lock it out—at least until you have scanned through the remaining banks where the call may be found. If this fails, reactivate them and listen again. If this doesn't work, then you have lost it or the caller has hung up. Again, remember that cellular calls are frequently very short because of the high cost.

Another factor to be considered is the time of day you are monitoring and the direction of vehicle traffic. In the morning, people move into the metropolitan area, in the afternoon they go back to the suburbs. When you intercept a call you want to track, listen carefully. Often the caller will say where he is or where he just left or where he is headed. Find his general location and direction on the map to determine the next cell he will enter. If the caller does not reveal any of this information, you still know which cell he is in by the bank number of the radio. The call is on a frequency programmed into bank three, which corresponds to cell C, which is outlined on the map.

Think about all this for a minute. What did you learn from this call? Did the caller say something that causes you to want to find him again? Perhaps you are trying to track drug dealers. Did they say something to indicate that they are selling? Did you make a note of the time and cell where you first picked them up? People who work in factories and offices use their phones mostly on their way to and from work. Dealers are out and about most any time of the day or night. All of these little things help make for more successful monitoring. If you concentrate on a few callers, you will get to know a lot about their life-style and be able to anticipate their calling habits.

A TEST DRIVE

OK, let's go over it again, as if you were actually monitoring. You are scanning through the cells and hear an interesting conversation. Quick—what's the first thing you do? How strong is the signal? Is it weak enough that you might lose it because of the signal strength?

When I was testing monitoring equipment, I noted the channel number, looked up the frequency, and punched it into an ICOM R7000, which has better sensitivity and can hear a conversation when some monitoring equipment cannot.

Turn the squelch down. This slightly increases the receiver's sensitivity and reduces the chance of losing the transmission. You do this automatically as you glance at the display to see which bank is active. The channel number isn't important, just the bank. Now glance at the map to see where the cell that corresponds to that bank is located. When the handoff comes, which is the most likely cell? Has the person given his location? Is it on a freeway? Have you drawn heavy lines over the main roads to make them easier to see on the map? What can you tell about the caller from the content of the conversation? Will that give you any ideas on where the caller might be going? With a little practice, this gets easier.

PORTABLE MONITORING

So far, this chapter has been about operating from a base, a fixed location. However, successful monitoring is possible from a vehicle or even on foot. In a vehicle, you might have the same equipment as in a base location and run it from the electrical system to eliminate the problem of batteries discharging—and there would be space for your maps and things.

From a vehicle, you can operate the same way as from a base (that is, using the forward channels), although reception will be limited because your antennas are closer to the ground, and the signal will sometimes be blocked by buildings and whatever else. But you have the advantage of being able to get close to the target phone. If you know who your target is and have a description of the car, or know where the person lives, you can visually search for him.

If you have the person in sight, you can probably receive him on the reverse voice channel, which is always 45 MHz lower than the corresponding forward voice channel. Forward channel 991 is 869.040 MHz, so the transmission from the vehicle will be on 824.040. If your radio is programmed with reverse channels, search through them, the same way as you would from a base location, using forward channels. Everything else is the same, except that the reverse channel signal is weaker than the forward.

If your map is not available, when you intercept the target, look up the frequency (remembering to add 45 MHz) in the tables and determine the group used in the cell that the target phone is transmitting from. The little diagram will tell you which cells (by group, A through G) the handoff can go to. Again, remember that the direction of travel narrows this down.

PRODUCT REVIEW: THE OPTOELECTRONICS SCOUT

I magine being able to follow someone walking down a street and intercepting him when he uses a cellular phone. This is possible with some of the commercial monitoring systems, some portable scanners, and also with the Optoelectronics Scout.

When I received a press release from Opto, I was anxious to try it out for any applications to countermeasures work, as well as its intended purpose: to record and determine unknown frequencies. I was also very anxious to try the reaction tuning feature. I borrowed a Scout and, after experimenting with it for a few weeks, realized that it would be of some, though limited, use in countermeasures. However, for finding unknown frequencies it is a gem.

My first impression of the Scout was that the manual could have been better. Some useful information is omitted; however, this is not a big deal because theinformation is in the product sheet and because the Scout is very easy to learn to use. The Scout looks good—the front panel is clean and not cluttered—and though it weighs only 8.5 ounces, it has a nice heft, like a good gun or tool.

CONTROLS

There are three slide switches and a push button. With the switches, the operator can select which of the four modes are to be used:

- *Normal:* In this mode, the Scout operates as a normal frequency counter.
- *Filter:* The filter reduces random counting, noise, and false signals. Only a solid signal will be displayed.
- *Capture:* With capture engaged, the Scout stores the frequencies it picks up in memory.
- *Recall:* In this mode the stored frequencies, along with the number of hits, are displayed.

The gate push button has a dual purpose: it scrolls through the stored frequencies, advancing one number each time you press it, and it also sets the gate time. This determines how accurately the frequencies are captured and displayed, i.e., the resolution. This has four settings from 10 cycles to 10 kHz.

PARTICULARS

The manual says that the Scout "is not a frequency counter in the traditional sense because it is not intended to be a measurement tool . . . it is actually a frequency recorder." It can store 50 different frequencies in memory and count the number of times each one was received (hits) up to 250 for each of the 50 frequencies. The recorded frequencies can be displayed on the backlit LCD screen.

I don't know of another product like the Scout. It comes with a little, stubby 1-inch antenna (others are available as options) that uses a standard BNC connector. It also has a built-in vibrator, like some pagers, to alert you when it receives a frequency. The significance of this should be obvious, particularly if you happened to have read *The Bug Book*. You see some . . . well . . . interesting people standing around trying not to look important . . . which is hard to do when one of them is wearing a suit, holding a two-way radio, and not smiling. You'd love to find out what frequency they are transmitting on, but you don't like the idea of standing around with an ordinary frequency counter in your hand.

With the Scout, this problem is eliminated. Just walk past the interesting people when they are transmitting, and when you feel the vibration, you hustle around the corner and read the display and then punch it into your portable scanner. Very nice. In a situation where one doesn't have to be so discreet, the beep tone can be used instead of the vibrator. One beep means another hit to a stored frequency; two beeps means that a new frequency has been received.

REACTION TUNE

Not only does the Scout find frequencies, it can also tune a radio to each frequency it detects. This function works with the Realistic PRO-2005 and 2006 if the scanner is equipped with the OptoScan 456 or with communications receivers that have the CI-V computer interface installed (e.g., the ICOM R7100). The idea here is that one can drive (or walk) around collecting frequencies, and the scanner tunes to the ones it has received automatically. Pretty nifty, I think.

PERFORMANCE

How well does the Scout work? Here are the results of some tests I made. I first tried out the Scout by placing it on my desk beside the radios. I used the Scout's stubby antenna and turned on both filter and capture. This was in the evening when the local radio traffic was at a minimum. I heard it chirp, looked at the display, and quickly punched 157.650 into the ICOM R7000 and heard a cab driver calling in. He was within 100 feet of where I was set up.

A little while later, I heard another chirp. I punched in 490.125 and heard a firefighter calling the dispatcher. I looked out the window and saw the flashing red lights about 150 feet away. Several other frequencies were displayed and verified, including a ham radio operator and a sheriff's car. There were some I could not verify, in the aircraft band of 108 to 136 MHz, and some that were vaguely familiar (e.g., cabs and ambulances). Since they stay on the air for such a short time, they were gone before I could tune the ICOM. This was before I got the OptoScan 456.There were no false signals that I saw and no interference from commercial broadcasting stations. Next, I fired up several transmitters to see whether the Scout would nab them, using various antennas. They were first checked on the R7000 to make sure they were working.

Transmitter: ICOM U-16 on low (1 watt) power setting. Different frequencies were programmed in, from 420 to 480 MHz. At a distance of about 25 feet, the Scout scored 100 percent. It grabbed and displayed every one of them.

Transmitter: Alinco dual band (2 meters and 440) amateur radio transceiver on low (1 watt) power setting, on various frequencies from 144 to 148 MHz. Same result as the U-16: 100 percent.

Transmitter: International MicroPower FM broadcast band wireless microphone at approximately 35 milliwatts. Using the stubby antenna (the wrong one) supplied with the Scout, I had to hold the antennas close to each other to get it to register. I switched to the rubber duck from the Alinco dual band and got the same result. Next, I used a long telescoping antenna, extended to half-wave, and the Scout logged it from across the room. The antenna makes a very big difference.

Transmitter: Cordless telephone base unit (49 MHz) with about 100 megawattts RF output, using the built-in antenna. With either antenna on the Scout, it would not register until the antennas were about 2 1/2 inches apart, with both vertically polarized. But when I switched to a telescoping type, Scout picked it up across the room.

Transmitter: Fisher-Price Wireless Baby Monitor, with estimated 50 milliwatts RF output. From across the room, the signal at 49.9 MHz pegged the "S" meter on the R7000, but the Scout didn't detect it. I had to place the antennas close together to make it read. After that, the Scout would beep every few seconds with a slightly different reading, which I assume is the instability of the transmitter; this didn't happen in any of the other tests. Using a 36-inch, telescoping, all-band scanner antenna, the range increased to across the room.

Transmitter: Cellular phone, Panasonic EB-3510 600 mw portable. Using the Scout's stubby antenna, from 25 feet away, it scored 100 percent. Every transmission was displayed.

Field Test
I took the Scout with me on a weekday and wandered around the city to see what I could find. I found much. Starting out, as I got on the Sutter Street bus, I picked up the driver using his radio to call in something that I couldn't understand—some weird terms and numbers that might have meant "the air compressor on this bus isn't working so I may not have any brakes," or "have a pepperoni pizza waiting at the end of the line." Whatever, the Scout grabbed the signal and displayed the frequency in the 480 MHz UHF band.

During the day, I logged police cars as they passed me, taxicabs, delivery trucks, and, in the financial district, tons of cellular signals. Most were the reverse channels, but a few were forward. If I had a portable scanner that can use the reaction tune feature, I could have monitored these calls.

I wandered around an area where there are dozens of messengers lounging about waiting for a pickup or delivery. When one of them used his radio, the Scout snagged the frequency.

Although I did not have a portable scanner to reaction tune or even verify what the Scout displayed, I knew it to be accurate from knowing about what it should display. The San Francisco Police Department came in on 465.050 to 465.550 MHz; messengers were in the 800 MHz area they use; ditto taxicabs and cellular.

CONCLUSION

The Scout is a fascinating device that I highly recommend. Although the low bands are not as responsive, above 144 MHz the Scout performed like a champ. Again, the type of antenna makes a very big difference.

The Scout is very easy to use, has good sensitivity, and rejects false signals such as intermod. Not only is it great for its intended purpose, finding unknown frequencies, it is also excellent for another purpose: monitoring what is happening in the immediate area.

This is something I like to be aware of, and I have my PRO-2006 programmed with the repeater input frequencies of the local police and fire departments and a few other services, but the 2006 has only 400 channels. With the Scout, I will hear any of these services if they transmit within 100 yards or so without having to program anything. The magic of reaction tune.

Indeed, the Scout is a fascinating device that I think anyone would be happy to own, consistent with the high quality you can always expect from Optoelectronics.

COMPUTER-AIDED SCANNING 15

As you have seen in the sections on monitoring, not having enough banks can be a problem. It is well and good that the new Super Belchfire 200B has 76,000 channels, but what the hell good are they if all of them are in only 10 banks? The answer to this problem is to let a computer control the radio. For this to work, the radio has to be connected to the computer, generally through one of the RS-232 COMM ports. Some radios have such a port built in; others require modification.

OPTOELECTRONICS

Opto has two CAS systems: the OptoScan OS-456 for the Realistic PRO-2005 and 2006 and the OS-535 for the PRO-2035 and 2042. The regular price at the time this book was written was around $300, but they are sometimes on sale for about $200. I bought the 456 for my PRO-2006.

What You Get

The OptoScan consists of a circuit board that installs inside the scanner and connects it to a computer. This works on practically any DOS computer; you don't need a Pentium. It runs fine on my 486 and will also run on a 386. It also runs on the Mac. Included is a well-done assembly manual, the RS-232 cable, and a disk with several demo programs such as Scanner Wear, ScanCat Gold, and Radio Manager.

Features

Depending on the software used, OptoScan increases the scanning rate to twice its normal speed and decodes and displays CTCSS, dual-tone multifrequency (DTMF), and DCS. Again, depending on the software, you can set up as many banks as you want, with as many channels in each as desired.

Assembly

Having a little mechanical ability in general and knowing how to solder are all you need—the manual makes it easy. I put mine together in about two hours, which included being distracted by one of my favorite old-time radio shows, *The Shadow*. In a nutshell, you remove the top and bottom covers and the backup battery compartment and mount the battery to the side of the chassis with the included double-stick tape. Next, you unplug four cables in the radio and plug them into the OptoScan board and then take the included set of cables and connect them from the Opto board to where they originally went in the radio. One minor problem is that you have to trim the edges of the connectors with an X-acto knife, otherwise they are too difficult to plug together.

113

This is the OptoScan system for computer control of a scanner, the Realistic PRO-2006.

Next, install the board. It fits in easily, although if you place it before you attach the rear panel (contrary to what the manual says) it goes together a little more easily. Then solder two wires (clearly illustrated in the manual) and install the rear panel. Double-check everything you have done, pop the covers back on, and it's done.

Connect the included cable to the radio and the computer and load one of the software demo programs that is supplied. In a little while, you'll be up and running, and a whole new world of monitoring will open up. The OptoScan is an excellent product with which I think anyone will be pleased.

DELTACOMM

According to the manufacturer's ads, this is a complete system: it includes everything you need to interface the radio to the computer, including cables and software. It is available for the R-7000, R-8500, and R-9000. The R-7000 requires modifying for the "S" meter and installation of the CI-V computer interface.

Also required is a software package (not included) such as ScannerWear, ScanCat, Scan Star, Visual Wavelengths, or Wave for the Mac. Call or write for details. For more information, contact:

Delta Research
P.O. Box 13677
Wauwatosa, WI 53213
Voice and Fax: 414-353-4567

SOFTWARE

There are several programs available, and in my opinion none of the ones I reviewed are as easy to use as they could be. They are all too intensive, too complicated. Someone should come up with a simple program that is set up with a step-by-step multiple-choice menu. Maybe something like this:

Welcome to the new Belchfire CAS Main Menu. You can program up to 500 entries.

First, select which entry, 1 to 500.

Next, do you want to program a list or a range of frequencies?

Enter the list with each frequency followed by the # key.

Enter the range of frequencies followed by the * key.

Hit the SAVE key on your main menu.

Now, hit the START SCAN key on your main menu.
To activate or deactivate (toggle) any entry, hit the ESC key and then the entry number, 1 to 500.

To display the contents of any entry, hit the CTL key and then the entry number; 1 to 500.

Why can't it be that simple? You could program the local police into entry 1, the fire department into entry 2, the FBI into entry 3, etc. Then you could program the local police and fire departments—but not the FBI—into entry 4 or all general mobile photo service (GMRS) and all local police and only the main fire department into entry 5, and so on. But no one has developed such a program, so we work with what is available. Some of these CAS programs are as follows:

Scanstar
This is a fairly easy-to-use program with a great many useful features, including the following:

- Having unlimited frequency and bank capacity
- Storing information settings for up to 10 radios
- Working on most popular radios
- Having output for CTCSS and DTMF decoders

There are a lot of choices offered in how you customize Scanstar and useful help files. Once done, you can set up as many "banks" as you want, with however many frequencies you want in each one. But keeping track of them, and switching from one to another, isn't easy. The program can't display the individual banks, the "entries," alone—each one displays all of the individual frequencies. So with many entries programmed, you have to scroll back and forth to find what you want to activate.

Among the radios it works with are the ICOM R7000, 7100, and 9000; OptoScan 456 PRO-2005, and 2006 conversion; various Yeasu models; and a lot more. To try it out, a demo copy is available free from the BBS. System requirements are a DOS computer, 286 or faster, 2 MB of RAM, a hard-disk drive, and a transistor transistor logic (TTL) to RS-232 cable. Some radios may require internal modification.

Wave Links
Wave Links is an intermediate-level computer control scanner program. It currently supports the Opto 456 and 535 and imports Scout Data. It is a comprehensive system that supports many modes of operation, such as Scan, Search Direct, and manual modes of operation—so sez the producer.

Visual Wave Links
Visual Wave Links adds a new dimension to scanning. Using the control features of Wave Links and the Visual Interface of Geo_db, scanner users can now localize the hits (transmissions received) on a computer map display. Users can configure the display to any level of detail, color, and labeling they desire. Icons are displayed, allowing users to click and display the hit location data. Accessing the visual display allows users all the features of Geo_db, which include loading and displaying data points. Again, so says the producer. I have not reviewed either of these products.

Wave Links is about $69.95 and Visual Wave Links about $129.95. They are produced by and available from:

Per-Con Corporation
Voice: 716-386-6015
Fax: 716-386-6013
E-mail: sales@perconcorp.com
www.perconcorp.com/

Probe 2.0

The producer of Probe, for whatever reason, did not want it reviewed in this book, so it is not. It has been reviewed in *Popular Communications*, and here are a few selected comments from that review:

- The strength of Probe is in its ease of use.
- Probe is designed for set and forget, whether scanning or searching.
- The informative screens provide a lot of information, most of which can be directly imported from the PerCon CD.
- Overall, the Probe is very impressive, and I use it almost daily. For computer control of a scanner it is hard to beat.

The entire article in *Popular Communications* was very positive, not a single criticism. Other reviews were similarly positive, pointing out that it is the fastest CAS program on the market. Note that this version of Probe (2.0) is for the Optoelectronics OptoScan systems for the PRO-2005, 2006, 2035, and 2042

SUMMARY

With these techniques and CAS programs, one can increase the effectiveness of cellular monitoring 1,000 percent over just programming a scanner sequentially with as many frequencies as it has channels. But tracking a particular call is still tricky. The next chapter is about commercial monitoring systems made specifically for intercepting a particular cellular phone and tracking it as long as it is within range.

COMMERCIAL MONITORING SYSTEMS

Sales of commercial monitoring devices are restricted, and possession is a violation of federal law. The Electronic Communications Privacy Act prohibits the manufacture and possession of any device made for the specific purpose of monitoring cellular radio frequencies. Part of the text of the ECPA follows:

Title 18 USC section 2512: Manufacture, distribution, possession, and advertising of wire, oral, or electronic communication intercepting devices prohibited:

(1) Except as otherwise specifically provided in this chapter, any person who intentionally:

(b) manufactures, assembles, possesses, or sells any electronic, mechanical, or other device, knowing or having reason to know that the design of such device renders it primarily useful for the purpose of the surreptitious interception of wire, oral, or electronic communications, and that such device or any component thereof has been or will be sent through the mail or transported in interstate or foreign commerce;

(iii) shall be fined not more than $10,000 or imprisoned not more than five years, or both.

In the first edition of *The Phone Book*, I wrote, "I do not know of a single instance where this part of the ECPA has been enforced. A number of manufacturers produce cellular monitoring systems, but since the federal and local law enforcement agencies buy most of them, this is probably why they have been left alone."

That has changed.

A few years ago, I worked for a company that made a commercial intercept system. Actually, three of them. I was a technician who built, tested, and demonstrated them. I even delivered them to an agency of the Mexican federal government and the now defunct Spy Factory.

Well, that company has since been raided by the feds. The owners of this company are presently under indictment and eventually will either go to trial or cop a plea. So, the feds are now getting serious about the sale of cellular intercept equipment—just as they are about surveillance transmitters.

Now, consider that the phrase "the design of such device renders it primarily useful for the purpose of the surreptitious interception of wire, oral, or electronic communications" may be subject to interpretation. Some of the equipment described here does more than just monitor and record cellular conversations, such as measuring signal strength and quality and monitoring and logging channel activity.

So, the manufacturers have argued in court, such functions qualify it as test equipment. The government says otherwise. One unit, the Cellmate, has been advertised for years as an interception system without any mention of it also being a "test instrument." I should know; I am the one who produced some of these ads. So the manufacturers' argument doesn't hold up. Also, some systems are sold in kit form, meaning that assembly is required, so this supposedly exempts them, including the Digital Data Interpreter that you will read about in this chapter. Whether it is an interception unit remains to be seen, but as far as I know it is still being produced.

So, should you desire to own one of these devices, be aware that you will probably be violating federal laws just by having it.

THE HARRIS TRIGGERFISH

Some of the first commercial cellular monitoring systems were made by the law enforcement products division of Harris, the semiconductor manufacturer. One of its units, the Triggerfish, a single-cell system, fits inside an attaché case and operates from a custom-made receiver and an Apple notebook computer.

The Triggerfish can also be configured as a multicell system. It was on display at the TREXPO (Tactical Response Exposition) in beautiful downtown Burbank in February 1994. This was a get-together for SWAT team people, local and federal law enforcement, and the military—the "Velcro guys." There were a number of workshops; since I was a guest speaker on electronic surveillance, I was allowed into the exhibition hall. I should have spent more time looking at the Triggerfish but got distracted by the displays.

There were enough submachine guns to win World War III; Uzis, MACs, HKs; dozens of Colt, Beretta, and Ruger pistols; lots of sound suppressers ("silencers"); all kinds of devices for breaking through doors, from simple battering rams to compressed air gizmos that spread the frame apart; and a video version of *Hogan's Alley*, the game where you use a laser pistol to shoot the bad guys on a wall-size screen display. After I blew away a lady pushing a baby carriage and the bad guys shot me six times, the operator kicked me out.

Anyway, the multicell system is about the size of a big-screen TV and needs a van to tote it around. Depending on how many "modules" are installed, it can monitor up to 21 control channels at one time and has an unlimited memory for specific cellular phone numbers. The cost is somewhere around $30,000. The guy who had it set up at the booth told me it is an excellent system, one of the best. For information, inquire on agency letterhead only. If you are not qualified, you will not get the information, but you might get your name in a computer file in Washington.

Harris Corporation
P.O. Box 91000
Melbourne, FL 32902

CUSTOM COMPUTER SERVICES' DDI

Custom Computer Services (CCS) manufactures the Digital Data Interpreter (DDI), which interfaces a personal computer and modified receiver. The DDI is a small aluminum box, about 6 x 5 x 4 inches, that contains firmware that decodes the Manchester signals sent over the cellular data channels and displays it on the computer screen. It works with any DOS computer and an ICOM R-7000, 7100, or AR-3000 communications receiver or a Realistic PRO-2006 scanner. When the DDI is assembled, the operator can monitor cellular transmissions and observe the MIN, relative signal strength signal quality, and various other information.

The ICOM and Realistic radios have to be modified. This requires some knowledge of electronics and is not for beginners; the 2006 requires drilling two holes in the back panel for the two connectors and soldering in a ribbon cable, as well as replacing several components. The R7000 modification requires soldering a ceramic filter to one of the circuit boards and tacking on a cable. Again, not for beginners. Once this is complete, plug the cables in, load the software, and make the initial settings. Configuring and operating the DDI is not at all difficult, but it will take an hour or so to get used to it, since the manual is unorganized and incomplete. Some of the functions are not even mentioned, but they can be figured out.

Once it is up and running, the DDI defaults to the general monitoring mode, in which it intercepts conversations as they are processed through the control channel it is tuned to. On the screen are displayed the MIN, frequency and channel number, relative signal strength, date and time, and the new channel when the call is handed off. It automatically tracks the call.

In the specific mode you can program 10 cellular phone numbers, and the DDI will lock onto them if they are used to make or receive calls within a certain geographical area. The DDI has a number of options, such as automatically activating a tape recorder, making and storing a log of all the calls it hears, which can be exported in ASCII and edited on any word processor. The user also has the option of changing the control channel, so the DDI does not have to be in the same cell as the calls it intercepts. If you are located in cell A and the person you want to intercept lives in cell D, you can select a control channel for that cell. The DDI is the only system I know of that intercepts the reverse data channel and decodes the information, which includes the MIN of the calling phone, the SIDH, manufacturer of the phone, and the number called.

Opinion
While working for CSI, I assembled and tested quite a few of these systems and found that it is the best and most versatile single-cell system I have used. It is easy to learn (despite the manual), has unlimited specific number storage (in banks of 10 each), and has a log that can record exactly which information the user desires, including reverse channel.

Options
CCS has a version of the software that does display electronic serial numbers, but it is for sale only to law enforcement agencies, and purchase orders are verified before the sale is made. The DDI unit includes the standard software package to operate it, and one program works with all listed radios. The company also has a "law enforcement version" that is simplified and has fewer commands for easier use in the field.

BLAH, BLAH, BLAH

What do you hear when you monitor cellular radio? The same things you would hear on landline phones if you tapped them: people talking about the things people talk about. Husband and wife fighting over who forgot to take out the garbage, business people who are plotting to screw other business people, drug dealers who are setting up buys, and, more often, just people staying in touch. These are usually short calls (because cellular is so expensive) like, "Clem, yew git yore ass home right now. An' don't yew be stoppin' fer any beer, either . . ."

"Yes, dear. Yes, Sadie . . ."

It is 99.9 percent b-o-r-i-n-g, and rarely will you hear anything that is of any real interest unless you have "tapped" the phone of a particular person. Your boss, your spouse . . .

119

The Portable Monitoring Station

Also restricted, this is a complete DDI unit built into a small suitcase. It includes the forward and reverse channel modules, a 486 notebook computer, and tape recorder. Additionally, it does the following:

- Works with both AMPS and extended total access communications system (ETACS) systems
- Monitors forward and reverse channels
- Scans 50 channels per second
- Has general and specific modes
- Stores up to 250 numbers in specific mode
- Works unattended
- Intercepts both odd and even at the same time

CCS is in the process of developing a multicell system, which will use a number of the RF modules and DDI boxes controlled with one notebook computer. This will probably be the lowest priced multicell system available. Sales are restricted.

Custom Computer Services
P.O. Box 11191
Milwaukee, WI 53211
414-781-2482
Fax 414-781-3241
www.ccsinfo.com

CES OKI 900

This is another system I assembled and demonstrated. It is comparable to the DDI, as it does essentially the same thing, but is not quite as sophisticated. It consists of an unmodified Oki 900 cellular phone, a DOS computer (any type), a software package, and an interface cable. Because I have not been involved in the production of this system for several years, I do not know whether it is still available.

The interface is made by a small company south of San Francisco and is resold exclusively, the last I heard, by Cellular Evaluation Systems, in Union City, along with the software. You provide the phone and computer. Assembly consists only of plugging the DB-9 end of the interface cable to the computer and the other to the Oki. The software takes only a few minutes to install, and it is ready to work. The following is from the manual I wrote:

Cell-Scan is a single-cell monitoring system that can be set to scan automatically through all or selected cellular voice channels, both Wireline and Non-Wire, or only to search for specific cellular (MIN) numbers that have been programmed into it. Ten numbers can be scanned at once, and any quantity of ten number files can be programmed, limited only by the computer's disk storage.

It operates from one particular control channel, which can be changed as desired, so the unit does not have to be in the same cell as the target phone(s).

As this unit, which I named Cell-Scan, can operate on a Hewlett-Packard palm-top computer, and the interface to the Oki phone is nothing but a small cable, this is the smallest cellular monitoring system that was available at that time. You can literally put it in your pocket.

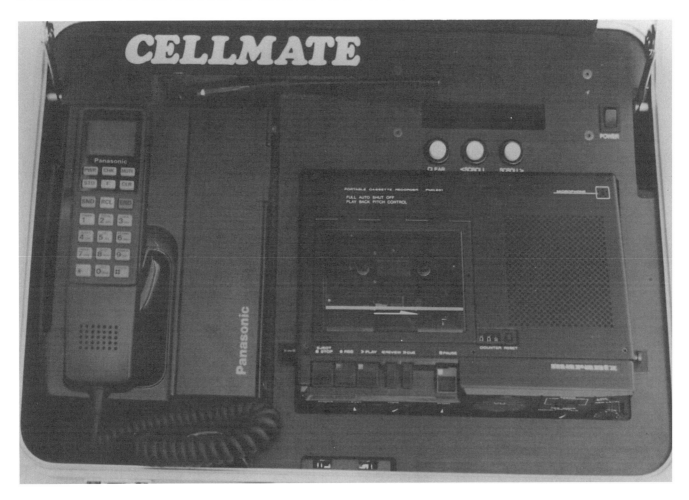

This is the Cellmate that was the impetus for the recent raids, arrests, and trials concerning cellular monitoring. I built more than 100 of them while working for the company that was then producing Cellmate. The window at the top is a DTMF decoder and display made by MoTron in Eugene, Oregon.

How well does it work? I demonstrated this system for a number of government agents on several occasions. It does indeed work. Quite a few specific numbers were intercepted, to the satisfaction of the agents, and a number of them were purchased. However, there are two problems with Cell-Scan. Because the interface cable plugs into the Oki jack where external power goes, you have to use the battery, which means you have to keep a spare in the charger as they last only a few hours. One of the demos I did involved five of these things working at the same time. While explaining the operation in my very limited Spanish, I was running back and forth switching batteries and placing them in the chargers. A very bad design flaw.

The other problem is that it sometimes stops working without warning, flashing a message that the "Oki phone is not responding." Fixing this takes only a few seconds by unplugging and reconnecting the interface cable, but whatever the operator was listening to is lost.

The last I heard, CES was developing the system to work with other Oki models and some by AT&T, and these two problems are being eliminated. All things considered, I think this is a very nice system, and well worth the price. The interface cable and software goes for about $400.

CELL-TELL

NOTE: The following address is from the first edition of *The Phone Book*. I do not know whether Cell-Tell is still available, but I doubt it. The phone number I have for the manufacturer has been disconnected.

Cell-Tell
Operative Supply
P.O. Box 2343
Atlantic Beach, NC 28512

Cell-Tell is based on a modified Panasonic transportable cellular phone that is fitted into a watertight Pelican hard-shell carrying case and includes a DTMF touch-tone decoder and cassette recorder. This is a completely automatic system; once programmed with the specific target numbers, it can be left unattended. When a call is intercepted, the built-in voice-operated transmitter (VOX) starts the recorder. The price of Cell-Tell was under $3,000 retail and under $2,000 wholesale. Discounts are available for quantity and prepaid orders.

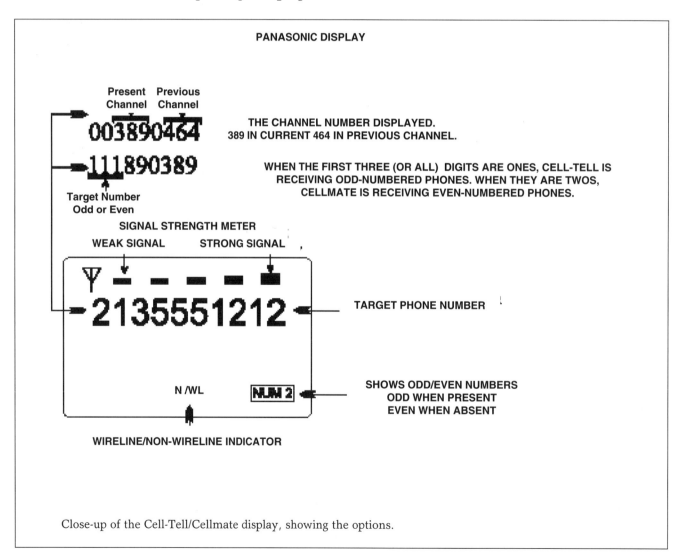

Close-up of the Cell-Tell/Cellmate display, showing the options.

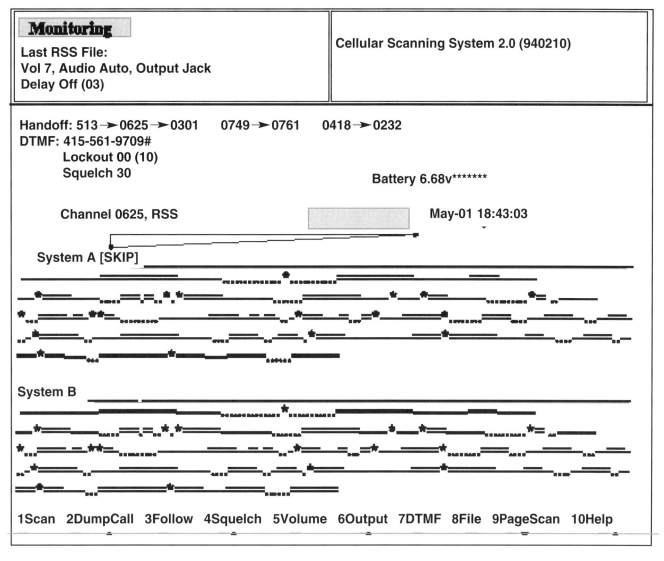

This is the main operating screen of the Oki 900 cellular interception system. When the company I was working for first started producing it, the boss asked me for a name. So I called it Cell-Scan.

The ad states that the Cell-Tell does the following:

- Monitors either cellular system, A or B
- Identifies unknown cellular mobile phone numbers
- Identifies the active channel by number
- Decodes touch-tone phones used to access voice mail, answering machines, etc.
- Targets one to ten mobile numbers for all calls made in or out
- Automatically records both sides of conversations
- Tracks hand-offs from cell to cell when following vehicle
- Tones decoder and autostart recorder
- Comes with connection cables for direct recording/decoding/monitoring of telephone landlines, watertight hard-shell Pelican case, manual, pocket cards, battery, charger, 12-volt cigarette cord, decoder and recorder AC adapters, all connection cables, and warranty

How It Works

The EPROM (eraseable, programmable, read-only memory) chip inside the phone that contains the programming is removed, modified, and replaced. Then a series of instructions, based in part on a random number and the phone's ESN, is entered to activate it. This prevents anyone from copying the chip and making his own Cell-Tell.

In the storage area (register) where the MIN would normally go, the user enters the number of the phone he wants to monitor. Then when a call is placed or received on that phone, Cell-Tell locks onto it and records the conversation, the same as if it were the target phone.

Opinion

Cell-Tell is a clone of the original Cellmate, which was designed by the company I worked for. Other than the case and model of tape recorder, it is the same, right down to the exact programming sequences.

SUMMARY

All of these systems work, but none of the ones I have used are 100 percent when it comes to intercepting specific numbers. Remember that any given cell has one to three control channels and these single cell systems operate on only one. So if a call in the cell being monitored is processed by one of the two data channels the system is not tuned to, it will not pick up the call.

Of the three, the Oki 900 is the smallest and most portable system, using a palm-top computer. It can be hidden in a coat pocket and is very easy to use. However, it sometimes quits working and has to be reset, and with the 900 model phone, you cannot use an external power supply. It runs only on batteries.

Cell-Tell and CellMate are completely automatic. Once the target numbers have been entered, both can be left in a hiding place in the cell where the target phones are. If in a vehicle, these phones can operate from the cigarette lighter with the included cable. Both are the easiest to use of all—an operator can learn it in 10 minutes.

The DDI made by CCS is the most versatile of all and the only one that will intercept the reverse channel. This is required if the operator needs to know the numbers being called from the target phone. It takes longer to learn and is a little tricky, so spend an hour or so with it to get used to the settings. It is not portable (that is, not battery powered) but can be powered by a vehicle cigarette lighter.

I think the Portable Monitoring Station from CCS is, all things considered, the best system available. It does everything the DDI does and is packaged in a fiberglass carrying case. It works on AMPS, total access communications system (TACS), and ETACS systems; has a built-in tape recorder; and can store up to 250 specific target numbers.

Frankly, I have little use for any of them. After a year and a half of building and testing and demonstrating them, I have found that cellular conversations are 99.99 percent b-o-r-i-n-g. Almost worse than television. You will hear small-time drug dealers, bored housewives and househusbands, working people on their way to and from the office, guys and girls bitterly and endlessly fighting over such trivial things as who was supposed to take out the garbage last night, people checking their voice mail and listening to messages that mean nothing to anyone else but them, such as a reminder of the meeting with Mr. Schnozzola in accounting. You might listen for months and never hear anything exciting. Why bother? There is a lot of action on the police and federal government frequencies.

Will Monitoring Ever Be Stopped Completely?

No. The laws mentioned above cannot be enforced, there is no way to know if someone is or is not listening, and there are hundreds of thousands (millions?) of scanners already on the market that cover cellular frequencies. And even those that "cannot be modified" have been modified.

There are also converters available that were made before the law prohibited them, radios that can intercept cellular on image frequencies (see glossary), and even old manually tuned TV sets that can pick up cellular calls. Also the law does not apply to "authorized" purchasers, such as law enforcement agencies, meaning that they can listen whenever they want to.

Since the first edition of this book was written, the technology for reconstructing cellular digital conversations has become available. It requires a fast personal computer, and, as of this writing, the software is available on the Web.

The code-division mulitple-access (CDMA) system, explained elsewhere in this book, will defeat all but the most determined and well-equipped listeners, but sooner or later someone will find a way to defeat the spread-spectrum modulation it uses.

What about Digital Encryption?

Later in this book you can read about digital and spread spectrum, as they apply to people who use scanners and communications receivers. However, this does not include those who use modified phones. I will explain. No matter what the cellular vendors do to their system or to your cellular phone to "scramble" your conversations, there has to be a way to convert them back to ordinary speech. Otherwise, you wouldn't be able to use it, right?

Whatever does this is inside (or received by and temporarily inside) the phone, and whatever is inside the phone can probably be analyzed and duplicated. It may be very difficult, it may take teams of engineers with powerful computers and high-end logic analyzers, but eventually it will be done. And that technology will find its way onto the black market and become available to those who have the right connections.

It is possible that there will be a two-part key (shared secret data) that, I believe, is based on Data Security's RSA algorithm. The RSA is explained in Chapter 24, but in a few words, if a long enough key is used, it is literally unbreakable and will be for years to come. However, such secure keys will not be available to the general public. The feds will not let us use anything they cannot defeat. And if the feds can do this, so can big corporations' industrial espionage experts. And, again, sooner or later this technology will be available on the underground market.

So, the answer is no; monitoring will never end. The feds will always be able to monitor the cellular, the landline, and the new PCS conversations. Big corporations will have the funds to set up the facilities necessary, but for the hobbyist, only the conventional analog cellular will still be possible to monitor.

TRACKING CELLULAR PHONES

Remember O.J.? How he was located through his cellular phone? This means that *you* can be located through your cellular phone. Yep. Whether you are using it or not, as long as it is turned on, it is sending out a periodic "registration" signal. And that's all that is needed to zero in on you: where you are and where you've been. Maybe you don't care. You aren't the subject of a manhunt. You haven't mailed any nasty letters to the White House or the FBI. No one is looking for you. So what do you care? But if you do care, if you don't like the idea of being tracked, then just don't use a cellular phone. If you must, keep it turned off except when you are making a call. Use a pager to alert you when someone calls and then call that person back.

HOW DO THEY DO THAT?

Cell site antennas have several elements on top of the tower. One is for transmitting, and at least two are for receiving. With two receiving antennas, when a signal comes in, the system can determine its direction, because it is receiving from two slightly different angles. If these two angles, or bearings, are projected from the antenna, the point at which they meet is the source of the signal. *You.* This is called *triangulation*. And since the registration signal from the cellular phone includes the channel number, the system also knows which cell you are in. One example of this is a special service (I don't know what it is called) that businesses can subscribe to. A dedicated phone line is set up from the office computer to the cellular switch, and the boss can use it to keep track of where the company vehicles are at any given time. Supposedly, this can be to within 100 feet.

The idea of using a cellular phone as a surveillance transmitter occurred to me while I was testing the Cell-Scan surveillance system that is based on the Oki 900 phone. With this system, the Oki can be used as a normal cellular phone, but when in use as a monitoring system the power switch is placed in the off position, so the display is blank. The phone is controlled, through the cable, by the computer.

So why can't the same thing be done without its being part of the Cell-Scan system? Why not modify it so it can transmit with the power switch and display turned off? Just bypass the power switch and replace it with another, hidden under the battery, along with a second one to turn the display off and on.

This is a fascinating idea, because it would eliminate the two main problems with a room audio transmitter: range and installation. Concerning range, unless a person has the chance to test a transmitter, he may not know for sure whether it will send its signal to the listening post. But cellular phones have no such limitations. With installation, instead of finding a place for the bug, find a reason to get into the target area, call a prearranged number, and just leave it there. It may run up a large bill, but this is insignificant when the stakes are high, such as in corporate espionage. And to eliminate the possibility of the phone call's being traced, it can be rented on a prepaid basis. Big deposit, no ID required.

There is another way to use a cellular phone for eavesdropping. Some phones, such as the Motorola Flip Phone, have an auto-answer feature. You are at a meeting where promotions are being discussed and want to hear what the others are saying about you. So you find an excuse to leave the room for a few minutes, hustle down to the nearest phone booth and call your phone, which you left lying on a chair. It auto-answers, and you can hear everything being said in the room. You might also set up a call-forwarding system in your home. You call there, and the system automatically calls the cell phone, and activates a recorder.

HOW I MIGHT DO IT

To make a bug out of a cellular phone, I would use both a pocket-sized model and a large, transportable one. The large phone would have the insides removed, and the small one, with the case removed, would be placed inside. The keyboard would be accessible through a hole cut in the space beneath the transportable's battery, and extra batteries for the small phone would be placed in the space left over. If anyone were suspicious, he might try to turn the transportable on, but nothing would happen, so he would probably assume it was defective or that the battery was dead.

So if someone should leave a phone in your office, be suspicious. Disconnecting the antenna may not stop it from working. Also remove the battery and see what is underneath. Another keypad? Switches? Go about damage assessment the same way as you would if you found a phone transmitter. Meanwhile, place the phone under a pile of rags in the custodian's closet and wait to see whether someone comes back to get it.

NO ASSEMBLY REQUIRED

Cellular phones are controlled by a microprocessor, the same as a computer. And there is an existing program, in another chip, usually an EEROM (electronically eraseable, read-only memory), inside that contains the instructions that the microprocessor controls.

It is possible to rewrite these instructions to make the phone do things is wasn't designed to do. Cell-Tell, for example, instead of switching the MINs would be set to listen for a certain code sent from the eavesdropper. When it was heard, the ringer would be silenced, the display turned off, and the phone would auto-answer. So if you were driving down a freeway and someone activated such a modified phone, that person would be able to hear what was being said in the vehicle. Theoretically, this could be done without taking the phone apart. The Motorola models, perhaps, could be modified by plugging a palm-top computer into the service jack and transferring the program while your car was being vacuumed at the car wash.

THE OLD BUG IN THE BATTERY TRICK

If you have read *The Bug Book*, you know that a surveillance transmitter can be disguised as, or built into, virtually anything. Audio Intelligence Devices (AID) in Florida makes a bug built into the clip of a 9mm pistol, and PK Elektronik builds them into ashtrays, picture frames, and light bulbs. So why not build one into a rechargeable battery? I recently heard that AID has such a bug, but I haven't seen its latest catalog. For obvious reasons, it won't send me one.

It wouldn't be difficult for the average technician to build a small bug into a cell phone battery. And cell phones are getting very cheap—like get one free when you fill your gas tank cheap. Just "forget" the phone as you leave the lawyer's office.

128

CELLULAR CLONING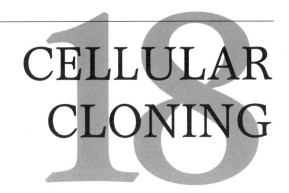

One evening several years ago, on a freeway in San Francisco, a black Toyota Camry was pulled over by San Francisco Police Department narcotics officers. One of the cops searched the car and found five ounces of cocaine in an aluminum Halliburton case. The driver was placed under arrest and taken to jail. Later that night, police searched the driver's home in the expensive Richmond district and confiscated a number of items, one of which was a printed list of numbers. But apparently, at the time, the police didn't know what the numbers were.

A few months later, the U.S. Secret Service raided a small business in Menlo Park, a city south of San Francisco. The business raided was the company mentioned earlier, where I was a technician. At the time of the raid I was in Hermosillo, Mexico, doing a demonstration of cellular intercept equipment, but I wasn't too disappointed about not being in Menlo Park.

Well anyway, the Secret Service confiscated most of the contents of two filing cabinets, a computer, and a quantity of cellular phones, and the two owners were later charged with numerous violations of federal law, including possession of counterfeiting devices (18 USC 2512).

It seems that the list of numbers that the San Francisco police found at the Richmond home ended up in the hands of the Secret Service—and the Secret Service *did* know what the numbers were: cellular telephone electronic serial numbers (ESNs).

Then another raid, in nearby San Jose, resulted in the seizure of a Porsche Carerra, about $14,000 in cash, several computers, and other electronic equipment, including a Curtis Electro Devices ESN reader. Three persons were arrested and arraigned in federal court. Shortly after that, because of the raids and for other reasons, I resigned my position as a technician with this company.

The newspapers called it "one of the largest operations ever to be broken." One person, the article said, was charged with "altering more than 1,000 cellular phones so that millions of dollars in calls were billed to unsuspecting owners of legitimate phones." In the *San Francisco Examiner* article, U.S. Attorney Michael Yamaguchi was quoted as saying, "It really was pretty ingenious. It takes a highly sophisticated individual to come up with the software and perpetrate a fraud like this."

One of the persons arrested, the engineer, maintains that he did not clone phones, he only sold a computer program that could be used for cloning. The jury thought otherwise. After the closing arguments, we left the courthouse to have lunch and hadn't been back more than 20 minutes when the bailiff came out into the hall and announced, "There is a verdict." The jury convicted the engineer, Ken Watson, on all three counts, and later he was sentenced to seven years in a federal prison. The raid apparently came as a surprise, but the people involved should have expected it; they did everything but call the Secret Service and invite its agents over.

129

- They kept a list of ESNs where it could easily be found.
- They kept large amounts of cash, and this attracts the feds like sharks.
- They threw away evidence, apparently incriminating, which was found by Secret Service agents who went Dumpster diving.
- They ordered the phones that were allegedly cloned through the company name.
- They rented a storage locker where the phones were kept in the company name.
- Someone talked too much.

This was but one cloning operation of many. The others are more careful. Nothing incriminating is easily found, records are either encrypted or not kept, the operation is kept small, and sales are through a third person who has no idea who is cloning the phones. So while sometimes the big dealers get caught, there are hundreds of small ones that do not.

Cellular cloning is big business. How big is big? Precise numbers are hard to get, because the cellular vendors don't like to talk about it. According to an article in *Nuts & Volts* magazine, the Cellular Telecommunications Industry Association (CTIA) claims that losses are a million dollars per day. I suspect that the numbers are exaggerated, but there is little doubt that the losses are considerable.

I called two cellular providers to ask about this and what percentage of their gross revenue losses amount to, but I got the same response as when I asked for technical information—no one would tell me anything. They kept referring me from one person to another, and when these endless referrals ended up back where I started from, I gave up. For a communications industry, they aren't very communicative.

Now hearing about these huge numbers, one might assume that it is the cellular service providers that are losing all this money. But, as Gershwin said, "It ain't necessarily so." The owner of the phone may be stuck with the bill. As part of the research for this book, I bought a portable phone. I made a "pattern" of calls, most to a handful of numbers. Then I used the phone for a few calls that did not fit the "profile" and that were in a different part of the state. I called the vendor to ask about this, but the person with whom I spoke was reluctant to talk about it. I persisted and finally the representative called the account records up on a computer monitor and told me that there was nothing unusual there. I had the phone deactivated and let it go at that.

Whatever the actual losses are, it is unlikely that the cellular vendors are going to absorb all of it. Even if it is only 4 or 5 percent of their gross income, it is still many millions—and as with any big business, this loss may be passed on to the customers. Like you. But many people have never even heard of cloning. They don't know what it is or that it could happen to them.

MORE MYTHS

The CTIA doesn't like to talk about cloning any more than Ma Bell likes to talk about wiretapping. Neither do the cellular phone dealers want to discuss cloning. No one wants to talk about it. If you go to a dealer to buy a cellular phone, that dealer isn't going to mention cloning. Here are some of the responses I got when I called a few retail vendors:

- "Cloning? Why, that's just something that happened a few times. The newspapers [are] making a big deal about it."
- "Cloning? Umm, I don't know what that . . . what did you call it? Umm, what does it do?"
- "Oh, I wouldn't be too concerned. The government has a law against that."
- "The [electronic] serial number can't be changed except by a team of engineers in a laboratory . . ."

WHAT IS CLONING?

Cellular cloning is the process of taking the MIN and ESN of one phone and placing them in another. There are two reasons why one would do this.

The first is so that they can have two phones on one account. A husband and wife or two business partners might want to do this to avoid having two separate bills to pay. This may or may not be legal; it is being decided in the courts. It's like it was back in the 1950s, when people were forbidden by law to own a telephone. In fact, people actually went to jail for having an "unregistered" phone in their possession. If you wanted an extension, you had to have it installed by Ma Bell and pay a monthly fee. At one time, it was believed that this law might be determined to be unconstitutional, but the enormous power of the CTIA indicates otherwise.

The other reason, which is very illegal, is to use someone else's numbers so that calls will be billed to that unfortunate person.

As you may recall from the section on cellular phone operation, when one makes a call, the ESN and MIN of the phone are transmitted over the reverse data channel to the cell site in which the phone is located. These numbers are compared to make sure that they match and are scanned through a database to determine that the phone has not been deactivated. After this has been done, the call is placed; the system has to do this for billing purposes. If the numbers do not match, the system will not place the call. So this means that to clone a phone, it is necessary to have both numbers.

According to the Electronic Industries Association (EIA) Interim Standard IS-3-B, Cellular System Mobile Station and Land Station Compatibility Specification (July 1984), "The serial number is a 32-bit binary number that uniquely identifies a mobile station to any cellular system. It must be factory set and not readily alterable in the field. The circuitry that provides the serial number must be isolated from fraudulent contact and tampering. Attempts to change the serial number circuitry should render the mobile station inoperative." It should. But obviously it does not.

OBTAINING ESNs

How do the "cloners" get these numbers? Aren't they "confidential"? There are ways. They can be stolen from a cellular phone sales and repair facility or copied from a label on the phone (which people don't realize they should remove). They can sometimes be found in Dumpsters or "snatched" from the airwaves.

The device that does the snatching is the ESN reader mentioned earlier. In newspaper articles, it is often described as being a "scanner-type" device—in other words, passive—and the operator waits on a freeway overpass or other location where there is a great deal of vehicular traffic. The operator turns the reader on, and it starts intercepting number sets.

Actually the ESN reader is not a passive device; it is a "miniature cell site." It sends out a signal on one of the cellular control frequencies, and if a cellular phone is nearby, it is fooled into thinking it is actually receiving a legitimate control channel. So it locks on to the reader, which intercepts and stores the ESN, MIN, and some other necessary information. The range is also exaggerated; 3 to 20 feet is more accurate, according to the manual of one such unit made by Curtis.

Recently, the technology of how to intercept ESNs by making some minor modification to a cellular "bag" phone has become available on the Internet. A cellular phone has to be able to read data as transmitted by the cellular site transmitter, including the MIN and ESN. So a cellular phone can be modified to display these data on a computer screen. This can be done by tapping into a particular place on the phone's circuit board and feeding the data into a computer, where a special program (I have heard that it is available on the Web) decodes the Manchester data into plain text.

As I understand it, this is something that can easily be done by the average electronic technician. However, I have not tried it—I have no need for, or interest in obtaining, this information. Also be aware that making such a system is a violation of 18 USC 2512 (possession of counterfeiting devices).

USING ESNs

Once a cloner has the numbers, it is not difficult to burn them into a phone, and here is where the quote from Mr. Yamaguchi breaks down. What he said is not entirely untrue, but it just tells only part of the story.

Some cellular phones store the MIN and ESN in an EPROM chip. To change the numbers, it is necessary to remove the chip and place it under a high-intensity ultraviolet lamp, which erases the information stored inside. Then the chip is placed in a programmer that is connected to a computer. Any DOS computer will work; nothing elaborate is required. A program made for "burning" in the new ESN digits is run, and the chip is replaced inside the phone. The ESN reader costs about $1,300, the EPROM burner about $200, and the computer a few hundred. So the equipment investment is well under $3,000.

Other phones use a different type of chip, which does not have to be removed. To change the programming, a cable is connected between the phone and a computer and a code is entered, which places the phone in "program" or "test" mode. The new numbers are entered into the computer and then are "burned" into the phone. No disassembly is required, the chip is not switched, and the whole thing takes only a few minutes. These programs were once difficult to come by; the manufacturers supplied them to the cellular service shops and no one else. Today, anyone with a computer and a modem can download them from any of hundreds of computer bulletin boards and through Anonymous File Transfer on the Internet.

This type of cloning is not ingenious or sophisticated. Some programs are menu driven, and the average computer user can learn them in half an hour. They may even contain details on the type of cable required, including the part number and where it can be purchased, or it can be put together from parts by any electronics hobbyist.

The latest and most versatile in the cloned phone line is the "lifetime phone." It requires that one chip be replaced (which takes 10 minutes), and then the user can enter the ESN and MIN from the keypad. This is done on the fly, as it were; no cable is required, and neither is a computer. The new chip is set up so that the programming mode can be accessed by entering a simple code, something like # 0 * 0 # 0 * 0 # 1, and then entering the numbers. Just that easy. The Panasonic EB-3510 pocket phone is one that can be converted this way.

To produce the program that is burned into the lifetime chip does require a knowledge of programming and electronics and the workings of the phone to be used, but there are any number of good programmers who could do it. They don't have to be "sophisticated," and the user doesn't have to be "ingenious."

PREVENTION

The manufacturers of ESN readers have been under heavy fire from the government, the cellular phone industry, and the media. One of the largest, Curtis Electro Devices, Inc., voluntarily agreed to modify its readers in such a way that they could not be used for cloning operations. One of the first things Curtis did was to install a circuit that requires a code number to be entered from the keypad of the phone to be read. In other words, to extract the ESN from a phone, it is necessary to have physical possession of that phone. Then Curtis instituted a policy that any reader sent to the factory for repair would have this new feature installed. Finally, it tightened restrictions on sales. Without verification that the purchaser is in the business of activating and repairing cellular phones, the sale will not be made.

Nippon Electric Company (NEC) is working on a voice recognition system. A sample of your voice is taken, digitized, and stored in the cellular systems computers. When you want to make a call, your voice is compared with the stored sample. If voice and sample don't match, the system will not place the call. This doesn't prevent the numbers from being intercepted, but it makes them useless.

NYNEX, the telephone company in New York, has set up a personal identification number (PIN) code, like those used with ATMs at banks. The PIN has to be entered before the call is placed, and ESN readers do not (yet) intercept the PIN. As does voice recognition, it makes the numbers useless if they are intercepted by an ESN reader, because it will not capture the PIN. However, sooner or later, commercial monitoring systems will be modified to display PINs, if they haven't been already. But it's a step in the right direction.

Q: What about the hundreds or thousands of old ESN readers that are still out there?
A: They're still out there.

Q: Meaning that they can still be used to intercept ESNs?
A: Yep.

Q: If they all "disappear" will this solve the problem?
A: Nope. Remember that some cell phones can be modified into ESN readers.

TRANSMITTER FINGERPRINTING

There is something about the phone that does not change just by installing a different chip. This is called the *transmitter fingerprint*. Whenever any transmitter, cellular phone, citizen band (CB), or whatever starts to transmit, the signal that is seen on the screen of an oscilloscope describes a unique wave form that can be compared with others and positively identified. This is because every transmitter is slightly different, even two of the same model that rolled off the assembly line together. Such a system, the Tx-ID-1, is manufactured by MoTron Electronics in Eugene, Oregon.

When you analyze almost anything carefully enough, you will find that it is different from anything else. Fingerprints, voice prints, and retina scans show significant (and identifiable) differences. Even the noise generated by the propellers of Soviet submarines were "printed" so that they could be identified by sensors (sonabuoys) placed on the ocean floor.

How It Works

Whenever a transmitter comes on the air, it takes a few milliseconds to stabilize. During that time it produces what is known as a *transient*, which is unique to that transmitter. It can be detected at the discriminator section of a receiver and digitized into a "fingerprint," which can be displayed on a computer screen and stored on a disk. This information can be called up and compared with an unknown transient to check for a positive match.

Say you are a NSA agent in New York, trying to find some bad guys who have built an atomic bomb. The bad guys have threatened to blow up, oh, the Chemical Bank, the Queensborough Bridge, or whatever. To communicate with each other, they are using lifetime phones.

You have managed to follow one of them in a surveillance van, and when he uses the phone, you intercept the transmission and record it. Inside the van is the Tx-ID-1, which makes a digitized record of the phone's unique fingerprint. This information is taken to Fort Meade, Maryland, for processing and is then programmed into one of the NSA's Cray supercomputers.

Unknown to the public, the NSA has set up cellular monitoring stations across the country, and every call made over the cellular system is relayed by satellite. The next time the phone is used, the Cray will flag it and its location will be pinpointed through triangulation to within a few hundred yards.

The Tx-ID-1 consists of a printed circuit board that plugs into the motherboard of a personal computer (a DOS 386 or faster), the software package, and a pretty decent manual. The card has an RS-232 interface for connecting it to a communications receiver such as the versatile ICOM R7000 and AR-3000.

Q: Will cellular cloning ever end?

A: No. It is being reduced through the modifications made to ESN readers, the use of voice recognition, and the PIN, but ways to defeat them will be devised. New techniques will be developed, and defeated. Encrypting the ESN will defeat many attempts at intercepting them, but there may be a way to defeat this. The phone has the program inside it, so it can be analyzed and duplicated and then modified so that a different ESN can be used.

Meanwhile, there are millions of cellular subscribers, the vast majority of whom won't switch to PCS for years to come, if they ever do. Such people will always be vulnerable to both monitoring and cloning. It's their choice, and though it is not their fault if this happens, they still could have avoided it by making the switch to PCS.

Q: Will it be possible to monitor and clone PCS?

A: As long as it is unencrypted digital, it will be possible to monitor it. Although no one I know of has developed such a system, it is inevitable. As to cloning, PCS will be a tad more difficult, I hope. Pacific Bell says a lot about its "smart" chip, implying that it cannot be cloned, but no one there was willing to talk to me about this.

Any time you use *any* telephone—landline, cellular, cordless, PCS—there is a chance that someone else will hear you. And the game goes on . . .

HEALTH HAZARDS OF CELLULAR PHONES

DO THEY CAUSE CANCER?

Does using a cellular phone pose a health hazard? David Reynard thinks so. His wife died of brain cancer, and he claims that the cause was her heavy use of a portable cellular phone. He filed a wrongful death suit against NEC, GTE, and the dealer who sold the phone.

A number of employees of companies that require them to use pocket cellular phones also seem to think so. They claim that the rate at which they develop brain tumors is much higher than the average. Global Communications Corporation claims that some cellular carriers provide cellular service that threatens both the public interest, via predatory pricing, and public safety, via radio frequency or RF radiation, according to *Telecommunications Reports* (June 21, 1993, p. 28).

A special report by Mark Fischetti in *IEEE Spectrum* June 1993 said, "A debate has raged in the media over whether cellular-telephone use relates to the etiology of brain cancer, even though the 'numerous studies conducted show no definite link' between the use of cellular phones and brain cancer. Scientists disagree over the results of some experiments, but users need to understand that zero risk is impossible to prove and that scientists can only say that extensive study does not indicate that there is any health risk."

According to Carla Lazzareschi, in the February 3, 1993, *Los Angeles Times* (p. 4D), the U.S. Food and Drug Administration (FDA) plans to release its "first advisory" on the use of cellular phones. However, Mays Swycord, head of the FDA's radiation biology division, says there is no proof yet of a cancer threat from the phones. The National Cancer Institute will conduct a study of brain cancer to see if there is any link to cellular phone use.

In an article by Lurie Silberg, in *The Weekly Home Furnishings* newspaper (February 1, 1993, p. 67), the cellular radio equipment industry is refuting claims that use of portable cellular telephones can cause cancer. The industry cited several studies showing that UHF radio waves posed no appreciable health risk.

A few months ago, there were some articles in the major newspapers stating that "while the energy from cellular phones does cause a slight heating of the brain, this is 'not a health hazard.'" So who do you believe? Statistics say whatever the statistician wants them to say, but so far there is no conclusive evidence one way or the other.

There is no question that electromagnetic radiation affects human beings. Radio waves at different frequencies cause heating of tissue exposed to them, from ultrasound used for relaxing muscle spasms to the old Diathermy machines of the 1930s, and, obviously, so do microwaves. Someone made the statement that using a cellular phone is akin to putting your head in a microwave oven, and though it is reasonable to believe that the radiation from cellular phones could have some effect, this is a gross overstatement: microwave ovens use hundreds of watts, and the output of a pocket cellular phone is less than one watt. Using CDMA, it is a fraction of a watt.

PCS and Ionizing Radiation

Ionizing radiation is, as I understand it, a type, or rather a frequency, of radiation that has a wavelength that causes molecular changes, the type of changes that results in cancer cells mutating from normal cells. The radiation from a cellular phone makes up only a small portion of the entire electromagnetic spectrum. It ranges from audio to radio waves to infrared and then visible light, ultraviolet, X-rays, and finally gamma and cosmic radiation from outer space. Some areas of the spectrum are known to be ionizing: X-rays and gamma rays. And now, it appears that long-term exposure to radio frequencies much lower in frequency than PCS (longer in wavelength) can also cause cancer—if the power level is high and the exposure is over many years. So even while the power level is very low, apparently it is possible that very long-term use of PCS might truly be a health hazard. The PCS system is apparently on the edge of the ionizing part of the spectrum.

So if this concerns you, then what do you do? Give up using a portable phone? Perhaps there is a compromise. With pocket phones, the antenna is very close to, if not touching, the user's head, but with the transportable phone, it is several feet away. RF energy decreases under the inverse square law. If you double the distance between yourself and the phone, the energy you are subjected to is reduced to one-fourth.

Another option is the NexTel by Motorola. This is a combination cell phone, pager, and two-way radio. It is a "flip" type that can be used like a phone (holding it like a regular cell phone) or a two-way radio where it is not held close to one's head. You can hold it 6 inches from your lips as you talk with the antenna pointing away from you.

There is something I thought of called the Off-tenna, a cellular antenna that flips out at the touch of a button and is offset from the phone by 6 inches or so. This would reduce exposure levels significantly.

There are antenna shields advertised in *Cellular Business* and other publications and available from some dealers. The ads claim that 80 percent of the signal is blocked. But then if that much of the signal is in fact blocked, then how can it transmit to the cell site? Perhaps only the part of the antenna that faces the user is shielded, in which case the device might be worth considering, though one would have to make sure he was facing in the right direction while using the phone. Maybe this will catch on—and in major downtown areas thousands of people will be doing something called the Cellular Circle—the high-tech version of (with apologies to Chubby Checker) The Twist—to get themselves pointed in the right direction. Maybe, to avoid attracting attention, these people will bring back the Hula Hoop and explain with a sheepish grin that it's the latest craze in mono-aerobic weight-loss technology.

Moving right along, remember the CDMA phone? It uses a fraction of the output power but works as well as or better than ordinary cellular phones. Perhaps this technology will soon become available in the PCS system.

So, there doesn't seem to be any conclusive evidence either way. If there were, I have little doubt that the cellular industry, and PCS, would try to clamp a lid on it. However, sooner or later the truth will be known.

136

CORDLESS PHONES

EASY TO MONITOR

An idea whose time had come, cordless phones solved the problem of users being tied to within a few feet of where the wire came out of the wall. Now it became possible for users to sit by the pool or in the front yard and communicate with people—more people than the user realized, since virtually every scanner made covered the frequencies the cordless phones used. The most intimate personal calls, drug deals being set up, plots being made to commit this and that crime—virtually everything that people talk about on telephones was being heard, and is being heard, on cordless frequencies. These are the same things heard on cellular phones, but in greater detail because cordless phones aren't expensive to use and people yak longer.

True, there are laws against monitoring—the Digital Telephony Act and some state laws—but don't let this give you a false sense of security. They don't prevent anyone from listening. With all the newspaper and magazine articles about cordless monitoring, people should know this, but obviously they do not.

They should also know that the range may be well over the advertised "900 feet" or whatever. Range is based in part on calculations made from FCC rules; the antenna on the handset cannot be more than 1 meter in length and the power output not more than 1/10 of a watt. But what about a person who has a sensitive communications receiver with a carefully matched antenna on top of a 50-foot tower? Or a scanner owner who lives on one of the highest floors of a tall apartment building, which can increase the range to more than a mile?

Being careful about what one says over a cordless phone is not the answer—the idea of any telephone is to be able to communicate what the user wants to. Collapsing the antenna to reduce the range is no good if someone across the street is listening. So what can a person do?

In Part 4 are the details of a number of cordless phones that provide a fairly high level of security. Casual eavesdroppers, hobbyists, most local law enforcement agencies, and even industrial espionage agents will be shut out, and only the most determined and well-equipped persons (e.g., employees of the federal government) will be able to defeat them. So don't count on a law that cannot be enforced. It is up to you to make your cordless conversations private. This is easy to do and not at all expensive. More on this to come.

The same arguments against monitoring cellular phones also apply to cordless phones, and though no one can reasonably expect such calls to be private, obviously some people do. Supposing you were plotting a crime to eliminate someone—murder one. Would you talk about it over a cordless phone? According to the December 30, 1994, *Memphis Commercial Appeal,* via a post on the Internet, a lady in Tennessee got a scanner as a gift last Christmas. She was trying it out when she intercepted a conversation where a woman and her boyfriend were plotting to kill her husband for the insurance money. It seems that they intended to fake a burglary, at which time the husband, worth more dead than alive, would be killed. The scanner owner called her daughter to listen with her, and her daughter recognized some of the names, so they called the Shelby County Sheriff's Office, whose officers questioned the two suspects. Later, the suspects allegedly confessed.

So one innocent person is alive, if not well, because someone was monitoring a cordless frequency. But this "someone" broke two federal laws: the ECPA and the Communications Act of 1934. If I were to hear such a plot I would anonymously call the news desk at a local paper, where there are always scanners. Let someone there check it out and call the cops. It is a sad state of affairs when citizens are afraid to report crimes, but look at what happened to Richard Jewell in Atlanta during the 1996 Summer Olympics.

No wonder we are seeing so many bumper stickers that read: I LOVE MY COUNTRY, BUT FEAR MY GOVERNMENT.

PART 3

DATA
COMMUNICATIONS

ONCE THERE WERE NO COMPUTERS?

Just as there was a time when there were no telephones or radios, there was a time when there were no computers, although the idea of finding a better way to manipulate figures probably predates recorded history. Perhaps it goes back to the time that man first developed a medium of exchange. Salt was once used as money, as were clams and waterballs, according to *BC*, and folks needed a way to keep track of how many of them they had.

The first mechanical counting machine was probably the abacus, and though it may seem primitive, an expert can total numbers as fast as on a 10-key adding machine. This was improved on, and in the 1930s the comptometer was developed. It was about the size of a bread box, weighed about 60 pounds, used a complicated set of gears and wheels, and could multiply as well as add and subtract.

Then some unknown person theorized that the diode vacuum tube could be used to make calculations, or rather several thousand of them could, which led to the first electronic computers. These room-sized monsters were used during World War II to calculate the trajectory of artillery shells and to try to break the German Enigma mechanical encryption machines. Actually, Enigma was broken by people, not a computer . . .

For the next quarter of a century, computers remained very large and very expensive—beyond the reach of individuals and small businesses, and then in the 1970s personal computers appeared.

The first was the Altair. It didn't have a monitor or even a keyboard; to enter data, the operator set a series of toggle switches on the front panel, using Assembly language. It might take several minutes just to add three and four, and if the switches were all flipped right, the answer just might be seven, displayed in ASCII on a row of LEDs. Such computers weren't able to store more than a few bytes and had no way of communicating with other computers.

A year or so later, Steve Wozniak came out with the Apple, and IBM released the first PC. Both of these had keyboards and monitors and disk drives. They became a sort of status symbol. Everyone wanted one. Tons of software and peripherals appeared almost overnight, including modems and programs with which computers could communicate with each other. Small businesses could computerize their records and access their systems from other computers.

COMPUTER HACKING

Just as there was fraud on the first mobile telephone system, there was fraud in data communications. Back then, any computer that was connected to a phone line was fair game, and as the use of small computers skyrocketed, so did the interest in something new called *hacking*.

I remember my first hacking experience. In 1983 there was a chain store in the city where I lived that set up one of the first computer BBSs. The idea was to advertise the store's products, but to get people interested the store had to offer something besides commercials. So the manager of the store installed a few games that could be played online. One of them was Pong. Remember Pong? Another was a text adventure game where the player was required to type in responses to questions. But, I soon discovered, that if I punched in a series of nines—999999—the Radio Shack Model 1 became confused and crashed back to the command line. From there I had complete control over the computer, the same as if I were at the keyboard. I could copy files, erase files, and read other users' "private" messages.

I didn't destroy any data, but I did read the private mail messages and set myself up with an account with which I could log on at any time and have the same access, and I did look through their entire customer list just for the hell of it. In analyzing the list, I discovered that this store provided a list of customers who purchased "certain items" to one of the three-letter government agencies on the first of every month. Hmmm. Well, this was many years ago, and I do not know whether the chain still does this or not, but this chain still pesters its customers for their names and addresses. I suppose it could be just to build their mailing list . . .

Soon this new breed of computer enthusiasts was getting into thousands of computers, and as the owners finally started to realize what was happening, they were less than happy. The idea that someone could access their records didn't sit too well with them, so they started looking into ways to keep unauthorized persons locked out. And the game that never ends began.

The first thing computer programmers did was to set up a password feature, but these programs were primitive in that they would just sit there, endlessly waiting for the right word. Since there was no limit to the number of passwords that could be tried and because the passwords consisted of only three or four characters, it was only a matter of time before the right one was discovered. For more than a few years, this was the extent of "security" until someone modified the operating system so that it would disconnect the caller after three attempts. But no matter what programmers did, someone found a way to defeat it.

A second password was added, but since some hackers already knew the computer's operating system, it was possible to get around this new "foolproof" security measure. Improvements were made and defeated, improved upon and defeated again. Soon these defenses became so sophisticated that it was virtually impossible to defeat them, assuming that they were used.

While I was researching *Digital Privacy*, a computer security consultant told me an interesting story. One of the businesses that hired him was concerned about break-ins. The system it had used was a program called Carbon Copy, with which company employees could access information from branch offices or their home computers. Fine, this is necessary, and Carbon Copy was a good program, except that the password needed to log on was never changed. The default password that comes with the program was still being used, and default passwords are known to anyone who has the same program. They are also passed around on some computer bulletin boards.

This company used its computer system for bank transactions, electronic fund transfers, and anyone who "broke in" might have been able to transfer funds to his personal account. But company owners weren't worried because they didn't "publish" the phone number used to log on to its computer. Apparently they didn't see *War Games*. This is not at all unusual. There have been a number of books written about famous hackers who "broke" into this or that system, and most of the time this was possible because no one bothered to change the default password. So if your system is invaded because of this, you have no one else to blame. On the other hand, if you set your system up so that both a password and a user ID are required, and three wrong tries will disconnect the caller, then it will be damn hard to break in without inside help. Eliminating direct access by modem is one way to secure your files and electronic mail, but there are other ways they can be invaded.

Physical Access

Anyone who has physical access can copy your files, such as the people who clean the office at night or someone who breaks in. Keeping sensitive information encrypted will defeat this. Any of the password programs available will defeat amateurs, and removable drives that hold sensitive information can be locked in a safe or removed from the area.

Meet Dr. Van Eck

Some years ago in Holland, a scientist named Wim van Eck demonstrated that it is possible to intercept what are called transient electromagnetic emanations, or the radiation coming from a computer.

From Part 1, you may recall that Maxwell discovered that a current flowing through a conductor radiated magnetic waves into space. It is the times when the current first starts flowing and when it stops that produce the strongest "signals." This is how radio works: the signal is of an alternating current, which turns on, builds to a peak, and then falls back to zero. The higher the voltage, the farther it radiates. The voltage in this case is the beam of electrons (remember that current is the flow of electrons) inside the cathode ray tube of the computer monitor. The principle is exactly the same as with a television set. The beam turns off and on at a high rate of speed and generates these magnetic pulses that can radiate from a few feet to, theoretically, several miles out into space. So at a distant location, these signals can be intercepted and converted back into what is on your monitor screen.

The equipment used to intercept this information ranges from crude, inexpensive, and displaying a very poor image to very sophisticated systems costing tens of thousands of dollars. So obviously the cost limits the number of people who might eavesdrop on your monitor. But the government has this equipment, and using it apparently is not a violation of the ECPA or any other law because these computer "signals" were not intended to be broadcast to anyone. It is also dirt cheap compared with attempting to break an encryption code such as the Data Encryption Standard (DES). Remember, it isn't yet scrambled while it is still on the monitor screen . . .

WHAT CAN YOU DO?

How can you prevent this type of eavesdropping? Since it is possible to intercept what actually appears on the screen of your system, encryption is of little use. So what do you do? First, you can purchase a computer system from Wang Laboratories that is shielded against this radiation. These systems are a bit more expensive, but how much is security worth to you? Otherwise, you can shield your system in a number of ways. Anything metal between the computer (particularly the monitor) and the outside will reduce the distance the radiation travels. This can be a sheet-metal box, metal foil on the inside of the monitor (leaving holes for air circulation), or a special type of wallpaper from International Paper that has a fine metal screen laminated inside it. Using connecting cables that have metal shields will also help.

How well you need to do this depends on your situation. If you are in a rural area and no one can get a van full of equipment within a quarter-mile, you have little to be concerned about. In an office building, someone might be monitoring through a thin wall in the adjoining room. Some more ideas are in *Digital Privacy*.

SECURITY GUIDELINES
PERSONAL COMPUTERS

COUNTERESPIONAGE CONSULTANTS TO BUSINESS AND GOVERNMENT

Every organization using personal computers (PC's) needs a formal set of security procedures. Our basic suggestions for a Personal Computer Security Program follow. You may reword it, and add items to it, to suit your particular needs.

• Obtain employee cooperation - Accomplish this by implementing your program slowly. Advise employees of procedural changes well in advance. Explain why the tighter security is necessary, and how it will be of benefit to them. Use examples.

• Develop a communal sense of responsibility by encouraging employee participation in the development of the program. Ask for suggestions. The effectiveness of your security program will be in proportion to the base of its support.

• Limit physical access to PC's – Computer systems or terminals should be left in the *off* and *locked* position when not in use. (You lock your desk, don't you¢) Install power switch locking devices if necessary. Secure the computer case so that internal boards, hard disks, etc. cannot be removed. Have an authorized users list for each machine. Verify identity and work orders of repair persons.

• Password access – A password code should be an integral part of the system access procedure. Advise users to: change passwords frequently, and use quality passwords (My/DoG - is superior to MY/ DOG - is superior to ROVER, for example). They must not to reveal, loan, or write passwords down. Some password programs automatically request users to change passwords on a regular basis.

• Secure PC related manuals, e.g. Instruction, Procedure, Passwords, etc. Even amateurs can read and learn.

• Never leave an active terminal. Always *log-off* and *lock* the terminal when not in use.

• Report altered data to the Security or department manager. Early detection of a virus, or forced access, will mitigate losses.

• Report suspected physical tampering to the Security department. Remember, *The data you save may be your own.* You work hard to compile information. It's valuable. Protect it.

• Remove sensitive data from the PC when not in use. Diskettes should be removed and securely stored. The PC should be turned *off* and *locked*. This will erase information left in most PC's RAM memory; check the manufacturer's manual to be certain.

• Memory typewriters should not be left with confidential information stored in them. Purge confidential data regularly.

> *To get back up and running, get running and back up.*

• Memory media, such as floppy disks, are very susceptible to destruction via physical abuse and magnetism. They should be backed up and stored in secure locations to prevent espionage or sabotage; one on premises, one off premises.

• Do not rely on copy commands. PC copy commands often move data by sectors, thus moving more than the specified file. Sensitive information may inadvertently be passed along this way.

• Do not rely on deletion commands. Usually the commands 'delete', 'erase', or 'remove' only open up an area of memory to be rewritten over in the future. Data remains intact until new information is entered. This data can still be read using one of the many "reconstruction" utility programs available. The *format* or *initialize* command will usually erase the entire disk.

• Erase diskettes before disposal or transfer to other use. One acceptable method is total degaussing (bulk demagnetizing), the other is the use of a data shredder program. If this isn't feasible, just destroy the disks and use fresh ones. Disks are inexpensive.

• Disconnect PC's from networks when not in use. Remote access to a PC can result in information loss, or data tampering. This can be prevented by not logging into the network unless necessary, and turning power off when the PC is not in use.

• Computers connected to phone lines need access protection. Use modems that have a call-back feature or employ high quality password protection. When transmitting sensitive files, use encryption. Do not leave computers attached to phone lines unless this type of use is required on a continuous basis.

• Do not use unsolicited or borrowed software. It may contain instructions or programs designed to capture, alter or obliterate the user's data (aka. viruses, worms, Trojan horses, etc.). Virus detection software and hardware are available at very reasonable prices. There is no excuse for getting *sick*.

• Back-up all hard drive data and programs on a regular basis. Store the back-up copy in a secure, and physically separate, location.

• Store floppy, removable hard drive, and optical disks in special data strong boxes, available for individual PC users. These specially made containers provide protection from fire generated heat, as well as the by-products of fires (steam and soot) — all very damaging elements. Although they lock, they should not be relied upon for protection against espionage. Media storage areas for confidential information require high security locks.

Stealing computer data and planting viruses are only two spy tricks. There are hundreds more. Remember — Espionage is Preventable. For further information about pro-active programs to combat espionage, electronic eavesdropping and wiretapping please contact us.   **PO Box 668, Oldwick, NJ 08858**

PAGERS

I remember an episode of . . .

"Uh oh, here he goes again. What's it gonna be this time—Perry Mason or . . . you guessed it, The Twilight Zone*?"*

. . . about a businessman who was commuting from the suburbs to The Big City and hating every minute of it. The commute, the job, The Big City; he wished it could be different. A different way of life. He drifted off, dreaming of another time, another place. He was a regular on the train; the conductors knew him, so they would awaken him when his stop came up. Until one day when he didn't wake up.

He didn't die, though. He just got off at another stop.

"Willoughby. Next stop is Willoughby, Indiana. Willoughby."

It was the turn of the century, an era of lazy summer evenings, ice cream socials, and band concerts in the park. Telephones were installed in some of the homes in Willoughby, but there were no pagers. They hadn't been conceived of, and even if they had been, it is unlikely that anyone would want one in that peaceful, unhurried little Midwestern town.

Would it really be so bad if life were a little more like Willoughby, Indiana, of the 1890s?

INTERCEPTING VOICE PAGERS

Now we approach the turn of the next century, millions of people carry the beeping vibrating devices. To some, they are a way to maintain communications. To others, they are an abomination that gives them no peace, no escape. Whatever the reason, some people never leave home without them. A security blanket of sorts, I suppose. And as they go about their daily lives, it never occurs to them that others can pick up the messages they receive.

"Why in the world should anyone care about that?" you ask. "Of what possible use could it be?"

Sound familiar? Well, to industrial-strength spies, these messages may provide some very useful information. You are the president of a manufacturing company that makes computer chips. Naturally, other manufacturers want to know as much about your operation as they can. Perhaps you are able to produce a microprocessor chip for less than they can. They want to know how. *Specifically how.* They already know a lot about your operation, your fixed costs, how many employees you have and their wages, but they may not know where you buy your materials. One way for them to find out is to intercept your pager messages.

Even if the content of the conversation is not available, sometimes it is enough just to know who is talking to whom.

So one of your competitors obtains your capcode (your pager's unique serial number) and sets up a system to intercept your messages. When your competitor sees on the computer screen that you have been given a number to call, he calls it himself to see who answers, or perhaps he just looks it up in a cross directory or one of the CD-ROMs that lists zillions of business phone numbers. And now he knows whom you are communicating with. OK, maybe it is only your secretary, reminding you of an appointment with your mistress. But maybe it is the secretary of a supplier of one of the chemicals (there are many) used in manufacturing chips. Aha! Your competitor now knows something useful. All these bits and pieces of information add up, enough of them paint a very revealing picture.

If you have a voice pager, all that is needed is a scanner. It makes no difference what frequency is used; most of the available scanners will intercept all of them. Unlike cellular radio, where the channel your phone uses at a given time can be any one of 395, your pager uses the same one all the time; it's crystal controlled and does not change. And unlike cellular, with its 395 voice channels, pagers have only a few dozen.

"Mr. Chelsingham," the answering service operator informs you, "please call Mr. Copperfield at Blotto Chemicals. The number is . . ."

Wonderful. Naturally, the competitor knows what Blotto makes—or will in a few minutes. Now he knows what you are buying from Blotto—and, with a little social engineering, how much you are paying.

There are also alphanumeric pagers. The message is spelled out on the tiny LCD screen: "Call Jack at Mayfield Machinery ASAP." A little more secure? Yes, but not much. It might work against the poorly equipped amateur who has only a communications receiver, but not against government agents using one of the commercial pager-monitoring systems or hobbyists who have constructed their own system. Remember, this is a one-way communication. On cellular, you can stop someone from saying something confidential, by interrupting him, but with pagers you have no control over what information is sent. Think about it as you read about commercial pager interception.

PAGERS AND THE LAW

Is it legal to intercept and decode pager transmissions? The ECPA excludes signal or tone-only pagers from its protection, so apparently it is legal. This law seems to cover voice pagers, but if it doesn't stop people from listening to cellular and cordless, it sure won't prevent them from listening in on your little belt-clipped black box.

WHAT ARE THE FREQUENCIES?

Pagers operate in every area of the radio spectrum, from low VHF to high UHF, 30 to 900 MHz. Here are a few, but this is far from a complete list.

035.220–035.66
043.220–043.64
152.030–152.21
157.740–158.10
158.490–158.70
454.025–454.35
459.025–459.65
929.000–932.00

PAGER INTERCEPT SYSTEMS

Signals from pager transmitters are more powerful than most others, such as police, trucking companies, or taxicabs. A delivery company might have output of 100 watts or so, but the pager company may well use 1,000 watts. This is one reason why the pager transmitters work virtually everywhere and other radio systems do not. So they are very easy to find. Back off the squelch control to reduce the sensitivity, and, since the transmitters send frequently if not continuously, virtually all of them can be found in a few hours of searching.

A better way is to use a commercial decoding system.

The Beeper Buster

The SWS Security Beeper Buster pager-intercept system is an electronic surveillance system that allows you to intercept and monitor all messages sent to pagers carried by persons under investigation. Digital, alpha, and voice pages can be monitored. The Beeper Buster permits unattended, automatic monitoring of up to 100 pagers simultaneously. The system is easy to use, extremely powerful, and versatile. With the Beeper Buster, criminals can no longer use pagers to hide their activities from law enforcement.

Specifications

The Beeper Buster pager interceptor allows authorized agencies to intercept, record, and display messages sent to target pagers. From your office you can monitor and record all digital and alpha messages sent to pagers carried by persons under investigation. This reliable, economical, and easy-to-use system was designed specifically for law enforcement operations from the most basic to the most advanced. The Beeper Buster offers performance and flexibility to meet any requirement.

Benefits
* Accurate, real-time operation; operates faster than the paging system to ensure no missed pages
* Pages not missed when the channel gets busy, in contrast to competitive units
* Inexpensive video terminal used; does not require a computer
* Menu-driven software for easy operation
* Turnkey packages available
* Ease of setup and use, most adjustments automatic
* Easy capture of capcode or search string or monitorinf of all traffic
* Password-protected operation
* Twenty-hour-hour telephone support included with purchase
* Two-year warranty
* Affordability—purchase and lease programs available
* Specific design for law enforcement operations
* Covert operation, no one knowing but you, and no coordination with paging carrier necessary
* Perfect operation at new fast 2,400-baud speeds where all other brands fail
* No add-on computer needed—immune to computer interference that plagues other units
* Decoding of all formats simultaneously: 512-, 1,200-, and 2,400-baud POCSAG, Golay, NEC
* Built-in parallel printer port for permanent hard-copy output
* System with receiver wired and adjusted—out of the box to operation in 5 minutes
* Wideband receiver for stand-alone use for other duties (500 kHz–1,800 MHz)
* Voice page capture option to external cassette recorder (special order, inquire)
* Storage of intercept sessions internally in nonvolatile memory; can review, save, or print
* Capture on all pages of up to 100 target capcodes or 20 message search strings

- Menu driven for instinctive, nontechnical operation
- Password-protected operations
- Capability of driving modem for remote or unattended operation
- Twelve-VDC operated/ 600 mA; ideal for portable or mobile operation; AC supply included
- Internal battery-backed time-date generator time-stamping of all messages
- Auto resume—unit resumes operation automatically after power failure (no missed pages)
- Small size— 6 x 9 x 1.5 in. (152 x 229 x 38mm)
- Compact, rugged, and portable
- Terminal disconnect and removal for security or convenience once the pager is operating
- Two-year warranty—the best in the business
- Lease programs, field installation/operation, and 24-hour toll-free support available

Single-Channel Pager-Intercept System
The single-channel system is part #7100. It comes equipped with the following:

- AC main power supply
- Whip antenna
- Video terminal interface cable
- Two-year warranty
- Instruction manual

Options include the following:

- #120 video terminal, Wyse model 30 +, includes interface cable
- #155 parallel printer (includes ribbon, interface cable, initial supply of paper)
- Spares/maintenance kit (quoted on request, inquire)
- Twelve-VDC mobile power cord
- Maintenance contract (quoted on request, inquire)

Multichannel Pager-Intecept System
The multichannel system is part #7100-4 for a four-channel system, and #7100-8 for an eight-channel system. It comes equipped with the following:

- Four- or eight-channel pager intercept system (decoder modules and receivers)
- AC main power supply for decoder and receivers
- Four- or eight-whip antennas
- Pentium computer, monitor, keyboard, mouse
- Windows 95 operating system
- Beeper Buster decoding software (not sold separately)
- Serial multiplexer unit for four or eight channels (installed in computer)
- Parallel printer, cable, and initial supply of paper
- Surge suppressor multi-outlet strip
- Two-year warranty on Beeper Buster, manufacturer's warranty on computer
- Instruction manual

Options include the following:

- #MC14 antenna multicoupler to permit use of only one antenna (four-channel system)

- #MC18 antenna multicoupler for eight-channel system
- Spares/maintenance kit (quoted on request, inquire)
- Laptop and mobile installation configuration (special order, inquire)
- Maintenance contract (quoted on request, inquire)
- Training, on-site setup/installation, and on-site maintenance/logistics quoted on request

The Beeper Buster is in use worldwide, with more than 300 units sold. It has been declared a critical defense item by the governments of Colombia and Turkey and is a major tool for the drug interdiction squads in those and other countries. Sales are absolutely restricted to government and law enforcement agencies.

An interesting trick: If you know the pager owner's number but not the capcode, you can call and send a unique message and then watch for it on the computer screen when it is transmitted. The capcode is intercepted and can be placed in memory so that any messages sent to that pager will automatically be flagged, displayed on the screen, and printed.

Power Fax System

Another pager interception system is made by Power Fax, in the Netherlands Antilles, two chains of islands in the Caribbean. This is the pager monitor described in the information sheet I received as follows:

The Pager Monitor is yet another state of the art system from PowerFax. It enables Law Enforcement Agencies to track down criminals using pagers for their communication purposes.

The Pager Monitor is a system that enables monitoring of paging messages. The unique design provides the capability to monitor multiple pagers at the same time on a single frequency.

As an optional feature, the Pager Monitor can also monitor capcodes in multiple frequencies simultaneously.

The Pager Monitor can also handle both numeric and alphanumeric messages. It has the capacity to recognize messages of both these types.

Like other PowerFax products, the Pager Monitor uses the IBM PC as platform to increase reliability and performance and more importantly to provide an AFFORDABLE SOLUTION.

Here are some of the particulars about the Pager Monitor, from the same brochure:

- Multitasking ability. The Pager Monitor has a multitasking scheduler that enables the user to perform various activities such as printing or adding new capcodes and other. operational activities without disrupting its regular activities.
- Hunting capability. To track down capcodes that are not known easily, the Pager Monitor is equipped with a hunt mode. This hunt mode allows the user to specify a message string to search for. The user then sends the pager a message starting with the specified string or digits. The Pager Monitor will track all installed channels for capcodes in which that specific message string is received.
- Is user friendly.
- Allows printing of messages.
- Context-sensitive help.
- Multilevel security.
- Multicapcode tracking.
- Multichannel capability.

Although this brochure does get the information across, it could be improved upon. I will elaborate. Pager Monitor consists of a DOS computer, IBM or clone, and one or more pagers that have been modified. It uses them to receive the signals rather than a communications receiver. One modified pager is required for each frequency, but any number of different pagers operate on the same frequency. The system, without computer, is about $1,600. Write for current prices.

DataScope

DataScope first became available in March 1995. It consists of a software package and an inexpensive interface unit. It interfaces a DOS computer (386 or faster) with a radio, such as the ICOM R7000 or PRO-2006 in either of two ways. The first is through a simple modification that is less complicated than that of the DDI interface. The second requires no modifying; the output is taken from the external speaker jack, through the interface, and into the RS-232 C computer serial port.

DataScope monitors POCSAG only, not Golay or Motorola; displays on the computer screen capcodes, and alphanumeric and text messages; and can be used for text. It also keeps a log of everything it receives. The price is about $250.

DataScope was designed as a diagnostic tool for technicians in the pager industry. Sales may be made to other legitimate buyers. Call or write for details:

JSoft Technologies
21414 W. Honey Lane
Lake Villa, IL 60046
Phone: 708-356-6817
Email: jsoft@mcs.com100

The POCSAG Decoder

Another system is available at a fraction of the cost of the above and as far as I know is just as good. It is the POCSAG Decoder, which sells in kit form for about $20 and includes a demo software package. The kit includes a small (1-inch-square) circuit board and a handful of components (a Schmidt trigger circuit) and the computer cable. On the disk are diagrams and assembly instructions. It takes maybe an hour to put together.

Once it is assembled, connect it between the computer and radio. You will need to find the discriminator output from the radio, which may mean opening it up and soldering a small cable in place. Step-by-step instructions are available on the Internet. You can start in the "radios" section of http://www.lysias.com, where there are links to sites that have this information, and then start the program. Tune in one of the pager channels and adjust the volume until text appears on the screen. It's just that easy.

How well does it work? Well, don't expect it to compete with the Beeper Buster, but most of the messages you see will be readable. There will always be a certain amount of garbage even when connecting the unit to the discriminator output of the radio rather than the earphone jack.

The Twilight Zone exists on television and in some people's minds, but in the real world, pagers are necessary to obtain information. But it is not necessary to let someone else take advantage of you. If you have a voice pager, consider changing to a tone-only type that works through an answering service so that no information is transmitted except the phone number. It is less convenient, but more secure.

FAX INTERCEPTION

In a world where we depend on high-speed communications, the facsimile (fax) machine has become indispensable. And for good reason: it is more efficient. When people talk on the phone, they tend to say more than when they put their communications in writing. They are inclined to come to the point instead of jaw-jacking about the weather or whatever else. It is also cheaper, so long-distance charges are less, and it lets the recipient read the communication at his leisure and consider a reply without the pressure of someone on the other end of a phone waiting for an answer.

The fax machine is nothing new; it has been in use since the 1920s. Newspapers used a system of photocells mounted on a large rotating drum called *wirephoto* to send pictures over telephone lines, and before World War II, the government used a similar system to send and receive maps and weather information. Anyone who likes to listen to short-wave radio has heard the roaring, buzzing sounds of wirephoto in the 81-meter band and the military facsimile transmission, which made many different strange and exotic sounds.

HOW FAX MACHINES WORK

A fax machine processes the document to be transmitted similar to the way information is displayed on a computer screen—in a series of small blocks or dots called *pixels*. As it passes through, a bright light, or series of small lights such as LEDs, shines on it, and the reflected light activates (or docsn't) a scrics of scnsors. The output of these sensors is converted to binary; a dark pixel becomes a one and a light area, where there is no printing, becomes a zero.

The binary code is then converted to audio tones, which are sent through the phone line. At the receiving end, the process is reversed. Where the binary code says there is a dark pixel, heat is applied to the sensitive paper, which turns it a yucky shade of almost black.

So the document you are sending, converted to audio tones, can be captured or intercepted anywhere along the phone line, the same as with a voice call. This puts confidential documents at risk. One way to intercept fax documents is to use Power Fax, a commercial fax interception system.

POWER FAX

Power Fax is user friendly, easy to set up, and easy to use. I have used and demonstrated it for government agencies in Mexico. It's a good system that does what it is advertised to do. It consists of a printed circuit board (card) that plugs into a full-sized slot in a desktop or "lunchbox" DOS

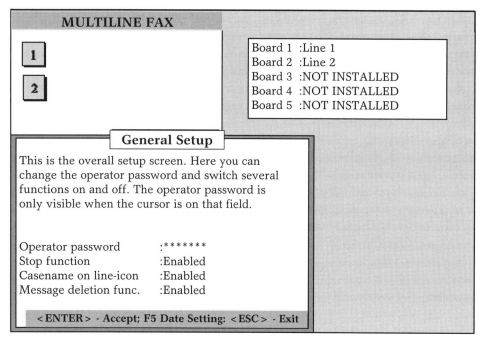

MULTILINE FAX

1

2

Board 1 :Line 1
Board 2 :Line 2
Board 3 :NOT INSTALLED
Board 4 :NOT INSTALLED
Board 5 :NOT INSTALLED

General Setup

This is the overall setup screen. Here you can change the operator password and switch several functions on and off. The operator password is only visible when the cursor is on that field.

Operator password   :*******
Stop function   :Enabled
Casename on line-icon   :Enabled
Message deletion func.   :Enabled

< ENTER > - Accept; F5 Date Setting: < ESC > - Exit

The main screen of the FaxMate system.

computer. An external version is under development so that it will operate with notebook types. A hard-disk drive is required.

Included are an interface cable, software program, and basic instructions. Although the help files are fine, this system could use a good instruction manual. But Power Fax is easy to use, so the operator can figure out what the instructions do not make clear.

To use Power Fax, install the card and the software and then, using the supplied cable, plug the card into the modular jack of the fax line to be monitored. It has a DB-9 connector on one end and a standard modular RJ-11 telephone plug on the other.

Installing the software takes only a few minutes, and learning to use it takes maybe an hour. There are just a few settings to make, and it is ready to work. This can be in the background, freeing the computer for other use. One card is required for each line to be monitored, but the cable can be moved from one fax line to another, and each line can have its own computer file.

When a fax is sent or received, Power Fax automatically intercepts it and stores it as a bit-mapped graphics file on the hard-disk drive. The file can then be viewed, shrunk, or expanded, reversed (black to white), inverted for when the sent document was inserted upside down, copied to a floppy disk for storage, and sent via modem to a remote computer. And, of course, it can be printed on a laser printer.

Another nice feature of this system is that it will intercept a multipage document that is already in progress, meaning that it does not have to be turned on or connected to a particular line when the initial handshaking occurs. This is because there exists something called a "mini-handshake" that is sent at the beginning of each new page. When the first edition of *The Phone Book* was being written, Power Fax was available from several vendors. However, as far as I know, it is now sold only by the manufacturer.

A HOMEMADE SYSTEM

Is it necessary to spend the money for a commercial interception system? If a fax transmission is only a series of audio tones sent through the telephone lines, then can't it be recorded and converted into a copy of the original document? Yes, this can be done, using a digital audio recorder. The recorder is attached to the line the same way as in the chapter on recording voice conversations in Part 1.

However, converting it is a little tricky. First, you rewind the tape to where the handshaking tones begin to get it ready to replay. Then connect the output to your voice phone line. Use it to call

SECURITY GUIDELINES
FACSIMILE MACHINES

C O U N T E R E S P I O N A G E   C O N S U L T A N T S   T O   B U S I N E S S   A N D   G O V E R N M E N T

Facsimile machines (fax) are a boon to spies. They provide an ideal method of transmitting information to the opposition. The internal spy does not have to photocopy documents, or risk taking paperwork from the premises. Some fax machines can transmit to 20+ locations with one scan! New security procedures are necessary...

• **Basic premise.** Confidential papers should not be transmitted by fax unless encryption is used.

• **Accountability.** In sensitive areas, fax machine operation should be entrusted to one responsible employee.

• **Double check.** Confirm the destination fax number... before transmitting.

• **Warning.** Notify the recipients of sensitive transmissions... before transmitting. Ask them to wait at their machine while the transmission takes place.

• **Be sure.** Directly dial the phone numbers for all sensitive transmissions. Speed Dial features, although convenient, are mistakes waiting to happen.

• **Handshake Part 1.** The first page of all transmissions should be a cover sheet which identifies the intended recipient, the sender, the total number of pages being sent, and a confidentiality notice. (Call us for sample wording.)

• **Handshake Part 2.** Have the recipient confirm the number of pages actually received. Note: On many fax machines, pages become stored in memory if the paper runs out.

• **Audit.** Review your fax machine's Transmission/Reception Audit Reports. Make sure that documents are being sent only to authorized locations. Added benefit: In addition to detecting document theft, this procedure will also detect unauthorized use of the machine.

• **Investigate.** Review the fax machine's speed dial numbers, especially the ones that are not marked as being in use. Look for unauthorized numbers which have been programmed in. It is very easy for the internal spy to make transmissions to unauthorized destinations, while legitimately using the machine.

• **Cheap insurance.** Fax machine transmissions can be intercepted via ordinary wiretapping techniques. They also provide an excellent hiding spot for other types of electronic eavesdropping devices. Any machine which handles confidential information should be part of your regular electronic eavesdropping detection program.

• **VERY IMPORTANT:** Carbon film piano rolls from some *plain paper* fax machines contain a perfect copy of **all** transmissions received. Don't toss these expired rolls into the trash where they can be retrieved by spies. Also, don't let secretaries send them to "carbon recyclers" – *this is an old espionage scam.*

Fax machine wiretapping and carbon roll theft are only two spy tricks. There are hundreds more. Remember – Espionage is Preventable. For further information about pro-active programs to combat espionage, electronic eavesdropping and wiretapping please contact us.   PO Box 668, Oldwick, NJ 08858

the fax number and, when it answers, start the recording. With a little luck, the fax machine will think it is another fax calling, and the handshaking will be successful. From there, everything will be as if it were an incoming fax.

This works—I have done it—but it's tricky. Timing and recording and playback levels have to be just right, and even then it doesn't always work.

If you seriously need to monitor the messages being sent from your office fax machine, invest the money in a Power Fax system.

SECURING YOUR FAX SYSTEM

Faxes containing sensitive information can be protected by encrypting them, using a commercial encryption system. Ricoh Corporation makes the Model SFX2800M, which uses the DES. No details were available when this book was completed.

SecureFX fax system, from Cylink, works with your existing fax machine or computer fax modem. Transmissions are encrypted using the DES, and key management is through the SEEK system. So if you are sending a fax in the secure mode, it will not be transmitted unless the sending machine detects another SecureFX system on the receiving end. This eliminates the mistake of sending classified information to the wrong person. It also works in normal unsecured mode.

PART 4

SECURE COMMUNICATIONS

SCRAMBLERS AND SECURE DATA TRANSMISSION SYSTEMS

Landline phones can be tapped. Cellular and cordless phones can be monitored. Fax messages can be intercepted, and, short of speaking face-to-face as did our distant ancestors, virtually every method of communication is vulnerable. Maybe you are concerned about this, maybe not.

As you have read, the chances of the "average person" having his phone tapped are very slim, whether by a business competitor or someone who selects him at random. There are hundreds of thousands of scanners that can monitor cellular telephone calls, but the chances of someone logging on to your communications are also very slim, and unless some entity, a government agency for example, has a serious interest in you, it isn't going to spend the money to use a commercial monitoring system to spy on you. Based on everything you have read so far, and what you are involved in that anyone else would want to know about, it is up to you to decide whether you should take some precautions to make your communications secure.

If you do decide to make your system secure, you may be faced with a bewildering array of products. What do you buy? Where do you get it? There are plenty of choices, but how do you know exactly what you are being offered? The salespeople in retail stores may or may not know the details of every product they sell, especially with hundreds of items in stock. Mail-order companies aren't much different. Their catalogs are designed to get across the most information possible in the smallest space and are often written by advertising specialists who probably don't understand the products.

Sometimes the information provided is misleading. One of the big mail-order retailers, The Sharper Image, recently advertised a simple phone tap detector as being more effective than a physical search. You now know that this is not true, and so do many others. The company received so many complaints about this advertisement that it was forced to retract the statement and change the ad. Maybe the manufacturer of this device misrepresented its product to The Sharper Image. At any rate, the ad was misleading. Such ads are not unusual, either. There are many "security" products available whose maunfacturers make claims that are flat-out bullshit.

This chapter is about different types of telephone scramblers and secure data transmission systems, how they work, and how safe they really are. Nothing in this book is misleading; I don't sell any of these products, and I don't get a kickback from sales generated by any of them, so I have no reason to be other than objective. Some of these products provide a minimum of security; like door locks, these security products keep honest people honest. Others are secure enough that all casual eavesdroppers will be locked out, as will most industrial-strength spies. A few products are so secure it is extremely unlikely that even the NSA would be able to defeat them in the next dozen years. And you may be pleasantly surprised to know that you don't have to spend very much money.

SUBCARRIER EXTENSION PHONES

Subcarrier extension phones are a clever idea. They eliminate the need for expensive wiring, long cords that get tangled up and tripped over, and conventional cordless phones that can easily be monitored. Just plug a subcarrier extension phone in to the nearest 110-volt wall outlet and talk. Your voice is sent through the power lines to an interface unit connected to your telephone line so that you can place and receive calls the same way as on an ordinary phone.

Indeed, they are a clever idea, but are they secure? Some of the catalog ads for these phones claim that they are. One such ad says that no one can "listen in outside 'your own' pole transformer." The implication is that each house has its own, which it does not. The transformers referred to change the transmission line voltage from 7,200 volts or so to the single-phase 220/110 volts that enter your home and are often located on telephone poles in the alley. One transformer provides sufficient power for about a dozen houses or maybe two dozen apartments. And anyone in any of the houses or apartments can intercept conversations from cordless extension phones by using the same type of phone.

An unconfirmed rumor is that there are devices that can extract the conversations from beyond the pole transformer, but I don't know of such a system. So if you want to use one of these phones, fine, but you might want to consider what you read here.

FREQUENCY INVERSION SCRAMBLERS

Frequency inversion is a process that allows communications to be scrambled by using a fixed base point, at which the frequencies are swapped. Anything above the base point is swapped with a low frequency and vice versa.

"The Scrambler"

One of the most widely advertised phone scramblers in the business is The Scrambler, made by Research Electronics, Inc., in Cookeville, Tennessee. The few remaining spy shops and related mail-order companies sell it. The Scrambler is a versatile device, it is completely self-contained, and it fits over a telephone handset and some cellular phones, with an elastic band. It is battery operated, and there are no wires to connect.

It is sometimes advertised as "giving you the advantage over all types of eavesdroppers, from the scanner hobbyist to the specialist in industrial espionage." It has, the ad says, 52,488 different "codes," the implication being that this is the number of different keys that would have to be tried to break the encryption system it uses, described as "a speech spectrum inversion technique." This is actually ordinary frequency inversion.

It is true, apparently, that one would have to try all of these thousands of keys to be able to listen in, if that person was also using the same unit. But if The Scrambler is being used with a cordless or cellular phone, and someone is listening with a communications receiver, he would be able to unscramble the conversation. The same is true if The Scrambler is used with a landline phone, and someone has tapped the line. All the eavesdropper would have to do is feed the intercepted audio through a frequency inversion scrambler, such as the TVS250 from Securicom, to decrypt it. I have tried this, and it works. Among other things, I heard two small-time drug dealers talking about stocking up on crack, getting ready for the first of the month, when the welfare checks come out.

The Scrambler is a readily available device that will keep out the casual listener, but not a

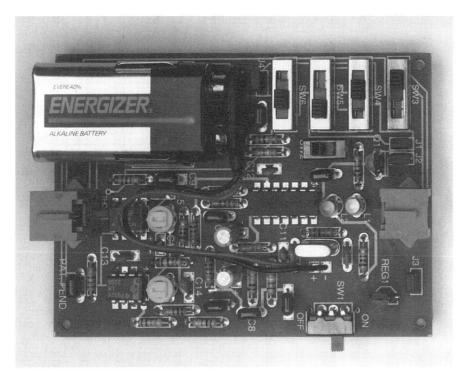

This is the TVS250 frequency inversion scrambler from Securicom.

determined individual who has read this book or other similar ones. One Scrambler is required for each end of the line, and it retails for $550 to $700 a pair.

The TVS250

The Securicom TVS250 scrambler is a frequency inversion type that plugs in between the handset and base of virtually any desk or wall phone. It does not work on one-piece, cordless, or cellular phones. Two units are required, one for each phone to be scrambled. It is sold in both assembled and kit form. I ordered one of each, and the package was delivered by UPS within the time I expected.

The first thing I noticed about the unit was the circuit board. It is a high-quality green fiberglass—and it is thick, unlike the ones in some other stuff made in Taiwan, for example. The silk-screening was of good quality. All of the printing was easy to read, and the placement of the parts was clear and easy to follow. I looked through the parts, and everything was there—nothing missing!—and of good quality. For example, the resistors are all 5 percent tolerance rather than 20.

Assembling the TVS250 was easy. It took me less than two hours (I have had a fair amount of experience building things), but a person with very little knowledge of electronics should be able to assemble it with little difficulty in one evening if he has had a little experience in soldering printed circuit boards. This is not at all difficult to learn, at least the level of skill required for the TVS250. There aren't any places where soldering the components is difficult, and there are no surface-mount devices.

The instruction manual is very well written. A clear, easy-to-read diagram of the board is on the right-center page, and on the left is a list of components. They are all identified by numbers or descriptions, so even for a beginner knowing what's what is not difficult. To make it even easier, it lists the order in which the components should be placed on the board. Also in the manual is a chart showing how to determine the value of resistors from the colored bands.

Once the scrambler is assembled, the manual has a test to perform to make sure it works, as well as troubleshooting tips just in case it doesn't. Then you are referred to the user's manual, which explains how to set the switches for the phone on which you will be using it. Most phones use the same settings, but with so many companies making different types, which are not wired the same, the TVS250 provides these switches to compensate.

Using the TVS250

The instructions are as easy to follow as the assembly manual. Just read it carefully, and you will be up and scrambling in a few minutes. To install it, just unplug the handset and insert the unit between it and the base of the phone. A short cable is included for this. It is powered by one 9-volt battery, for which there is a clip-type holder on the circuit board, or a 110-volt adapter can be used. Two switches are provided to turn the power off and on and change from scrambled to clear mode. Both have a bright LED to show the condition.

There are two gain (volume) controls, for the microphone (mouthpiece) and earphone of the telephone receiver. Setting them is a little tricky at first (it takes a minute or two), but after that it works fine.

Sound quality is very good: in the clear mode the phone works as if the scrambler were not even there, and in the scrambled mode sound quality is also very good. You will easily recognize and understand the person to whom you are talking, although it's not 100 percent as good as in the clear, but perhaps 90 percent or so. There is always a slight change in sound with telephone scramblers anyway, even the high-priced ones.

How Secure Is the TVS250?

With frequency inversion the higher portions of sound are swapped with the lower frequencies. This is not the same as more sophisticated and secure digital types (nor is it misrepresented to be), which cost eight to ten times as much. Frequency inversion will prevent nosy neighbors and landlords from knowing what you are saying, but it can be defeated the same way as with The Scrambler. The TVS250 was not made for high-security applications, and it is not advertised as such, but it does provide enough security to defeat the casual listener.

Conclusion

The TVS250 is easy to assemble and use, is made of high-quality components, and does exactly what it is advertised to do at a very reasonable price. In kit form it is about $85, and assembled and tested it is about $110. Write or call for the latest information.

The Motorola "Secure Clear" Cordless Phone

"Cordless phone eavesdroppers are everywhere," says pro golfer Lee Trevino, in a brochure promoting Motorola's cordless phone line. "But with my Motorola Secure Clear Cordless Phone, my private conversations stay private." This also is plain old ordinary frequency inversion. Motorola produces some of the most secure telephone and two-way radio systems in the world. From DES to Digital Voice Protection, Motorola is an industry standard. Therefore, Motorola should know better than to misrepresent frequency inversion as "secure."

Transcrypt International

Located in Lincoln, Nebraska, Transcrypt International makes three models of frequency inversion scramblers. One is essentially the same as those described above, but the other two are not. The principle is the same, but then they do some magic that makes these two units very secure.

Again, ordinary frequency inversion uses a fixed base point, at which the frequencies are swapped. Anything above the base point is swapped with a low frequency, and vice versa. Now suppose the base point were changed periodically. Anyone trying to descramble the speech would have to know how often it changed and what frequency it changed to. This is what Transcrypt has done. The more often it is changed, the more difficult it is to decode. Exactly how often the base point is changed, Transcrypt asked me not to reveal, other than to say that it is many times a second. So to convert it back to clear speech would require a fast mainframe computer and a great deal of time to determine the sequences.

If you were listening to one of these units on a communications receiver, you would hear sounds similar to ordinary frequency inversion, in that you would know it was speech. Listen carefully for a

few minutes and you will even think you can make out a word here and there, but you can't. It just seems like it. Every half-second or so, there is a loud knocking sound, which is a data burst—the two units sending information back and forth to keep them synchronized.

The three models of Transcrypt International scramblers and their retail prices (each) are:

Model	Level 1	Level 2	Level 3
PX	$370	$435	$500
LX	$740	$805	$870
CX	$250	$315	$380

The PX is for Motorola MicroTAC phones, the LX for landline desk phones, and the CX for cellular transportables. The LX and CX are plug-in types, using standard modular RJ-11 connectors. The PX has to be installed at the Transcrypt factory. This is included in the price.

Level 1 is ordinary inversion. Level 2 uses a changing base point and a certain rate. Level 3 uses a much faster change in base point. Two scramblers are required, one for each end of the line. This is for both cellular and landline phones, meaning that someone on a home or office phone can talk to someone using a cellular phone and the system will work. When the connection is made, the scrambler system goes through what is called "handshaking"—each scrambled phone sends out a signal looking for a signal from the other end. If a phone using this scrambler does not hear the signal, then it automatically works in "clear" mode, meaning that it is compatible with any other unscrambled phone.

If the signal is heard, the phones automatically go into scrambled mode. It is not necessary to arrange for a key ahead of time; the system selects a one-time key for each conversation.

There may be other phone scramblers that are similar, but this is the only system I know of that does not require a prearranged code to be used. That, along with the security level, makes this a very desirable and affordable product for those who are serious about secure phone communications.

For security in commercial two-way radio communications Transcrypt makes a wide variety of products, from encryption to portable repeaters to computer control systems and more. Transcrypt is the actual manufacturer, not a reseller. For more information, phone, write, or fax (necessary information is in Appendix 2).

900 MHZ CORDLESS PHONES

The FCC has approved the frequency band of 902 to 928 MHz for use by no-license devices, wireless modems, and cordless phones, sometimes just called "900 cordless." However, just changing the frequency does not make them any more secure than their VHF counterparts. In fact, the user may have a false sense of security by believing that these frequencies are out of reach of scanners. Once, a few years ago, that was true. Most scanners didn't cover beyond 512 MHz. But many communications receivers and most of the newer scanners do. So much for ordinary "900" phones. But there are two other types that offer a fairly high level of privacy.

Spread-Spectrum Technology

This technique was first used in World War II for secret communications and to protect against jamming. The reasoning was that since conventional transmitters used a narrow bandwidth signal, it was easy for the enemy to zero in on that signal and transmit a stronger signal on the same frequency, thus interfering with it or jamming it. Bandwidth refers to how much of the radio frequency spectrum a particular signal occupies. Most two-way radios have a bandwidth of plus and minus 5 kHz, or

5,000 cycles. Commercial television stations have a bandwidth of 6 million cycles, or 6 MHz. More than 1,000 two-way radio channels would fit into the space used by one television station.

Now if it were possible to modify a radio transmitter so that its signal was much wider, then the enemy would not be able to jam it easily. This is what spread-spectrum technology does. It "spreads" a signal over a much larger portion of the spectrum, from 500 kHz (half a MHz) to about 5 MHz. Not only is it much more difficult to jam such a signal, it is also very difficult to intercept it and understand what is being transmitted. To add to the confusion, many transmitters can be operating in that portion of the bandwidth at the same time. Another advantage of spread spectrum is that even at UHF frequencies, it has greater penetrating power and isn't blocked by walls, ceilings, and other obstructions in the signal path; it is similar to low frequencies used in international shortwave broadcasting.

Technical Stuff

There are different types of spread spectrum, two of which are frequency hopping and direct sequence. With either method, the signal to be transmitted is first converted to digital "bits" to ones and zeros. Then the bits are assigned slightly different frequencies. The ones might be 10.0001 MHz and the zeros 10.000. It is also possible to break the ones and zeros into small parts and assign each a slightly different frequency.

In frequency hopping, the frequencies of both are changed, perhaps to 12.4251 and 12.4250 and then again to another frequency, so they "hop" around within the wide bandwidth. This change can occur hundreds or even thousands of times per second, and without knowing the sequence of the changes, it is very difficult to extract the conversation from the signal. The faster it changes, the harder this is.

The direct sequence method is similar, except that the frequency does not change, or hop, which makes it a little easier to crack, but it is still very difficult. Many companies have been established to improve on spread spectrum, both making it more secure and breaking it. Granger, ESL, Lawrence Livermore Laboratories (where atomic weapons are developed), and some other labs are involved in this never-ending game of spy versus spy.

How Secure Is It?

Spread-spectrum technology was classified as secret until 1985, but it is now available to the public. How secure is it? Can spread spectrum transmissions be "broken"—i.e., is it possible to intercept a spread-spectrum signal and extract the conversation or data being transmitted?

This is difficult to quantify. It is, I am told, possible to break the direct-sequence method with a very fast personal computer or workstation, using a program such as Fast Fourier Analysis or Digital Fourier Transformation, depending on the bit rate and whether the bits are broken up. It requires someone who knows what he is doing and, still, this can take a great deal of time. The frequency-hopping method is much more difficult.

The three-letter government agencies may be able to break spread spectrum, and possibly some industrial-strength espionage specialists can too, but not hobbyists, private detectives, local law enforcement agencies, or most electronic technicians. Unless some very powerful people want to know what you are saying, there is little need to worry about it.

Vtech

Vtech, of Beaverton, Oregon, makes several models of 900 MHz cordless phones. I have not used any of them, so this is based on the information I was sent and a comment by a trusted associate who does have one. This associate bought his about two years ago and has never had a problem.

"Range is much better than on my old [low-VHF] Duo-Phone, and the sound quality is excellent," he says.

One model, The Regency, uses spread-spectrum technology. It has a lot of nice features, including multihandset capability: up to eight handsets can be used with one base unit. It has handset-to-handset intercom, 20-number memory, call hold, and something called multilink. The literature the manufacturer sent me doesn't say what this is; perhaps it is the handset intercom. Whatever it is, it offers a personal identification code feature to limit access to certain handsets.

Vtech also makes the 900DX with "up to five times conventional cordless telephone range" (which could be well over a mile under the right conditions) and many other nice features. This model is digital, and the brochure promises "Digital Voice Encryption System—Prevents Scanning for Total Security." Any kind of digital encryption system, even the simplest, will prevent the casual eavesdropper using a scanner, from listening in, as well as most hobbyists and electronic technicians and even local law enforcement agencies. However, I doubt that the method used will stand up to attack by federal intelligence agencies. But details of the encryption method were not available when this book was completed.

A third Vtech model is the 902 Platinum two-line phone, with a whole bunch of features. Digital voice encryption, an LCD display that shows the number called, three-way calling, caller ID display (requires that caller ID is available from the telco), automatic 10-channel search and select, speaker phone, hold, flash, mute, and redial.

Although I haven't tested or used any of Vtech's products, I am inclined to believe that these are high-quality telephones from the brochures sent by the company.

SPREAD-SPECTRUM WIRELESS MODEMS

New developments in electronics, as well as competition among manufacturers, bring down the price of electronic communications products, and much of the technology used by government and big business has become available to the consumer and the small business.

Global Integrated Network Access

One such system is the Global Integrated Network Access (GINA), made by GRE America in Belmont, California. GINA is a stand-alone, self-contained, high-UHF transmitter/receiver system that uses spread-spectrum technology to send computer data to a remote location. Two models are available: the 8000N operates in the 2.4 GHz band and the 5000N in the 902 to 928 MHz band, which you know is assigned by the FCC for low-power devices. No license is required to use GINA on either band.

GINA interfaces to any computer through an RS-232 serial communications port, the same as a standard landline-based modem. It is self-contained. To install it just connect the power cord, computer serial cable, and included antenna, and it is ready to go to work. In other words, install it the same way as you would an ordinary modem. Everything you need is included with your GINA, including the software, power supply, antenna, connecting cables, and an unusually well-written, easy-to-understand manual.

How Secure Is GINA?

You already know that spread spectrum is not easy to break, but what if one person is using a GINA and someone else has one set up in the signal path? Would the other party be able to intercept what is being transmitted?

In addition to having 21 channels, GINA has a user-selected code for each channel with 99 different settings. So if someone set up 2,100 GINAs and 2,100 computers, at a cost of about $4 million, and had enough people to operate them, perhaps. But remember that the data sent through GINA can also be encrypted. Use PGP (Pretty Good Privacy) or double-encrypted DES and you need not be concerned about interception. No one would be able to do anything with the intercepted data.

SCRAMBLERS AND SECURE DATA TRANSMISSION SYSTEMS

Range

This depends on several factors. With a clear signal path, no obstructions, and the antenna mounted on the roof of the building, you can expect a solid signal for at least one mile. Perhaps more.

Options

A voice option allows you to communicate verbally with another GINA using a telephone-type handset with a push-to-talk button. It connects to GINA with a standard RJ-11 (modular) connector, which is supplied with the handset. Just plug it into the front panel.

Specifications, Model 6000N

Operating range	905 to 925 MHz or 2.4 GHz
Radio technique	Direct-sequence spread spectrum
Output power	725 MW
Channels	21 user selectable
Power requirements	10.5 to 13.8 DC
Power consumption	10 W max
Dimensions	1.42 x 4.17 x 5 in.
Weight	16 oz.
Voice option connector	Standard RJ-11
Included	Detachable antenna and AC/DC power supply
Price	Under $800 per unit; two required

Opinion

GINA is an important and necessary product in an age of unrestricted government eavesdropping, industrial espionage, and interception of confidential information by casual listeners. GINA should be given serious consideration by any company or individual who wants a secure method of data transmission.

"GINA is a fine, reliable workhorse—try one!" says Randy Roberts, publisher of *Spread Spectrum Scene*, in the April/May issue. His fax number is 415-726-0118.

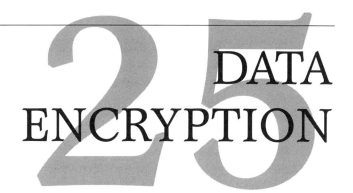

25 DATA ENCRYPTION

here is one way—and only one way—that you can send data from one place to another, or have telephone conversations and know that the content is absolutely secure: encrypt it. No matter how secure a phone line may be, there is always the chance that it could be tapped. As you have read, using a spread-spectrum wireless modem for data transmission may be more secure than other measures, but there is still the chance that the signal could be intercepted by government agents and the information recovered.

Sending confidential information through e-mail on the Internet is very risky, because it can be intercepted at many locations in its circuitous route from origin to destination. It might be bounced from fiber-optic cable to microwave relay tower to orbiting satellite to copper telephone wires, and may pass through various gateways before it is finally delivered. At various points along the way there are people who could read it.

As with other methods of intercepting information, this is very unlikely. At least it used to be. There are tens of millions of messages flashing through cyberspace every day, and the people who maintain the many systems through which they pass have little time to browse through random messages, even if they wanted to.

But, what with the government's constantly escalating war on privacy, there is always the possibility that your e-mail will be intercepted. The feds have special supercomputers (more on this) built by Cray that are designed to scan through e-mail, looking for certain words and phrases. If one or more of them are in your messages, they get flagged for further investigation.

ABOUT ENCRYPTION

First, I want to explain the common misconception that many people have about "breaking" a code. This is not the way it usually works. Strong, reliable ciphers, codes (such as the DES, DES-X, RSA, IDEA, and PGP) cannot be "broken." There is no secret way to decrypt any message that uses these ciphers—no "trapdoors" or anything like that.

It is true that there have been codes that had these built-in weaknesses, but they soon disappear from the market because no one will use them.

The way an encrypted (ciphertext) document is usually converted back into its original form (plaintext) is by somehow obtaining the key or password. Sometimes this happens when people leave the key where it can be found or use something dumb like their name spelled backward or their phone number. Another is when the keys are sent to another person through an unsecure channel.

Believe it or not, people do this; they call their secretary on their cell phone and reveal the key to anyone who is monitoring. Lacking this easy method, the persons or agencies trying to reconstruct the message will try any of several methods of attack.

"Dictionaries"

Those seeking to break a code might build a "dictionary" on the person who encrypted the message, which includes various bits and pieces of information about the encrypter. So someone trying to be clever uses the serial number of a gun he once owned or the name of his dog, Phydeaux, or whatever. If it is a matter of "national security" the government will be very thorough in compiling such a dictionary. It will include the obvious—name, Social Security number, addresses, license numbers, names of friends and neighbors—and also such obscure things as terms and names and locations from the college they attended, as well as names of instructors, buildings, off-campus businesses, etc.

Then all of these words, names, and numbers, individually and in various combinations, will be tried as possible keys. There may be tens of thousands of them, but this is a drop in the bucket compared with the alternative, which is brute force.

Brute Force

This is the process of trying every possible key until the right one is found or the possibilities are exhausted. Depending on the code used, this might be quick or it might be impossible. When the DES came out, it was considered totally secure against the brute force attack, and for many years it was. Then as computers increased in speed and special DES chips were developed, the DES became very much at risk. A technique called "massive paralleling" was created in which thousands of these DES chips work together to find the key.

In his paper *Efficient DES Key Search*, Michael Wiener states that a single encrypted DES key can be found in 3.5 hours, using a custom-made computer. This machine would use 5,760 of the VLSI chips in a "frame," and 10 frames, along with the programming, power supply, etc., could be built for a million dollars.

Today, it is believed that the NSA, the CIA, and probably other agencies can find a DES key in about 27 minutes. This is according to a telephone conversation with Phil Zimmermann, inventor of the encryption program Pretty Good Privacy (PGP, which provoked the federal government to try to outlaw it). So, no matter what key you use, if the cipher is weak it might well be broken, and if a weak key is used with a secure cipher, the key might be determined.

Plaintext-Ciphertext Pairs

This is mentioned only in passing because an explanation is beyond the scope of this book. Essentially, it is a way of recovering the key used for a message if both the plaintext and the encrypted versions are available. Using the DES as an example, this reduces the effective keyspace slightly.

EXAMPLES OF DATA ENCRYPTION PROGRAMS AND DEVICES

Now, a look at some of the programs, ciphers, mentioned so far. Some of them can encrypt data— a message, a file, whatever—so securely that the data cannot be decrypted with the technology that exists today within a "reasonable" amount of time. Plain/ciphertext pairs, brute force, dictionaries notwithstanding, they cannot be "cracked" within years to come. Probably not in your lifetime. Maybe not in the next trillion years. That's how secure they are, and that's why the government, the NSA in particular, is trying so hard to keep people from using them.

168

A more detailed description of these programs is in *Digital Privacy* (from Paladin Press), but here is some basic information on some ciphers.

Private Line

Little needs to be said about Private Line, produced by Everett Enterprises, because it is an uncomplicated DES encryption program that can be mastered in 20 minutes. The latest version, 7.04, is menu driven and has all of the choices laid out in an easy-to-follow format. Absolutely nothing about programming or encryption needs to be known to effectively use Private Line, although the user can learn the program in more detail, since it has a help file that is not technical.

It offers automatic erase after encryption and can call up the file to be scrambled from wherever it is on the disk—you don't have to copy it to the Private Line subdirectory.

Now, since the DES is at risk, what good is Private Line? Much. First, remember that it takes a very expensive machine to find the key used, and this is limited to those who have them: government and big business. Second, Private Line has what is known as "double encryption," which is very secure. (I'll discuss this more later, or you can see *Digital Privacy* for more details.)

IRIS

IRIS was produced by Peter Moreton of Digital Crypto in the United Kingdom, and on the program disk are a number of programs, including the DES, the RSA, Playfair, Vigenere, Littlefield, and Vernam. Some of these are of historical interest thoughand not secure, as they were before computers, but the RSA is probably the most secure program that exists. As an oversimplified example, the RSA can use keys of unlimited length (depending on the power of the computer doing the processing) with a key of 1024 being typical with the PGP program. The largest key that has been found (factored) is something like 132, and this was done with a number of Sun UNIX workstations working together over a period of several months.

The reason the RSA is not used for encryption is that it is so slow that enormously complex calculations, called *numbers crunching*, are required. What is important about the RSA is that it is the basis of the public key system.

The Private/Public Key Concept

Earlier in this chapter you read about the dangers of sending the key, the password, for a secure encryption system to another person at a distant location. It might be safely transferred if it is handwritten, given to the other person in a dimly lit cocktail lounge in one of the seedier parts of the city, and then memorized and swallowed. Chased, perhaps, with a shot of tequila?

For many years, this was the dilemma. Until the RSA private/public key cryptosystem was developed by three geniuses named Rivest, Shamir, and Adleman. It was named RSA from their initials and solved the problem of getting the passwords to the right people without them falling into the wrong hands.

Again, it is beyond the scope of this book to present a technical discussion of how the system works. Suffice it to say that it is based on a very simple mathematical formula (which is public knowledge) that involves some extremely heavy number crunching. A few years ago, Peter Moreton stated that the possible key combinations of his cipher are more than the atoms in the known universe. The speed of computers has increased by an order of magnitude since then, but so has the complexity with which data can be encrypted. In other words, there will always be a lag because it is millions of times easier to encrypt than it is to decrypt.

Pretty Good Privacy

This public key program was written by Philip Zimmerman and combines the international data encryption algorithm (IDEA) cipher and the RSA. The actual message is encrypted with IDEA, and then the IDEA key is encrypted with the RSA. That is an oversimplification, but that's basically how it works.

PGP has been out for several years, and, so far, no one has been able to find a weakness or trapdoor to break it. PGP has rapidly gained acceptance among Internet users—few of us on the Internet trust the federal government—so PGP has become something of a standard as the people's encryption program. Several levels of security are included, the highest being what Zimmerman calls "military grade"—and indeed it is. If the government has the capability of breaking PGP, it would take years to do so.

The original version of PGP was not menu driven; you had to enter everything from the DOS command line. Then a few years ago, someone wrote a "front end" called Win-PGP, so that it could be used from Windows. Now, PGP Inc. in the San Francisco Bay Area has produced a program, PGP Mail, that runs on Windows and is very easy to use. It has become the industry standard and probably will remain so for many years to come. Unless the feds finally outlaw it and force us to use something they can easily defeat. And believe me, they are trying to do just that.

Data Encryption Standard

The DES was developed by IBM as the secret Project Lucifer in 1971, and in the years since has proven itself to be secure. There are no weaknesses, no trapdoors, no secret ways to crack it. The most important thing about any cipher is that it has withstood the test of time, and DES has. As stated above, there is no doubt that the NSA can use the brute force attack to derive a DES key, and there is little doubt that other agencies (e.g., the FBI, DEA) can easily afford such a system—as can big corporations and some rich individuals. However, there is something, mentioned earlier in the section about Private Line that can be done to make the DES many times more secure: double encryption. Here's how it works.

Tech Stuff

The DES uses a key that is 56 bits in length (called a "keyspace") or 56 ones or zeros. Like the following: 10010011001100111001110111000111000111000111000011100011. The total number of ways these 56 bits can be arranged is 2 to the 56th or $7.2 \wedge 16$th. Seven point two quadrillion.

Now, when you use a DES program, it is not necessary to type in or remember this long string, the actual key is entered in plain English, eight characters long, such as "enfjtsml" or whatever the user decides on. The program converts these eight characters to the binary ones and zeros. Since each (ASCII) character is made up of eight binary bits, this adds up to 64. Of these, 56 are used for the key, and the remaining eight are used as something called "parity," an error-checking system. It is this that the NSA can allegedly crack in 27 minutes. Or maybe 2.6 hours or three days or whenever—the NSA can get it done.

Now supposing that we encrypt something with a certain DES key, called "A," as is normally done, but then we decrypt it with a different key, the wrong key, called B. Then to further confuse things, we encrypt it again, this time using key A again, which is also the wrong key, since it was decrypted with B. That something is now so scrambled that the only way to decrypt it would be to reverse what we did. This is called double, or sometimes triple, encryption, and the key length (keyspace) now is $2 \wedge 112$ or $5.19 \wedge 33$rd.

If the brute force machine the NSA has can derive a DES key in 24 hours, to derive a key from triple-encrypted DES would take something like 1,974,180,658 thousand centuries. The numbers are approximate, so suppose I am off by a factor of one billion. Then the key could be found in only about 2,000 centuries. Suppose even that is off by a factor of 1,000. Then the key could be found in only 200 years. Maybe I am off by yet another factor, say 10. It would still take 20 years, and by then the information would no longer be of any importance. If you use the triple-encrypted DES, you don't ever have to worry about anyone's deriving your key, and your grandchildren probably won't be too concerned, either. Just don't leave it lying around where it is easy to find.

What Can I Use for What?

Different ciphers are used in different devices, for different purposes. For sending and receiving computer data, you can use Private Line, IRIS, or PGP. This can be for sending e-mail or encrypting to a disk to be mailed somewhere. The same ciphers can be used for secure storage on your computer.

For landline and cellular phones, you are limited to what is available on the market. For most of us, just the DES is secure enough—who are we that the government or some big corporation has any interest in? But if you think it might, you can use PGP for e-mail and telephone calls made through the Internet.

Should you not have Internet access, you might be interested in knowing that you can make and receive telephone calls using PGP. You can also set up real-time video conferences with the audio portion scrambled with PGP. Again, PGP has become an Internet standard.

Programs *Not* to Use for Anything

As far as I know, those programs listed above are the only ones available to the general public that can be trusted. There may well be others that I don't know of, but before using them, you should know for sure just what they are. An example from Digital Privacy is the algorithm used in version 5.1 of WordPerfect. This is a simple exclusive-or process, or XOR, which is very easy to break. But does the manual tell you this? No. You are left with a false sense of security, by being told that without the key, the file can "never be recovered." Bullshit. Access Data of Orem, Utah, makes a program that will recover the password used in WordPerfect. I have this program, and it works perfect (pun not intended).

Some programs use what is called a proprietary algorithm, meaning that the actual cipher is confidential, proprietary information and is not available to the purchaser. In this case, you have no idea what you are getting, and such a program should absolutely never be trusted. True, it might be as secure as the triple DES, but you don't know that. So there is no reason to take the chance—especially when PGP is available free on many bulletin boards and the Internet, and the new PGP Mail for Windows is available and affordable.

Remember: The strength of a cipher lies in its keys and not in the cipher itself. If the source code of any cipher is not made public, then it should not be used—you don't know what it is.

SECURE LANDLINE PHONES

Another product from Cylink Corporation is SecurePHONE, a complete unit that connects to any standard phone with an RJ-11 modular cable. It uses either the manufacturer's proprietary algorithm or the DES and generates a random key, which is used only once and then erased when the call is terminated. It works with another Cylink phone using something called Secure Electronic Exchange of Keys (SEEK) so that both units use the same key. One SecurePHONE is required at each end.

SecurePHONE takes only a minute to connect and measures 2 x 9 x 10 inches, so the phone can be placed on top of it. It has an LED to indicate secure mode and works in clear mode with other telephones. Cylink is a large company that makes many products for secure communications, including wireless modems, wireless local area network (LAN) and wide area network (WAN) systems, encrypted modems, and secure fax systems. Call or write for details, keeping in mind what you have read so far.

SECURE CELLULAR PHONES

Ordinary cellular phones use a system called advanced mobile phone service (AMPS). This is an analog system, meaning that your conversation is transmitted unchanged like an ordinary two-way radio system. It is not digital or encrypted, so it can be intercepted with a communications receiver or one of the commercial monitoring systems. This system has been used by the cellular vendors since the beginning of cellular communication 10 years ago, and the vast majority of cellular telephones also still use it, perhaps 99 percent. In the past few years, several other systems have developed and are being integrated into the present AMPS.

Narrowband AMPS

Narrowband AMPS (NAMPS) is also analog, but it uses a narrower bandwidth so that three conversations can fit in the space of one channel. Other than that, it is the same as AMPS and is no more secure.

Time Division Multiple Access

Time division multiple access (TDMA) is the digital cellular system and also the new PCS. Conversation is converted, inside the phone, to a series of bits, the ones and zeros language computers speak, and heard over a scanner, it is an unintelligible hissing sound. This does not mean it is scrambled or encrypted, at least not for the purpose of making it secure. The TDMA system does shuffle the bits around, but this has to do with equalizing the signals and not making the transmission secure.

Even the simplest of digital transmissions shut out the casual listener, but as mentioned above, this type of transmission can be restored to normal speech with a fast Pentium or Power Mac using software that is available on the Internet. So, obviously, the government can easily monitor digital cellular/PCS calls using this technique or just intercept your conversations at the CO where it has been converted back to normal speech. And as you read in Part 4, this is about to become very easy.

Most of the cellular vendors have equipment that works with both ordinary analog and digital, so if you buy a digital phone and are in an area where there is no digital, it will still work as an analog phone. I tried out a digital phone at one of the dealers and found that although the sound quality is not quite as good as analog, it isn't at all bad.

Code Division Multiple Access

Code division multiple access is a form of spread-spectrum technology, the direct-sequence method. Once used exclusively by the military, CDMA cellular is already installed in some areas of the United States and is becoming available in more areas every month. I have heard but not confirmed that AirTouch, CellularONE, and NYNEX are all working on setting up their equipment for CDMA.

I don't have the specific details, so there is no way to put numbers on it, but I have been led to believe that CDMA is more secure than the spread spectrum used in cordless phones, and it has some other advantages. It is as effective as analog while using a fraction of the power: 1/ 25 to 1/1000. This is encouraging for anyone concerned about the alleged health hazards of cellular. The bandwidth of CDMA is 1.25 MHz, in which space more than 40 analog signals would fit, and the conversations are spread throughout this space in some 4.4 trillion different ways, making CDMA extremely difficult to monitor.

Integrated Services Digital Network

Integrated services digital network (ISDN) is a service of various telcos. With this system, one can have two high-speed 56 kbs (thousands of bits per second) data "channels," so data can be transferred at 128 kbs through one ordinary copper-wire phone line. Either channel can also be used for ordinary voice calls. There is also a third channel used for control purposes.

This system consists of a converter unit and a printed circuit board (card) that plugs into a computer mother board, and the cost to set it up is about $250 for the "terminal adapter" and $500 for the computer plug-in card. There is also a setup fee and monthly charge. The voice transmissions are not made any more secure than normal, but the data transmissions are at 56 kbs, which makes it inaccessible to anyone who does not have a similar system.

IT'S UP TO YOU

As you have seen, there are dozens of products available that increase the security and privacy of your communications. But remember that while one device or system may provide protection against one type of electronic spying, there are other devices. So, each may need to be used in conjunction with some others. Using a secure fax machine defeats wiretappers, but not a spy in your office who steals copies of the sensitive documents. Using the Transcrypt Motorola STU phone system will make your telephone conversations very secure but isn't much help if there is a bug in your office. Securing your inside lines will prevent an inside tap but it won't stop a professional from climbing a telephone pole.

Again, no single product, no single technique, will guarantee you total security. Each situation is unique and has to be analyzed as such—and then the right measures must be taken. *Digital Privacy* has information on various types of computer security, and *The Bug Book* is a comprehensive manual on defeating room audio surveillance transmitters.

All this information, all this technology, is available to you, most of it at moderate cost. But, as you will see in Part 5, the world of surveillance, of privacy invasion, is dynamic and ever changing. To achieve the security you want in the present you need only take advantage of what is there, but to maintain that security, it is necessary to know what lies ahead and stay on top of what is available. Current information will be posted periodically on my Internet Web site (http://www.lysias.com) where I also provide answers to your questions.

Now a look at what lies ahead of us in the government's never-ending war against privacy.

VULNERABLE PATH ENCRYPTION, ENCRYPTION AT HALF THE COST?
BY MURRAY ASSOCIATES

Scrambled phones have the disadvantage of requiring one at each end of the conversation. If you want to call someone who also has a scrambled phone, fine, but if the other party does not, then you cannot use yours. But there is a way to encrypt only one end of the conversation. Say you are using a cellular phone and are concerned that someone is monitoring you, but less concerned that anyone has tapped the line of the person you want to call.

To use this technique, set up a second scrambler in your office, connected to the PBX system. When you call in, the PBX will recognize the scrambled signal (yours) and feed it to the other scrambler, which will convert it back to normal speech. From there, a line will be opened up, and you will be able to dial out to the person you want to call. The outgoing call will be in the clear, unscrambled, mode, but you have protected your end from cellular monitoring, and as you read in Part 1, since a PBX system uses whatever line is available, this helps defeat anyone who might be trying to tap your office lines.

If interested, contact Murray Associates for details.

PART 5

THE FUTURE OF
COMMUNICATIONS

BIG BROTHER IS (STILL) WATCHING

26

I do not believe that the kind of society I describe necessarily will arrive, but I believe that something resembling it could arrive.

—George Orwell

Such a society is most definitely arriving.

I have said this before and I will say it again: slowly and insidiously, the government is attempting to monopolize communications technology and prevent We The People from having any secrets. Big Brother, mainly U.S. Customs and the Secret Service, has raided and shut down nearly every "spy shop" in the United States. Surveillance devices, bugs, and wiretaps are becoming very difficult for the average person to obtain—as will, one day, countersurveillance devices. Big Brother has already enacted legislation that bans scanners and communications receivers capable of tuning into certain frequencies, such as those used for cellular telephones.

Now, Big Brother has introduced legislation that would prohibit the manufacture, import, and sale of any scanner or communication's receiver that can pick up transmissions of virtually any two-way mobile radio system—meaning those of police, fire departments, medical emergency services, and just about everything else.

The following is excerpted from the Grove Enterprises Web site http://www.grove.net/mtnews7-97.html:

> We have just received a copy of a legislative proposal which, if passed, could well lead to the elimination of scanners, as well as the scanning receiver portions of commercial and amateur radio transceivers. Not surprisingly, the new sanctions come from the office of Edward Markey (D-MA), the privileged member of last February's Congressional Subcommittee on Telecommunications hearings who, upon being shown that his previous lawmaking efforts were defective, forewarned that we would "see scanner sales drop precipitously." And now he's making that promise good.
>
> What is surprising is that, in spite of Markey's record of flawed rule-making efforts, Congress has once again entrusted him with more rule making. Predictably, his new proposals are ill-considered, sweeping, and reactionary, as if to punish the radio communications industry.
>
> The Bill, HR1964, begins by reforming the Internet, a section which, by itself, is already generating considerable ire from the telecommunications industry, but it is the scanner portion

of the bill which we shall address here. Markey proposes to ban all of the frequencies allocated to the newly defined Commercial Mobile Radio Services (CMRS) on future scanners.

The frequencies, in MHz, that would be banned are most of the bands from 30 to 43, 137 to 162, 216 to 222, 399 to 512, 806 to 941, and 1525 to 1990. And that's just the beginning.

As it is, HR1964 would remove access not only to the mobile radiotelephone services which was its superficial intent, but also weather satellites, Military Affiliate Radio System (MARS), Civil Air Patrol (CAP), many Experimental/Developmental frequencies needed for scientific and commercial purposes, low power industrial, itinerant, and many others as well.

It is the intent of some that the censoring not stop even at this. We have learned from a high-placed government official that law enforcement representatives are requesting the elimination of public safety frequencies from scanners.

Such legislation has already begun, and, like book burning, there is no end to it. Although the enormous opposition to this bill will no doubt defeat it, it will be back in modified form. And a little at a time, such legislation will make more and more frequencies illegal to monitor.

One day, we may find that it is a felony to own a shortwave radio for listening to overseas stations such as the BBC, Radio New Zealand, and the many others that transmit on the low bands. This would be criminalizing a fascinating hobby that I have been involved in since I was a kid and a neighbor gave me an old U.S. Army surplus BC-342-M receiver. It is historically significant that another nation did the very thing that the United States is now considering: in the 1930s, Germany passed laws forbidding the possession of any radios except those approved by the führer, Adolph Hitler.

A politician who introduces legislation does not necessarily know anything about the subject matter of that bill. Maybe yes, maybe no. I suspect that Markey does not know (or care) how many times we scanner enthusiasts have aided law enforcement in apprehending criminals who otherwise might never have been caught. After all, the majority of crimes are never solved.

I doubt that he knows how much assistance we ham operators have provided to the community in diverse ways from emergency communications to crowd control. Yet his bill would eventually make it a felony to possess much of the equipment that we amateurs have—and for which we have paid a great deal of money.

I doubt that Markey gives a damn.

Current information on the proposed legislation affecting communications will be on the Grove web site, as well as mine. Please check in now and then to see what is new and what you can do to stop this tyranny.

THE LIFETIME NUMBER?

A few years ago, the Bell System came up with an idea: you keep the same number permanently, no matter where you move or what kind of phone, voice mail, pager, PCS, or whatever you use. Bell explained it thus:

The ability of the public networks to efficiently route and deliver electronic communications is heavily dependent on the efficient allocation and use of a limited resource—the pool of 10-digit telephone numbers. In recent years, the proliferation of telecommunications services and providers has placed increasing demands on this resource. More importantly, new requirements such as demands for personal mobility, whereby communications services are provided to individuals, rather than to fixed geographic locations, and number portability, whereby customers are able to change service features and providers quickly without needing to change their telephone number, will significantly alter the way we manage the numbering resources.

Having a lifetime number would indeed simplify the telco operations—and also a few other things, including the government's ability to know where we are at any given time. No warrant is necesssary to use a PIN register that maintains a record of when a phone is used, the location, number called, etc. Making a call creates a record.

Having a lifetime number would mean not being able to change it to avoid being harrassed by persons known or unknown. And it might affect your ability to get additional lines with different numbers. Thanks, Ma, but no thanks.

THE DIGITAL TELEPHONY ACT

Known formally as the Digital Telephone and Communications Privacy Improvement Act of 1994, this law, signed by President Clinton, is filled with the usual legalese, but it doesn't really say much about the technology involved.

> The purpose of this Act is to clarify and define the responsibilities of common carriers, providers of common carrier support services, and telecommunications equipment manufacturers to provide the assistance required to ensure that government agencies can implement court orders and lawful authorizations to intercept the contents of wire and electronic communications and acquire call setup information under chapters 119 and 206 of Title 18 . . . "and" . . . in particular, nothing herein is intended to enlarge or reduce the government's authority to lawfully intercept the contents of communications.

Section 3, paragraph 4 is a little ominous: "The ability to receive, in a generally available format, the intercepted content of communications . . . at a location identified by the government distant from the facility that is the subject of the interception access point."

In other words, to be able to monitor communications from a location of their choosing.

And "a provider of common carrier support services or a telecommunications equipment manufacturer shall make available to a common carrier . . . any support or service equipment, including hardware and software, which may be required so as to permit compliance with the provisions of this Act." Again, it doesn't say anything specific about this "support or service equipment" or what it is or what it will do. A blank check drawn on your account at the Bank of Personal Privacy.

One part of the bill states that common carriers, meaning the providers of landline and cellular telephone service, are required to have personnel on duty to implement their eavesdropping system at all times. This implies that these carriers are necessary to make it work, that, as the way it is now, someone at the telco does the actual wiretap, the bridging connection. But something that the FBI director, Louis Freeh, said casts some doubt on this.

The following is from a congressional hearing of the Technology and Law Subcommittee of the Senate Judiciary Committee and the Civil and Constitutional Rights Subcommittee of the House Judiciary Committee (too damn many committees!). Louis Freeh, is being questioned by Sen. Patrick Leahy (D-Ver.).

> Mr. Freeh: "That's exactly part of it, and that's why we're here today because the technology is running at such a pace that we could be out of the wiretap business in a very short period of time. We're already suffering instances of impediments which are preventing the enforcement of court orders."

"If you think crime is bad now, just wait and see what happens if the FBI one day soon is no longer able to conduct court-approved electronic surveillance."

—FBI Director Louis Freeh May 1994

"None of the FBI field offices has yet documented an instance where a lawful intercept was frustrated as a result of advances in digital technology."

—*CPSR v. FBI* 92-2117 DDC

Senator Leahy: "But we may end up also holding back technology for that same thing. I mean, we're talking about the federal government paying for the various costs. You've got one provision in your proposal to require telephone companies to designate personnel to be on call 24 hours a day to activate the government's intercept order. Are we going to pay for that on-call person? I mean if you're dealing with the local telephone companies, say, here in Washington or in New York City or something like that, it doesn't seem like a big problem . . ."

Mr. Freeh: "Well, I think . . ."

Senator Leahy: "Are we going to pay for them?"

Mr. Freeh: ". . . I think we do pay for that, but I don't think those costs are excessive at all. If you're talking about 919 wiretaps in the whole United States by every federal, state, and local authority, that's a very small number of wiretaps, which is precisely why the access is so critical, because we select out only the most important, dangerous cases to use the technique for."

Senator Leahy: "So if the Topsham Telephone Company in Topsham, Vermont, which has five employees, get concerned, we can tell them that if they've got to have somebody on there you guys would pay for it?"

Mr. Freeh: "I think if they have the right software package that they could probably design much cheaper than the federal government they could be home sleeping at night and we could still get the access we need."

In other words, the government would be able to connect the wiretap by remote control without any help from the telco. Or without them necessarily even knowing about it. Or anyone else knowing about it. And without leaving a record: the entire operation could be deleted from the computer when the operation was complete. It's freaky, the idea that the feds can punch some keys on a computer keyboard and zap! someone's phone is tapped. Anyone's phone is tapped. *Your* phone is tapped.

The Digital Telephony Bill was withdrawn because of enormous public protest. So the sponsors came back with another idea: to be able to tap a certain percentage of phones within a particular geographical area. That, too, was shot down, but they'll be back with something else. Again and again . . .

And it's not just the United States that is part of this ever-increasing plan to eavesdrop on anyone the government chooses to bug.

PROJECT TAP (TAP ALL PEOPLE)

A report issued on February 24, 1997, by Statewatch, a London-based advocacy organization, shows that the FBI has been working with its counterparts in the European Union (EU) for five years to create a "global tapping system." The report reveals the existence of a memorandum of understanding (MOU) to ensure that surveillance of all existing and new technologies is compatible and coordinated with the FBI's efforts to advance its "digital telephony" agenda in the United States.

The FBI's plan is to facilitate wiretapping worldwide by pressuring countries to harmonize national laws on interception, increase cooperation of telecommunications providers, ensure that equipment has interception standards incorporated, and create de facto global standards by persuading as many countries as possible to cooperate and by providing compatible equipment to nonparticipating countries.

To achieve these goals, the FBI and its EU counterparts wrote a resolution adopted by the Council of the European Union on "the lawful interception of telecommunications." The council issued the resolution on January 17, 1995 (unpublished until November 1996) and an MOU on the requirements that need to be adopted into all laws. The MOU has been signed by the 15 member countries of the EU and the United States. There have also been "expressions of support" from Australia, Canada, and Norway. The FBI and EU have also pushed the requirements as standards before the international telecommunications standards bodies such as the International Telecommunications Union and pressured other countries to adopt them.

The requirements are almost exactly the same as the FBI's demands for digital telephony. They include "real-time access" to the "entire telecommunication transmitted" sent to a "law enforcement monitoring facility," access to all associated call data, geographic location information for mobile phone users, decrypted information for all operator-provided encryption, and response times "in urgent cases within hours or minutes."

The report notes that even countries that do not agree will be affected: the strategy appears to be to first get the "Western world" (EU, United States, and allies) to agree to "norms" and "procedures" and then to sell these products to Third World countries—which, even if they do not agree to "interception orders," will find their telecommunications monitored . . . the minute such communications hit the airwaves.

THE CLIPPER CHIP: JUST SAY NO

The Clipper chip is aptly named, as it clips the wings of individual liberty . . .

—William Safire, *N.Y. Times*

On April 16, 1993, the White House announced the Escrowed Encryption Initiative, a "voluntary program to improve security and privacy of telephone communications while meeting the legitimate needs of law enforcement." The Clipper chip was just that, a microchip, that contained an encryption program called Skipjack. The chip was made in such a way that no one could break into it and extract the Skipjack program, which is classified as top secret. It was made to be used in telephones, computer data networks, and two-way radio systems.

How Clipper Works

Someone using a telephone that incorporates the Clipper chip decides to have a private conversation with another person using the same kind of phone. He makes the call and once connected sets up what is called a "session key" (KS), a unique key used to scramble this conversation. This key can be anything the user wants it to be, any word or combination of letters and numbers. The session key is sent from one phone to the other in the clear before encryption begins.

Then the phone sends this session key to the Clipper chip inside the phone. Clipper encrypts the session key using the chip's built-in "unique key" (KU). This key is different for every Clipper chip and is broken into two parts. One part is to be held by the U.S. Treasury Department and the other by the National Institute of Standards and Technology. The two keys, the KU and KS, are combined to form the Law Enforcement Agency Field, LEAF, which is sent to the other phone. The actual encryption is done with the KU. Then the encrypted communication can begin.

If a government agency, or industrial espionage organization with the right contacts, wants to decrypt the conversation, it records it and feeds it into a "decrypt processor," which determines whether Clipper was used for the encryption. If it was, then the processor would reveal the LEAF. With the LEAF information, the agency can obtain the two parts of the key and turn the conversation back into plain English. These keys are good for the life of the chip, regardless of the session key used, so the agency would then be able to decrypt any future conversation made from that telephone. In other words, once the agency had the LEAF, it could use it any time it wanted.

How Secure Was Skipjack?

According to the EPIC *1994 Cryptography and Privacy Sourcebook*, the Cray YMP supercomputer can do 89,000 encryptions per second. At this rate it would take 400 billion years to try all possible Skipjack keys. Thus, it may be safe to say that Skipjack is very secure, unless there is a trapdoor. And those rascals at the NSA would do something like that.

Why the Clipper Chip Should Not Have Been Accepted

Among all the controversy and the massive amount of data created, I can filter out a number of reasons why I believe that Clipper is not in the best interests of the American people.

Clipper Has Not Withstood the Test of Time

Whenever a new cipher is developed, regardless of who created it, it is greeted by the scientific community with healthy skepticism—to say the least. Why? For no other reason than its newness. Before any cipher is accepted, it has to withstand the test of time, during which it will be taken apart and analyzed and put back together again many times. It will be scrutinized to the finest detail by experts who will devote a great deal of energy to try and find a weakness, a trapdoor, any method by which it can be broken. A cipher that stands up to preliminary analysis only whets the appetite of those who are determined to see how secure it really is. It becomes a challenge.

The DES, which began life at IBM as the Lucifer cipher in the 1970s, took years to be accepted, and it now has become an industry standard. Philip Zimmerman's PGP was initially distrusted but now is rapidly being accepted as a safe (very safe) program for "the people." But it took a while. If for no other reason than the fact that it is so new, the Skipjack cipher inside the Clipper chip should not be trusted. But there are other reasons.

The Source Code Is Kept Secret

To repeat myself, the strength of a cipher lies in the keys, not the cipher. Of the many ciphers that exist, there are three that have gained almost universal acceptance—RSA, DES, and IDEA—and they all have one thing in common: the source code is available to anyone who wants it. The source code is the actual program as written by the programmer in its original form. Having it does not weaken the cipher, and unless there is a weakness in the cipher, there is no reason to keep the source a secret. The NSA has classified Skipjack top secret. On one occasion, a number of experts were allowed to briefly examine it, but something this complex would take a great deal of time to analyze thoroughly.

Why does the NSA keep it secret? There is only one reason: NSA wrote it with a hidden weakness, a trapdoor, through which its employees can easily decrypt messages coded with it. Nothing else makes any sense at all. If the agency didn't have something to hide, it would release the source code.

Clipper Has Already Been Shown to Have Flaws

You will recall that to get the escrowed keys, the LEAF field is needed. But what if it wasn't there? What if it had been replaced with a bogus field that contains only random characters? There wouldn't be any escrowed keys to get, the conversation would still be scrambled, and the whole thing would be useless to the government.

This has been done and is explained, in technical terms, in the paper *Protocol Failure in the Escrowed Encryption Standard,* by Matt Blaze, for the proceedings of the Second ACM Conference on Computer and Communications Security. The details are too complicated for the average person to understand, which includes this writer, so they are not reprinted here, but the paper by Dr. Blaze and many other documents are available from the Electronic Privacy Information Center.

Now, it is true that this method of defeating the LEAF is not something that the average person is able to do on his home computer. But it is also true that at one time changing the ESN of a cellular phone was not something the average person could do with a PC. It is only a matter of time until someone writes a user-friendly routine that allows anyone to just connect the Clipper's circuit board to a personal computer via an RS-232 cable and punch a few keys.

Since this was demonstrated by Dr. Blaze, the NSA has started working on a way to make it more difficult to defeat the LEAF, and this may make it too difficult for a personal computer. But a mainframe will probably still be able to make the changes. An underground network will evolve, where people can take their phones and computer cards to have them modified.

Sooner or later someone will obtain the source code for Skipjack. The Clipper chip is made in such a way that this cannot be done directly. Most chips can be accessed to reveal what is in them, but the Clipper has something like a tiny fuse built in. Once it is programmed, this fuse is burned out; therefore, direct access is not possible.

However, the information still has to get into and out of the chip, and by analyzing the chip, the source code can be extracted. This is a big-time job; many hundreds, if not thousands, of hours spent with a sophisticated logic analyzer and a fast computer would be required, but that can be done. And when it is, the code will spread like wildfire, and copies will be on thousands of bulletin boards all across the world. Experts will have the chance they have been denied: to analyze it and find out just what Clipper really is. And then, as far as the U.S. government is concerned, it will be useless. So various government agencies will spend billions to develop something new, and the same thing will happen all over again.

Businesses that use encryption have invested millions of dollars in computers and related equipment that use the DES and RSA. Banks, for example, use the DES in electronic fund transfers. Software companies, such as Lotus Development Corporation, use the DES and RSA in their programs. But Clipper is not compatible with any of them, so the hardware would have to be rebuilt at enormous cost, and in order to encrypt software, a printed circuit board would have to be added to every personal computer, a card that has the Clipper chip built into it, because the chip is not available in software form. If security and cost were the main concerns, then the new triple-encrypted DES could be used with minor changes in the software and hardware.

Foreign governments and private businesses are not likely to use Clipper when our government holds the keys. Following World War II, captured German Enigma mechanical encryption devices were sold to other countries, without telling them that the U.S. government had already broken it. This is a good reason for other countries not to trust Clipper. So if it is used in computer and communications systems, other countries aren't likely to buy them. They will buy from producers in other countries, and U.S. companies will lose sales, billions in sales, of both hardware and software.

The Clipper chip was produced by the NSA, which claims that its employees are never involved in domestic surveillance. Why, then, does this agency want Americans to use it?

Can the government force us to use something like Clipper? Not directly. Government agents can't escort us into Circuit City and point out what we can or cannot buy. What they can do is take away any alternative. They can arrange for the FCC to cause endless delays in issuing type acceptance to any manufacturer of secure communications devices, and, without it, the devices cannot be sold. A manufacturer isn't going to spend the money to make something that it cannot market.

Indeed, Clipper is dead, but attempts by government to force us to use what its agencies produce are alive and well, as explained in the following that I received via e-mail.

ALERT FROM *CRYPTO-NEWS*

To: crypto-news@panix.com
From: shabbir@vtw.org (Shabbir J. Safdar)
Subject: ALERT: Show Your Support for Privacy on the Net During August
Date: Tue., 29 Jul. 1997 15:11:22-0400
Sender: owner-crypto-news@lists.panix.com
Reply-To: crypto-news@lists.panix.com

This alert brought to you by The Voters Telecommunications Watch, the Center for Democracy and Technology, the Electronic Frontier Foundation, EFF-Austin Americans for Tax Reform, and *Wired* Magazine.

WHAT'S HAPPENING RIGHT NOW

The FBI, CIA, NSA, and other law enforcement agencies are pressuring Congress to pass legislation to force anyone who wants to protect their privacy on the Internet to use programs with built in "key recovery" features—virtual back doors which would allow law enforcement (and anyone else sophisticated enough to find a weakness) access to your private communications.

This effort by the Clinton Administration to force the domestic use of government approved "key recovery" encryption represents a very real threat to your privacy and security in the Information Age.

Fortunately, a bill known as the "Security and Freedom Through Encryption Act" (HR 695) is making its way through the House of Representatives. The bill, known as SAFE, would help protect privacy and security on the Internet by:

- Prohibiting the government from imposing key recovery or key escrow encryption inside the United States or abroad.

- Allowing Americans the ability to use whatever form of encryption they choose.
- Encouraging the widespread availability of strong, easy-to-use encryption technologies by relaxing cold war-era export restrictions.

SAFE enjoys support from a bipartisan majority of 250 Members of the House of Representatives, and has been endorsed by civil liberties and public interest groups from both sides of the political spectrum, as well as a broad cross section of the computer and communications industries. The SAFE bill has recently cleared two key House committees and is expected to be voted on by the full House of Representatives in September.

WHAT YOU CAN DO NOW

Consider sending a letter or making a phone call to your Congressman's home office. Whatever you can do to show your support for privacy and security on the Net will make a big difference when the issue is voted on by the full house in September.

1. Visit http://www.crypto.com/member/
    Simply enter your ZIP Code to:
    - Find the name and contact information for your Representative
    - Sign up to join the Adopt Your Legislator Campaign;
    - Learn about your Congressman's voting record and positions on the encryption issue;
    - Tips on how to set up a meeting and contacting your Congressman;
    - Links to background information on the SAFE bill, and more.

2. Forward this ALERT to your friends and colleagues. Urge them to join Adopt Your Legislator campaign at http://www.crypto.com/adopt/

Two years ago, the Internet user community responded in overwhelming numbers to the threat of censorship and joined together to defeat the Communications Decency Act. The ongoing debate over US encryption policy reform is no less important, and will determine the future of privacy and security in the Information Age. Now is the time to join the fight, before it's too late.

WHAT'S AT STAKE

Encryption technologies are the locks and keys of the Information Age, enabling individuals and businesses to protect sensitive information as it is transmitted over the Internet. As more and more individuals and businesses come on-line, the need for strong, reliable, easy-to-use encryption technologies has become a critical issue to the health and viability of the Net.

Current U.S. encryption policy, which limits the strength of encryption products U.S. companies can sell abroad, also limits the availability of strong, easy-to-use encryption technologies in the United States. U.S. hardware and software manufacturers who wish to sell their products on the global market must either conform to U.S. encryption export limits or produce two separate versions of the same product, a costly and complicated alternative.

The export controls, which the NSA and FBI argue help to keep strong encryption out of the hands of foreign adversaries, are having the opposite effect. Strong encryption is available abroad, but because of the export limits and the confusion created by nearly four years of debate over U.S. encryption policy, strong, easy-to-use privacy and security technologies are not widely available off the shelf or "on the Net" here in the U.S.

A recently discovered flaw in the security of the new digital telephone network exposed the worst aspects of the Administration's encryption policy. Because the designers needed to be able to export their products, the system's security was "dumbed down." Researchers subsequently discovered that it is quite easy to break the security of the system and intrude on what should be private conversations.

This incident underscores the larger policy problem: U.S. companies are at a competitive disadvantage in the global marketplace when competing against companies that do not have such hindrances. And now, for the first time in history, the Clinton Administration and members of the U.S. Senate have proposed DOMESTIC RESTRICTIONS on the ability of Americans to protect their privacy and security on-line.

All of us care about our national security, and no one wants to make it any easier for criminals and terrorists to commit criminal acts. But we must also recognize [that] encryption technologies can aid law enforcement and protect national security by limiting the threat of industrial espionage and foreign spying, promot[ing] electronic commerce, and protecting privacy.

What's at stake in this debate is nothing less than the future of privacy and the fate of the Internet as a secure and trusted medium for commerce, education, and political discourse.

For more information on this issue and the various legislative and administration proposals to reform U.S. encryption policy, visit http://www.crypto.com/ or any of the following:

Center for Democracy and Technology—http://www.cdt.org/
Voters Telecommunications Watch—http://www.vtw.org/
Electronic Frontier Foundation—http://www.eff.org/
EFF-Austin—http://www.eff-austin.org/
Americans for Tax Reform—http://www.atr.org
Wired Magazine—http://www.wired.com/

For more information, visit http://www.crypto.com/about/
end alert 07.29.97

This is a sample of the advisories you can receive from *Crypto-News* if you ask to be on its mailing list. They are posted whenever the government starts with new legislation that threatens privacy and free speech. Please contact it to stay on top of all this legislation.

THE INFORMATION
SUPER SPYWAY?

If you have not yet experienced the magic of the Internet, I hope you will consider doing so. It's an adventure the likes of which you cannot imagine. And, as you just read, it is something that might one day become a government-controlled nightmare. By getting connected and adding your voice to the millions of others who defy governmental control, you might help prevent this from happening. Please do.

WHAT IT IS

A network is an interconnection of computers. It might be as simple as two or three individual computers in a small office, or it might be a very large network at a corporation that has dozens of computers tied together. The Internet is a vast network that connects hundreds of other networks, including privately owned systems, universities, military installations, and government facilities. The users can access such different functions as sending and receiving electronic mail on USENET, sending and receiving files through Telnet, conversing in real time through the Internet Relay Chat, using Gopher to find files on virtually any subject, downloading information on what Congress is up to, and reading electronic books through the Library of Congress, just to name a few.

On the Internet, you can send and receive messages (e-mail) or speak by voice—like on a regular telephone—with any of the estimated 40 million people worldwide who have Internet access. And you can do so using encryption programs that will defeat Big Brother—without paying a cent in long-distance charges. At least for now. Ma Bell and her babies are attempting to force legislation through so that they can charge Internet users by the minute.

HISTORY OF THE INTERNET

The Internet began life back in the 1960s, during the so-called Cold War, as the Department of Defense Advanced Research Projects Agency (DARPA) network. The idea was to have a medium through which the DOD could quickly share information with defense contractors, research labs, and universities involved in government projects. It was designed so that any facility could connect directly to any other, so if one or more were destroyed by a nuclear bomb, the others would still be connected. Funding was provided by the National Science Foundation, and a few years later DARPA evolved into the Internet, the Net of nets.

For more than a decade, the Internet was a well-kept secret, and access was limited to such facilities and the few individuals who knew how to access. This was before the World Wide Web and information, at locations called Gophers, was searched for using tools such as Archie, Veronica, and, yes, even Jughead.

Then the Internet was "discovered," and within the past few years it has exploded into a system that defies description. And naturally there are those who are not too terribly happy about this. Such as Big Brother.

So if you decide to go online, please keep in mind what you have read here. Remember that Big Brother intends to take over and dictate what we can or cannot say and to whom we may or may not communicate. The government intends to take away any method of making our conversations and credit card transactions private. The feds intend to have the Internet totally under their control.

Going online really isn't difficult, as you can learn in the rest of this chapter.

An interstate highway system? Do you realize how much interstate crime that would facilitate?

—J. Edgar Hoover, 1938
(I wonder how "Speed" would have reacted to the mention of the Internet.)

GETTING STARTED

To get on the Internet, you sign up with an Internet service provider (ISP, sometimes referred to as a server), of which there are many. Some are small businesses and are inexpensive. For about $15 a month, you can have unlimited access (as many hours as you want) to the complete Internet. Others, such as Prodigy and America On-Line, offer only limited access and charge an hourly "connect time" fee. This can get very expensive, hundreds of dollars a month for heavy use.

With some ISPs you can set up your account by phone and pay by mailing a money order. Others require that the applicant have a credit card and may, I have heard, run a credit check, even though by requiring payment in advance they aren't extending credit. Some are purported to monitor and censor the users' electronic mail, but I have no evidence to support this assertion. There are ISPs listed in the yellow pages under Internet Services.

As a beginner, you might want to decide on a server that provides you with a software package. Most of them are very easy to install and use; it is mostly a multiple-choice process.

You'll get a rush the first time you log on and see the "CONNECTED" message on the computer screen, just as everyone does, and within a few hours you will be easily able to search the Web for information and send and receive electronic mail.

AND THEN ALONG CAME THE NSA

To repeat what I said earlier, not everyone is thrilled about this explosive growth of the Internet. Some that aren't, to name a few: the NSA, Defense Intelligence Agency, DEA, FBI, Secret Service . . .

Every day there are hundreds of millions of communications flashing across copper wires and fiber-optic cables, relayed by microwave towers and bounced off satellites. More and more people are using e-mail for personal and business messages instead of telephones and fax machines for two reasons: there are no long-distance charges to pay to AT&T or Sprint, and electronic mail is delivered almost instantly.

All of these transmissions are digital (both e-mail and Internet telephone), and since digital communications cannot be monitored as easily as ordinary analog (audio) telephone calls, the feds are very concerned. Add to that the ease with which such communications can be encrypted, and it probably has the feds climbing the walls. But they keep trying. They do the best they can. After all, some of this electronic traffic may involve organized crime. Since the Cold War is over, the feds need something else to justify their trillion dollar witchhunts: now instead of Russians it's terrorists. Massive new computers are being built to monitor these electronic messages, scanning those that are not encrypted for key words that will alert the operators to stop and investigate further.

According to *Government Computer News*, the Cray model 3 Super Scalable system, using something called *processors in memory,* was to be ready in 1995. This one is designed to recognize patterns in data, which means that it will be set up to flag certain words and phrases sent via electronic mail. Mention the word *roach* and perhaps the DEA will come knocking on your door. If the words *president* and *gun* are used in the same message, maybe the Secret Service will kick your door down and take you away. But if we of the Internet use encryption, such as PGP or DES-X (triple-encrypted DES), for our e-mail messages, these monster computers can't decrypt them. So the government's only choice is to try to prevent people from being able to use them.

INTERNET CENSORSHIP

Another way that government can prevent privacy on the Internet is through censorship. Here is more on the so-called Decency Act mentioned earlier.

The Exon Bill

In February 1995, Senator Jim Exon (D-Neb.) introduced Senate Bill S.314, the Communications Decency Act (CDA), in the U.S. Senate. In an effort to stamp out "digital pornography," this bill would have made all telecommunications providers doing business in the United States (from the telephone companies all the way down to offices that use LANs) liable for the content of anything sent over their networks.

The Exon Bill was an amendment to the Communications Act of 1934, which says that anyone who "makes, transmits, or otherwise makes available any comment, request, suggestion, proposal, image, or other communication which is obscene, lewd, lascivious, filthy, or indecent" would be liable for prosecution. To avoid the possibility of tens of thousands of dollars in fines, confiscation of their equipment, and up to two years in jail, service providers would be forced to police their networks and monitor all messages sent over them.

They would also have to view every graphics file received and become the judge of whether it is "evil" and delete what is so deemed. The ISPs don't have the time or the personnel to do this. So graphics would start to disappear from the Internet. The great works of art. Diagrams showing how to examine a breast for lumps. Scanned photos of missing children.

If the same law that Senator Exon wants for the Internet were applied to the rest of society, virtually every museum, library, theater, and bookstore would be shut down and their doors sealed with the chains of tyranny and oppression.

The Blue Ribbon Campaign

The people of the Internet reacted to the Exon Bill en masse. Tens of thousands of e-mail messages poured into Washington protesting this attempt at diluting the First Amendment. On the World Wide Web, hundreds of thousands of people blacked out their opening screens in protest, and the campaign swept across the Web like wildfire. Thousands and thousands of Web sites proudly displayed the Blue Ribbon on their opening screens or elsewhere.

Many more thousands of Web sites that previously had no "adult" or "vulgar" material started including long lists of words that Senator Exon and company would have found objectionable.

Last year, three federal judges ruled that the CDA was unconstitutional and set it aside. But now "they" are back, claiming something like "one person's free speech on the Internet interferes with another person's free speech on the Internet," therefore no one should have free speech on the Internet except those of whom the government approves. Once this starts, there will be no end to it. I don't know about you, but I'll be damned if I am gonna sit through a half-hour of Bible study before I get to read my e-mail.

Once again, I hope you will discover the magic of the Internet and join forces with millions of others who resent the government's attempts at denying us freedom of speech and a secure way to communicate.

THE LAST WORD

Privacy versus the right to defend. There was a time back in the 1940s and early 1950s when electronics surveillance equipment was very difficult to obtain. Bugs were all but nonexistent because they, like other transmitters, used vacuum tubes, which made them bulky, and they consumed a lot of power. They were handmade, a few at a time, by specialists and government agencies.

With the introduction of the transistor, this suddenly changed. As kids, we built small AM transmitters that operated on the 50–54 MHz band and soon discovered that we were sought out to make them for people who had other uses in mind. From there, the "industry" exploded. It wasn't long before surveillance transmitters were being advertised in magazines such as *Popular Science* and *Radio Electronics* and spy shops were opening all across the country. Anyone who wanted surveillance devices could have them. Now, in the late 1990s, they have all but disappeared.

Federal agencies, mainly the U.S. Customs Service, have put virtually every spy shop in the United States out of business; therefore, transmitters are no longer available in retail stores. Agents have also raided some of the smaller manufacturers in their war on surveillance devices, and it won't be long before all of them have disappeared.

Deco, manufacturer of some of the best low-cost transmitters in the United States, has discontinued them, as has Audio Investigative Equipment. Both have told me personally that this was their decision and not due to pressure from the feds.

Sheffield, maker of some of the better transmitters, has moved to Ireland, and the high-end devices (the good stuff) that the public could buy are disappearing quickly. There are still several manufacturers of high-quality stuff, but unless you have the right connections you can't buy it—most people have never even heard of these companies. One can still buy FCC-approved wireless microphones from Electro Voice and Sony, but they are expensive, from $500 to well over $1,000.

The handwriting is on the wall: the government does not want "We the People" to have this technology. The feds want it all to themselves.

Does this mean you will be safe from thy neighbor bugging thee?

No.

The government has "banned" heroin and cocaine; yet these and other drugs are openly sold on street corners of all of the large cities in the United States as well as in many small towns. Banning anything just increases the people's desire for it and, of course, creates a black market. The price goes up, but the merchandise is still readily available.

There are many true stories of how people, ordinary people, have used electronic surveillance in their own defense. In *The Bug Book*, you can read about a beautiful young woman who was being terrorized by her ex-husband and was helpless to do anything about it—until a friendly technician came to her aid with electronic surveillance and ended the torment. If he had not been able to access this technology, she might still be a victim of this drunken brute who had beaten and raped her for several years.

PRIVACY VERSUS THE RIGHT TO KNOW

The only sure bulwark of continuing liberty is a government strong enough to protect the interests of the people and a people strong enough and well informed to maintain its sovereign control over the government.

—President Franklin D. Roosevelt, 1938

People should have the right to privacy in their telephone calls, including cellular. But the cellular industry was not willing to spend the money to make it secure (and most cellular customers are not willing to spend the extra money to get secure communications), so this gigantic multibillion dollar industry is forcing the FCC to restrict the types of radios we may own. And, to repeat myself, like book burning, once it starts (and it has) there will be no end to it. The incident where House Speaker Newt Gingrich had a cellular conversation monitored and recorded has fanned the flames of government control, of placing the responsibility on the people rather than where it really belongs.

PRIVACY VERSUS BIG BROTHER'S RIGHT TO KNOW

What does Big Brother have the right to know? Well, it depends on the definition of *right*. The government says that its minions should have the right to intercept any communication of any kind at any time—all phone calls, all e-mail messages, everything. Otherwise, the government would not keep trying to enact legislation with which it could do exactly that. Nor would it have those special Cray supercomputers made specifically for searching e-mail messages.

So, OK, there is a need for legal wiretaps in some criminal investigations. But there are fewer than 1,000 court-ordered wiretaps in the whole country every year. Installing them does not require the equipment and the technology that the government wants. It simply is not necessary. Nor is cost a factor. The average federal surveillance installation costs something like $65,000, and the cost of the equipment is maybe a few hundred. The only reason the feds would even ask for the legal and physical means is to use them for massive illegal wiretaps. And anyone who believes the feds when they say they never unlawfully spy on U.S. citizens is very naive.

THE LAST WORD

In reading this book, you have learned something about surveillance. You have read about how surveillance technology can be used in self-defense. You know the basics of how it is done and what equipment is required. You know how such spying can be defeated and how to do so, without spending very much money. You know that although the odds are against it, you could be placed under electronic surveillance. And by now, you should realize that the government is, and has been for many years, spying upon its citizens, sometimes unlawfully.

Many thousands of people have joined the fight against government intrusion and have established the Electronic Privacy Information Center, Computer Professionals for Social Responsibility, the Electronic Frontier Foundation, and other such organizations dedicated to defending our ability to communicate without Big Brother's listening in.

Someone once said, "I don't want to find myself an old person sitting in a rocking chair, watching the world go by, and wondering if I might have made a difference." You can make a difference by adding your voice to the hundreds of thousands of others who are fighting this massive invasion of our privacy and wholesale destruction of our Constitutional rights.

What you do, whether or not you make a difference, is up to you.

—M.L. Shannon
July 1998

PART 6

ON A SWEEP

29 HOW A SWEEP IS DONE

This chapter is about how a sweep, a search for surveillance devices, is conducted by a team of surveillance countermeasures (TSCM) specialists. Every company has its own way of doing things, and some of the particulars are considered proprietary, so the team (of which I was a member) that this chapter is based on has requested that some details not be included. They are not. What is important is the result: that nothing is overlooked, and no listening device is missed. So while the order of things and a few other details may vary, this is an accurate representation of how a sweep is done.

THE CONTACT

One of the senior partners of a midsized law firm has just made an appointment with the CEO of a computer peripheral manufacturing company, which wants to buy out a smaller manufacturer that makes some of the specialized components used in its peripheral devices. However, a competing company that makes the same kind of peripherals is also interested in acquiring the small company. Both the attorney and the CEO are aware that the competing company would like very much to know the details of their plan to acquire the small company. The attorney has been consulted to work out these details, and therefore there is the possibility of electronic eavesdropping. Because of this, the negotiations will take place at the lawyer's office rather than the manufacturer's office, and the law firm that the CEO has consulted is kept secret. Just in case, the CEO suggests that, this being a multimillion dollar deal, the law offices might be checked for surveillance devices. The attorney doesn't know where to find a reliable sweep team but has read in *The Phone Book* that its author is a technical advisor to an experienced TSCM company and can arrange the initial contact.

So the attorney goes to see a trusted friend, explains the situation, and arranges to use the friend's unlisted home phone number. He writes this number on a plain slip of paper and mails it to the author. A few days later, the lawyer's friend receives a call from someone who identifies himself as "your old classmate Chuck from Boston." Without saying anything about the sweep, the friend invites the caller to have lunch at a restaurant near the lawyer's offices. A tentative date and time are set. The friend then calls the attorney pretending to invite him to lunch the same time and place, and mentions that "Chuck" is in town. If this is also agreeable to the attorney, nothing else need be done; the appointment will be kept. One other item of information is passed on, so the team leader and the attorney will recognize each other. It may seem that these precautions are extreme, but when millions of dollars are at stake no chances are taken.

CAVEAT EMPTOR

I know one "private eye" who will take one piece of equipment (a $1,000 bug detector, which, as far as it goes, is quite good) and spend 15 minutes walking through the area and waving the wand antenna around and then declare that there are no listening devices present. No physical search, no phone lines checked, just the RF detector. Ask about microphones and wiretaps, and he says, "My equipment finds all that stuff." For $500 all you get is a false sense of security. Having read this chapter, you can prevent that from happening to you.

References

The attorney understands, from having read *The Phone Book*, that there are businesses claiming to be well-equipped experts in countersurveillance, but which are not. He knows nothing about electronics or surveillance, but from *The Phone Book* he has learned several things to ask of the representative of the company he is considering hiring: references, a sanitized copy of the report of a previous sweep, and a list of the equipment that will be used. He takes his copy of the book and some notes he has made, so that when he gets to the meeting he is prepared.

The next day, one of the company owners, who will be the team leader in the sweep, takes a few pieces of equipment with him and makes the drive down to the restaurant, where he meets the CEO and the attorney to discuss the sweep and the reason for it over lunch. When asked for references, the team leader informs the attorney that he will contact three clients, all in the practice of law and ask if they may be used as references. He explains that the clients names are confidential and will not be divulged without their permission and that the same confidentiality will be extended to this attorney. The attorney is asked for some specific information (detailed later); a list of all phone numbers at the offices, including fax and computer modem lines; and floor plans and a diagram of the electrical wiring of his building. Last, the team leader gets a secure number where he can reach the attorney and a mail drop for the references.

The attorney asks about the equipment that is to be used, referring to *The Phone Book*. The team leader tells him that it is essentially the same as is detailed in that book, plus a few items he had asked me not to include in the book. After the attorney is cautioned not to mention the sweep while in his office, they go there so the team leader can look the area over to see how many rooms there are, the general layout, and the perimeter. What is around the law office building—other offices, unimproved areas, parking lots, shopping centers? The team leader is looking for potential listening posts. Once this is done, the team leader and the attorney walk out to the parking lot, where the details are settled. The attorney pays a deposit, and they agree on a date for the sweep. After the attorney goes back inside, the team leader will do some preliminary testing in the area.

THE CALL

The sweep will take place the following weekend when no employees (who do not need to know about the sweep) will be present, the offices will be quiet, and the team can work without interruption. This work requires concentration.

The team leader calls his specialists, advising them of the job—when it will be done, the approximate location (the exact location is not divulged until the team is already on the way there), and how many days it will take. Three of the specialists are available at the time of the sweep, and they receive their instructions. Each member is to prepare a "ready bag," a small suitcase containing enough clothes and personal effects for several days and hand tools. Also some precautionary measures will be used. The team will be taking $100,000 worth of electronic equipment with it, and we like to be able to protect it—and indeed we can.

THE EQUIPMENT

The equipment is always maintained in a state of readiness. After each job the equipment is unloaded from the van and taken into the shop, where it is calibrated as necessary. Accuracy is checked against several known crystal-controlled sources, sensitivity measurements are made, and fresh batteries are installed or the gel cell types recharged. Forms that will be used in the sweep are restocked, as are fresh rolls of film. Everything is done one step at a time following a checklist. Everything is organized, and there is a specific place for each item, which is labeled. All equipment fits into a snug layer of foam plastic to prevent damage during transport. In a separate suitcase is the Eagle Plus countermeasures receiver, because it is used first.

When it is time to go on the call, the equipment is loaded back into the van. It consists of several footlockers and a number of boxes and cases that weigh half a ton before the sweep and three tons when the job is done. (After all the climbing and crawling and lifting, at least it seems like it.) That is a lot of electronics, but a well-equipped team has to be ready for any eventuality. A partial list of the equipment is as follows:

General Equipment

- Transmitter detection
- Eagle Plus countermeasures receiver with a notebook computer
- Scanlock countermeasures receiver
- TSA Range Lock
- TSA CompuScan for the Scanlock
- Tektronix spectrum analyzer that covers up to 20-plus GHz
- ICOM R-71A communications receiver
- ICOM R7000 communications receiver
- DC440 Optoelectronics decoder for the R7000
- Optoelectronics 3000 frequency counter
- Optoelectronics Interceptor
- TSA SA-5 spectrum analyzer
- Fifteen antennas of various types and several tripods
- Microwave detector
- Two TV monitors

Telephone Equipment

- Several telephone line analyzers, including models from ISA and TSA, and a load coil detector for checking the phone lines
- Tektronix Time Domain Reflectometer
- Hewlett Packard 77M telephone test probes
- Teletone 600 LS line tracers
- CCR continuous-carrier current receiver (also for phone wires)

Audio Equipment

- Five audio amplifiers, for different purposes
- Four tape recorders; two Marantz, a Panasonic, and a modified 10-hour-long play model
- A calibrated sound meter to measure audio levels
- Two audio oscillators for activating RF surveillance transmitters

Other Equipment

- Garrett battery-operated metal detector
- Every kind of patch cord and cable imaginable
- Two ladders; one 4 foot and one 16 foot
- Five MagLites with spare batteries
- Three battery-powered ultraviolet lights
- Two volt-ohmeters—one Simpson 260 analog and one Fluke digital
- Three battery-powered screwdrivers for opening switch plates, etc.
- Wireless communicator headsets for the crew to talk to each other
- 35mm camera with wide-angle and normal lenses, filters, flash units, film, and extra batteries
- Two power supplies that provide 3, 6, 9, and 12 volts DC
- Assorted other tools and equipment

THE SWEEP

Depending on the size of the area to be swept, the team may consist of three to six specialists and the team leader. Some will ride in the equipment van, which goes to pick them up at prearranged places. The others will drive their personal vehicles to the job. Everyone gets together at the last pickup point for a short briefing, so that when the team goes in, everyone will know what to expect and what to do.

The lawyer's offices are located in a city 115 miles away. Little is said during the journey, because most of us are only half awake; it's still only 4:15 in the very A.M. These trips are usually quiet anyway. Everyone is ready, and there is little to say. Occasionally one of the crew checks the map, but the driver knows the way.

The cars are usually right behind the van, except in the case of a sweep at a high-security installation. In this instance, they will be pacing the van half a mile or so in front of and behind it, looking for anyone who may be tailing the van. Periodically, the drivers of the cars check in with the van on cellular phones, using phrases that would mean nothing to anyone who happened to be listening. The Scanlock, connected to one of the antennas on the roof of the van, sits between the bucket seats. Should anyone be following us and using a two-way radio or cellular phone, we will hear him. Other listening devices may be used.

The First Stop

About half a mile from our destination we stop in a convenient place. The team leader sets up the Eagle Plus countermeasures receiver and scans through its coverage. Everything it picks up (and there is little it doesn't) is stored in its first memory. The reason for this is to eliminate signals from commercial broadcasting stations, and the half-mile distance is such that the Eagle is out of range of any surveillance transmitter that might be in the search area.

The Arrival

Across the street from the law offices is a small shopping center that includes a McDonald's. From the parking lot we have a clear view of the building. From the back of the van, which has a reflective film on the windows, we watch the building through binoculars and a 20-power spotting scope and take pictures, while suffering the indignity of McDonald's food. Once again everyone swears that they will get up a little earlier and make breakfast next time. The coffee is even worse, but there was no time to fill a thermos with some good Colombian. I request a cup of plain water also.

Below: The inside of the van showing cases and footlockers. I don't know where the 7-11 T-shirt came from.

Bottom: Some of the cases in the motel room where the sweep team was staying.

The Perimeter

We are looking for several things, including people who seem as though they should not be there. It is Saturday morning, and few people should be around. At the first meeting, the team leader asked the attorney about the other tenants. The attorney said that all the tenants are lawyers or work in other businesses that are closed on weekends. The attorney was not aware of any kind of construction or remodeling going on in or around the building, so it should be pretty much deserted.

We are also looking for disguised transmitting antennas and anything that could be a surveillance device. Some examples are contact microphones placed in the corners of windows, wires leading from windows to the roof or inside signs, ventilation ducts, etc. If this building had been swept before, we would have photos of the outside to refer to. If anything is different, we would notice it. We see nothing suspicious. As I plop-plop, fizz-fizz the Alka-Seltzers I keep in my ready bag, the team leader announces that we will now drive around the perimeter for another look and take more photos. Having been relieved of McHeartburn, I am ready.

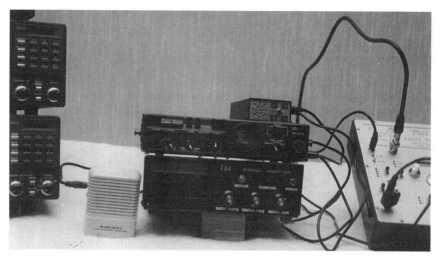

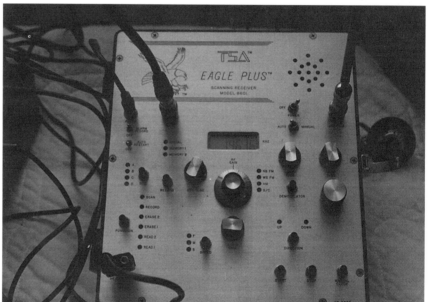

The six photographs on pages 202 and 203 illustrate the equipment set up for a sweep. The signal monitor shows the wave form of intercepted signals, and the ICOMs are used for verifying frequencies that could be from a surveillance device.

Page 202
Top: The TSA Signal Monitor.
Middle: Close-up of the Eagle Plus countermeasures receiver.
Bottom: Compuscan, which controls the Eagle Plus.

Page 203
Top: Phone-line analyzer and signal monitor.
Middle: Scanlock, signal monitor, and range-lock.
Bottom: Eagle Plus, signal monitor, and ICOM receivers.

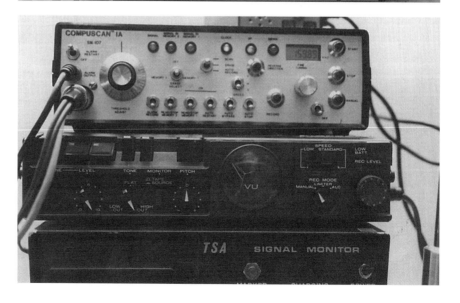

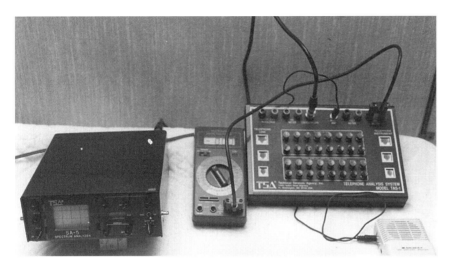

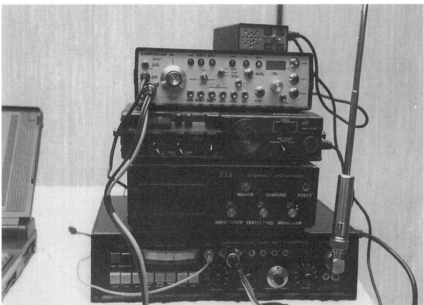

We are there 15 minutes or so before the agreed-on time and wait outside for the attorney, or whomever the attorney has assigned to be the contact, to come out to the van as was arranged, just in case something has happened in the offices to delay the sweep. If the contact were to arrive as we are waiting, we would call him on his car phone and, when he answered, punch an agreed-upon combination of keys. Nothing would be spoken. But this is not necessary; the contact is already inside.

The Premises
There is an underground garage at this building, and the contact has instructed the weekend security guard to let us in. The gate swings open, a faint screech emanates from hinges that haven't been oiled recently, and we roll in. The driver parks the van at the elevator, which opens almost immediately.

Out steps a distinguished-looking man with sculpted silver hair. He is wearing jeans and a sport shirt, but looks as though he belongs in a three-piece lawyer costume, which on weekdays he does. He turns a key in the elevator control panel to keep it at the parking garage level. We pile out, throw open the side and rear doors, and start removing the footlockers. All are on wheels, and we roll them into the waiting elevator, observing with some relief that we will be able to get everything in one trip.

"We Go Silent"
The elevator reaches the right floor, and we roll the equipment out and start down the long hallway. At a certain distance before we get to the door, the team leader states: "We go silent now." This means no talking until otherwise advised, which may be for just 20 minutes or as long as several hours, depending on circumstances.

Inside
There are nine private offices for the lawyers, a reception area, a conference room, the library, the communications room, three rest rooms (two of the senior partners have their own), a small break area with refrigerator and microwave oven, and a stock room where office supplies are stored. We will need a way to identify the various rooms other than as what they actually are. In other words, "Mr. Jenkins's office" might be called "site six" or something like that. (The actual way we do this is proprietary, so I can't include it here.) Meanwhile, one team member starts out on a circuit, dropping off some proprietary forms that we use in each room to be swept.

Hazards
The number and types of possible hiding places for surveillance devices are limited only by the imagination. A bug can be disguised as, or hidden inside of, virtually anything. Some are a permanent part of the area and are called *fixtures*. Others are items that have been brought into the area and are called *artifacts*. Anything that is a potential hiding place for a surveillance device—whether fixture or artifact—or other possible breach of security is called a *hazard*.

For example, potted plants are artifacts and hazards, because a transmitter can be hidden in them in a few seconds and someone who may come in periodically to water them can change the batteries. A wastebasket can be a hazard because it can be replaced with one that has a false bottom that contains a bug and can be switched by a custodian or cleaning person as the batteries need changing. A burned-out light bulb is a hazard—PK Elektronik builds bugs into them. Chandeliers and smoke detectors are fixtures and hazards.

Breaches of security, while not hiding places for surveillance devices, are such things as computer passwords or safe combinations left where they are easy to find, sensitive files that are not in locked filing cabinets, and doors that have weak locks or hinges on the outside. These, too, are hazards. Every possible hazard has to be checked thoroughly. This is done in six phases (with requisite reports):

1. *Electromagnetic radiation (EMR) frequency sweep.* This is an analysis of radio frequency emissions for the discovery of concealed "active" radiant radio transmitters that may have been planted in the area.
2. *Telecommunications diagnosis.* For the eavesdropper to access and monitor telecommunications traffic, a bypass, removal, alteration, or modification of the standard system has to occur. This procedure consists of an electronic analysis for the detection of a possible penetration.
3. *Wire link inspection.* All electrical facilities are opened and examined visually, electronically, electromagnetically, and with a carrier current receiver for the detection of devices.
4. *Audio leakage evaluation.* This determines whether a conversation taking place within the target area can be overheard.
5. *Physical search.* A physical inspection is conducted for the express purpose of locating hardwire microphones and all "passive" devices while in an inactive mode.
6. *Reports.* Upon the completion of the search, an oral report is provided with an overview of the hazards encountered. This is followed within 10 working days by a comprehensive written report with photographs of hazards (where found) and recommendations.

Setting Up

At the initial contact, the team leader had walked through the area and made a determination about what equipment would be brought in during the actual sweep—or rather what equipment would *not* have to be brought in.

We have brought most of our equipment with us, and once inside the building, we begin setting up. we refrain from talking and do everything as silently as possible and with practiced, experienced motions. The place for the EMR equipment to be set up, which has already been decided, will if possible be away from the reception area, just in case someone should come in. This will probably be the conference room or one of the attorney's offices. For our own reasons, we try to make it as close to the center of the suite as possible.

One specialist places a blanket on the table, to protect the surface and deaden the sound of the equipment being placed on it. Then the whole crew starts connecting things to other things. The Eagle is first. It works with the signal monitor and the notebook computer. The ICOMs are placed one on top of the other and connected to the SA-5 spectrum analyzer. The Tektronix spectrum analyzer is a stand-alone instrument. Then the antennas are connected, including a large discone type mounted on a tripod. There will be four different receivers and three spectrum analyzers operating.

A power cord with multiple outlets is plugged into a wall socket, and the cords to the equipment are laid together, ready to plug in. But first one specialist checks to make sure that the equipment is turned off, the speakers are disabled, and the volume controls are set at minimum. If someone were listening through a microphone and the receivers all came on, he would recognize the sounds and know that the area was being swept. If an RF transmitter were operating, the Eagle would pounce on it almost instantly and the howling sound of feedback would be a dead giveaway. Headphones are plugged into all equipment that produces sound.

The EMR Sweep

Although each specialist has his own area of expertise, all are cross-trained and able to work in some of the other phases of the sweep so that members are able to work as a team. Specifically, what each member will do depends on a number of factors, which will not be discussed here. One specialist operates the Eagle. It again scans through its entire coverage, picking up and storing the frequencies of anything transmitting in the area, except that it ignores those signals it stored when first activated outside the sweep area. The frequencies of any new transmissions it receives are dumped into the computer and verified with the ICOM communications receivers.

The Tektronix spectrum analyzer, which has been warming up, is adjusted by another specialist to receive different areas of the RF spectrum called *windows*. This piece of equipment is a sophisticated radio receiver that displays the signals it receives on a small screen like an oscilloscope. It covers 100 kHz to 21 GHz and can display any signals it intercepts, whether they are AM, FM, or sideband.

While this is happening, the telephone specialist has set up his equipment and starts analyzing the phones and the lines. Each phone, one at a time, is activated or taken off hook. If an RF transmitter is attached to any of the lines, the analyzers, the spectrum analyzer, and the Eagle will detect it.

The last step in the EMR setup phase is to activate the alarm feature of the Eagle. It will operate until the sweep is completed and is the last to be broken down. If the Eagle hears a new signal, it measures the length of the transmission. If the signal lasts for a certain length of time, as an illegal surveillance transmitter would, the Eagle will activate a tape recorder and capture a certain number of seconds of the transmission. Then it continues searching. The reason the Eagle waits this particular time is to eliminate false signals such as the cellular phone from a passing vehicle or the radio from a police car or taxicab. It will operate automatically until the second part of the EMR check, during which time we will be doing other things.

Now the CCR-3 (Carrier Current Receiver) is used. Everything electrical in the offices is turned on. Computers, lights, typewriters, fans, everything. This is because a special type of transmitter that uses the power lines to send its signal might be concealed inside one of these things. The receiver is so sensitive that it may even pick up a nearby AM radio station, and if a carrier current transmitter is present, the room sounds will come through the headphones.

Next, the two video monitors are used. These are similar to the Eagle, in that they sweep through the frequencies they cover, but are looking for video signals from a hidden camera. They are moved throughout the area, using a sophisticated antenna system.

While this is going on, one specialist has been analyzing whatever signals were picked up by the Eagle. When they have been identified as harmless, the TSA SA-5 signal monitor is connected to the ICOM receivers, which are tuned carefully through their entire range, which is 100 kHz to 2,000 MHz. This operation is one of the more time-consuming ones.

In some areas, a great many signals will be heard, and the specialist has to be able to determine that they are not hidden transmitters. This requires experience. A background in amateur radio and shortwave listening is invaluable here; such a person develops the ability to accurately identify various radio transmissions. While listening, the specialist is also watching the screen of the signal monitor and spectrum analyzers, and glancing at the "S" meters. The eye reacts slightly faster than the ear.

Once the silent phase is completed we can talk, but this is limited to necessary conversation. We don't tell jokes or war stories. Depending on circumstances we may or may not be issued headsets—short-range, two-way radios—to communicate with the other specialists. The types we use have been modified.

Now, we turn on one of the audio oscillators, which make a loud, warbling sound, and repeat the EMR search. Before, we were silent. There were no room sounds for a hidden transmitter to pick up, so it would be sending only an empty signal. Such a signal, an unmodulated carrier, is more difficult to detect than one with sound on it. There is another type of transmitter that sends no signal at all until it picks up sound. Now we have something to listen for: the warbling oscillator will be picked up by any bug in the area, and we will hear it in the headphones of the radios and spectrum analyzer. When this is done, the alarm on the Eagle is reset.

Telecommunications Diagnosis

The telephone system used in this facility is a PBX with 12 lines, voice mail, and intercom, working through a console at the receptionist's desk. A secondary console is installed in the communications room. Because the attorneys are concerned about hackers breaking into their phone system, precautions have been taken. They have conferred with AT&T-trained specialists and placed what is called a barrier on each line. This prevents them from being used for outgoing long-distance calls. The voice mail system is protected by requiring all users to have a minimum-10-character password.

But in spite of these precautions, we discover that three of the senior partners have private direct lines that do not go through the PBX. From Part 1 of this book, you know that this is an unnecessary hazard. Later, the team leader will mention this to the contact person, and it will be included in the report.

Earlier, the telephone specialist had finished helping set up the EMR equipment and started on the phones. They are unplugged and reconnected through the telephone analyzers. Either the ETA-1, made by Information Security Associates, or the TSA-1, by Glenn Whidden of Technical Services Agency, may be used, depending on some particulars. One of these is the type used for this phone system.

This will affect incoming calls only when each individual line is being checked. Otherwise the phones ring as they normally do. Unless otherwise advised by the contact person, we don't answer them. As far as the individual phones, they may be spread all over the table in several pieces, which makes them a little difficult to answer anyway. The pieces are checked thoroughly, and the specialist knows what to look for.

The lines are checked for audio signals that should not be there, such as infinity-type transmitters, and for RF signals from a telephone line transmitter. A number of other tests are made, including a measurement of the line voltage and current, and then all lines are checked with the time domain reflectometer (TDR). When the inspection is done, the phones are put back together.

The next step is to do something to the phones so that at a later date the attorneys can check to make sure they have not been switched. The easiest way to install a listening device inside a phone is to first determine the type used, obtain the same type and color, install the device, and switch them. It takes only a few seconds. What we do prevents someone from doing this to the phones in the attorney's offices.

Next, the lines have to be carefully checked from the phone to the point of demarcation, just as described in Part 1. If necessary, a line tracer is used, and if the lines are not identified at the 66 block, the universal ANI number is used to verify them.

Wire Link Inspection

In this part of the sweep all wiring is physically inspected and tested with several electronic instruments. This includes the power lines, cable TV, wired intercoms, phone lines—every kind of wire, whether it is connected to anything (that we can see) or not.

In the case of a pair of unknown wires, we will use the meters to make some measurements, voltage and resistance, and then may use one of the amplifiers to send a certain type of signal through them. Then we see what happens. This is a very powerful signal, and if a microphone, speaker (which doubles as a microphone), or other device is connected, it will "sing" to us; we will hear the oscillations and follow the sound to find whatever it is.

On one sweep of the penthouse of an apartment building, we found an unused pair of wires and used the amplifier to determine what they were. It turned out that the wires were part of an old security system. The system had been replaced with a newer one and the sensors in the apartment removed, but the old control console was still in place. The assistant manager had no idea what was going on, but was most upset about the "incredible racket" emanating from the old console.

Next, the TDR is used to measure the distance to the end of the wires and to anything connected to them (e.g., any splice of other wires or electronic device). Then, knowing the distance, we would know where to look as we follow the wires.

Audio Leakage Evaluation

The purpose of this test is to determine to what degree the walls of the rooms are soundproof. The Panasonic cassette player is placed on a desk in the lawyer's offices so that it is as close as possible to the point from where the voice of a person sitting at the desk would emanate. A recording of a well-known actor is played, and the volume adjusted to a normal speaking level of 70 dB. This is checked with the sound meter.

Outside the room with the door closed, the specialists listen with their ears to the wall and then with a contact microphone to determine whether they can hear anything. What we can hear from the hall can also be heard by someone in the next office. The results are included in the client's report, along with any recommendations.

Physical Search

If a specialist is good at his work, he can make a very good wage, and in the physical search, he will earn it. This is the most difficult part of the sweep. It is also the most effective. Even though we have the most sophisticated equipment available, there are some things it may not find.

Remember inductive taps from Part 1? A remote-controlled transmitter will not be detected if it is turned off and not transmitting. There are other devices that may escape detection, such as the burst transmitter. They are extremely rare, but they exist. Hard-wired microphones are another example. They may lead to a listening post somewhere or a transmitter on the roof of the building to give it more range. Remember, the microphone, transmitter, and antenna do not have to be in the same place. So the physical search must find anything the electronics did not. Anything. That means that every inch of the area has to be searched thoroughly. There is no margin for error here, no excuse for mistakes.

The actual procedure for the physical search depends on the team and the team leader. Some teams will draw up a "hazard chart," a drawing listing everything that is to be checked. Others may use small colored adhesive dots made by Denison or Avery. A red dot is placed on every fixture and artifact to identify it, and after it has been examined, a blue dot is placed beside the red one to check it off. If a floor plan has been provided by the contact, searchers may refer to it as they search.

Each specialist carries a toolkit of one kind or another, usually a leather pouch of the type used by electricians and telephone installers. It contains several screwdrivers (including a battery-powered model because there are a lot of switch plates to remove and replace), pliers and wire cutters, a magnifying glass, Mini-MagLite, a dentist's mirror, a battery-powered ultraviolet light, a darning needle, a tape measure, pens and pad, and other items. At least one specialist will have a battery-operated laser measuring device—an electronic tape measure as it were.

(While conducting the physical search during a sweep of another building, one of the specialists reported to the team leader that something didn't seem right. He wasn't sure what it was, just that "the walls didn't seem to fit." He was an experienced man, so his remarks were taken seriously, even though no one knew what the hell he meant. So the laser was used to make some measurements.

After comparing them with the floor plan, we discovered that there was something in the suite that did not appear on the diagram. At the point where the corners of four offices came together, there was a little room about 3 feet square. It was completely hidden; there were no doors or windows, and no one even knew that it was there. If someone could get into it, it would make the perfect place to set up audio, video, and RF surveillance equipment. The contact wanted it checked out, so we broke through the wall. There was nothing inside it.

Speculation about the room was rampant, but the most likely explanation was that the draftsman had made a few minor errors in the building plans or the carpenters had read the blueprints wrong when they framed the building, and by the time the errors were discovered, the building was too near to completion to change, so they just put the Sheetrock and paneling in place, and no one said any more about it. That was just speculation, of course; no one knew for sure what happened. (Of course, the room could have been used for surveillance, and if not for an alert specialist and the laser measuring device, it might never have been found.)

The first thing we do in the lawyer's office is examine the carpeting along the walls carefully. We are looking for bits of acoustical tile from the drop ceiling and chips of paint from the walls. Their presence may indicate that something has been tampered with, such as a hole drilled in a wall for a tiny microphone or video camera, a picture frame removed to conceal a bug, or the ceiling panels removed and replaced. Later we will move the ceiling panels, picture frames, etc., anyway, but we want to know whether someone else already has done the same thing. This means crawling around on our hands and knees.

At the same time, we are looking for tiny wires pushed under the carpet edge or behind baseboards that may lead to a hidden microphone. These wires can be almost as fine as a hair.

The lights are dimmed, and flashlights are held so the beam shines along the surface of the walls. If a tiny hole for a microphone or fiber-optic video camera is present, we will be able to see it. Try it yourself and see. Any irregularities in the surface will cast tiny shadows, and by moving the beam up and down, the shadow changes its angle, making them easy to pinpoint. Typically, such holes will be about the same as one those made by a thumbtack. If anysuch a hole is found, and it is believed there is a microphone inside, the mike can be disabled by jamming in a knitting needle. The hole is then photographed and marked to be plugged and painted over.

The plastic plates of every switch and wall plug, TV cable, and phone cable are removed. Each one is carefully inspected using a powerful flashlight and dentist's mirror so that the entire insides can be clearly seen. If anything is there that isn't supposed to be, the one who finds it halts the search and advises the team leader that he has found a serious hazard. This is done quietly, just in case. Whatever is there is carefully documented and photographed and will be included in the report.

Many offices have one or more of what are called *designer cubes*. Usually made of pressed particle board painted in bright colors, these cubes may be 12 inches on each side or larger and have lamps, plants, or whatever else on placed on them. And they are used to hide surveillance devices. Because they are hollow, there is room for virtually anything: for example, a high-powered transmitter capable of several blocks' range that could be powered for six months with a car battery, or a complete video system with a transmitter capable of sending images 1,000 feet or more. These cubes are taken apart and inspected and then resealed with cyanoacrylate (superglue).

Cabinets of all kinds are another favored place for hiding transmitters. So all drawers are removed, emptied, and checked inside and out, especially on their bottom. Then the inside of the cabinet is checked with flashlight and ultraviolet light.

One of the most effective places to hide a bug is inside a block of wood that looks as though it belongs where it is, such as part of a window frame, the underside of desks and chairs, or the inside of cabinets. If a spy is able to get inside the target twice, he can have a look under furniture and know the type of wood or paint to use. Then he will be prepared when it is time to make the drop. However, the wood may not match perfectly, because of type and age, and we are looking specifically for this. Also the glue used to hold it in place will be different and will show up under the ultraviolet light.

Some cabinets and drawers may be locked, and if instructed to by the contact, we may open them—we are prepared to do that. The senior partner may suspect one of the attorneys of leaking information and want to see whether he is hiding anything. Opening any locked object requires a written authorization to protect us, just in case.

Books are another good place for hiding an RF transmitter, because they can be switched quickly. They may be hollowed out, or the transmitter may be placed in the spine. During a search, every book has to be removed from the shelves and inspected. In a lawyer's office, this is a lot of work: there are so many books, law books are heavier than ordinary books, and

TRACKING AN INTRUDER

One particular attorney has a cleaning crew carefully vacuum the carpet in his office every night so that if anyone walks on it, that person will leave footprints. As he has for years, the attorney believes that a snoop comes into his office at night to look at his files. (It is a good thing that we have a vacuum cleaner with us on our sweep!)

getting them all back in the right place is tricky unless the specialist reads legalese.

Upholstered furniture is inspected carefully for an indication that the tacks have been removed or the fabric cut and repaired. The metal detector is used, and the ultraviolet light shined over the entire surface, including underneath. Lamps and potted plants, the bottom and underside of wastebaskets (hollow bottom?), desk organizers, picture frames, staplers, and anything else that could hide a bug are checked carefully. Office equipment is checked, underneath and behind, and the open areas of printers and typewriters are inspected. The acoustic panels of dropped ceilings are lifted and the area inside inspected very carefully. Although this is not the easiest place to access, it is one of the best places for hard-wired microphones. If something suspicious is seen, it may be necessary to crawl inside, and this is tricky. (On a sweep once, a specialist stepped where he shouldn't have and came crashing through one of the panels, making a helluva mess.)

Window frames are another favored place to hide transmitters. A window that faces the listening post is preferred, and there should be nothing to block the signal path except a pane of glass. A bug can be slipped inside the lining of drapes through a small cut and hung by the antenna wire in a few seconds. Curtain rods make excellent antennas if the transmitter has an adjustment for maximum power transfer, such as with the Deco VT-75, and installation can be done in a few minutes.

When the search is done, everything is put back as it was, and the area is cleaned up. We use a vacuum cleaner to remove dust and particles that result from moving ceiling panels, switch plates, picture frames, and the like.

The Adjoining Areas

If possible, the adjoining offices—all four sides, above, and below—are checked. These may be good places to hide contact or spike microphones or pinhole video camera lenses, depending, of course, on access. If the rooms are vacant and the attorney can arrange with the building manager to borrow the keys, we will check these areas. But we will not enter an occupied office.

The Photo Record

All specialists are required to be able to use a 35mm camera with electronic flash and to understand bracketing. This means taking several shots of the same thing from the same angle with the lens opening at different settings. This prevents the possible loss of a picture from under- or overexposure. When the sweep is complete, a photographic record is made of each hazard the team has found plus several shots of each room showing artifacts and fixtures.

The Benchmark

The report and photos provide a record called a benchmark, which shows "due diligence of the law firm above and beyond what is reasonable to ensure peace of mind and protection of privacy of their clients." The benchmark could play a crucial rol in settling a legal argument, should it arise, over whether the law firm had done everything possible to ensure clients' confidentiality.

There is another reason for the benchmark. Supposing a listening device is found during a future sweep or perhaps by one of the office personnel. If it is hidden inside an artifact, the photos will show whether the artifact was there when the sweep was made or was brought into the area afterward. If it is in a fixture, the report will show that the fixture was physically and electronically searched. This narrows the time that it may have been operating, which is useful in damage assessment.

Reports

When the sweep has been completed and the equipment is being packed away, the team leader makes a verbal report to the contact. He informs the contact whether any kind of surveillance device has been found and explains that a comprehensive written report will be delivered within 10 working days, which will include a computer list of hazards and recommendations. Since this sweep was only 115 miles from the company location, the report will be delivered by hand.

Damage Assessment

In this case, a surveillance device was found. The team leader advises the attorney of this and explains his options.

First, he can leave it in place to feed false information to the eavesdropper and maybe even draw out the person who placed it there. He can set up a time-lapse video camera and wait to see whether someone comes in to change the batteries. It can also be partly disabled, perhaps by placing something in front of the microphone so that the spy may attempt to repair it and be caught in the act. This is rare, but it has happened.

Second, the attorney can choose to have the device disabled and removed. But it should not be destroyed, because it may provide other useful information. It can be analyzed to figure out the type of person or organization that installed it. For example, the FBI wouldn't use a cheapo $20 wireless microphone, and a secretary who wanted to get something on her boss probably wouldn't know where to get a state-of-the-art spread-spectrum bug.

The chemicals in the battery (if it is discharged) can be analyzed to determine the approximate period when it would have been transmitting. Also, a new battery can be installed, the frequency determined, and an area check made to determine the battery's range. This helps narrow the location of the listening post. (For more on this, see *The Bug Book.*)

Another option, which the contact often wishes, is to call in the police. There probably isn't much the police can do because most departments don't have the training or personnel to deal with such things. Fingerprints usually deteriorate in a few days unless they are "plastics"—i.e., are left on a surface that preserves them, such as the adhesive side of electrician's tape. There are new laser techniques that may be able to recover the prints, but a local law enforcement agency isn't likely to have this equipment. If the attorney is determined to bring in law enforcement, it is suggested that he call in the FBI, whose crime laboratory is capable of near miracles.

Whatever action is to be taken, however, is decided by the attorney. The team leader only makes suggestions and has the attorney sign a waiver saying that he was advised that the device was found.

If Nothing Is Found

Most sweeps are negative—approximately one in ten will turn up a surveillance device, so it is no surprise when nothing is found. If nothing is found, the team leader reports this verbally to the client or contact, along with an explanation of what was done and what was checked (everything) and an assurance that a written report will be forthcoming.

Recommendations

Part of the responsibility of the team is to point out hazards and areas where the client is most vulnerable. It is up to the client to arrange for a construction crew or others appropriate to make repairs or modifications; the team does not recommend anyone.

The team leader explains to the client about van Eck computer eavesdropping, the wisdom of keeping floppy disks with sensitive information locked inside a safe, and the dangers of having safe combinations and computer passwords written on paper and placed under drawers or on the back of monitors, unlocked file cabinets, sensitive documents lying around, and anything else appropriate.

Next, the team breaks all of its equipment down and places it back in the footlockers, everything in its place. The lockers are wheeled back to the van and the ladders and antennas replaced.

Debriefing

There is always a certain exhilaration from having gotten the job done without any problems, such as falling through a dropped ceiling, but it has been a long day and we are anxious to have a bite to eat and go home. As we leave, someone reminds the team leader that it is not the wee small hours and there is a choice of places to go. We find a decent restaurant, where there is a booth big enough for all of us and where we can watch the van through a window. Each specialist makes a verbal report and submits any notes he may have made during the sweep. Any particular feelings someone might have had are related to the others, but it was a well-done sweep and everyone is satisfied.

Later That Night . . .

The team leader or one of the specialists stays overnight at a hotel or motel, where he works on the reports. The following day, he returns to the scene of the sweep to retrieve and evaluate the equipment that was left in place to see whether anything new developed through the night. Any last questions the client may have are answered, and a check for the fee may be collected.

Then the leader drives back to the shop, dropping the film off to be developed. This will be at a custom lab some distance from the sweep site and not a one-hour-type photo-finishing place, for several reasons. With a custom lab you'll get better results, there is less chance that the film could be ruined or lost, and fewer persons will see the pictures. The last is an extra precaution to protect the identity of the client. When the photos are developed, someone on the team tags and numbers them. One set is placed in plastic holders to be included with the report to the client, and the other goes in the team leader's files.

The Last Step

Within 10 days after the sweep, the team leader returns to the law offices to deliver the report. This document, which may be 20 to 30 pages long, is printed on a laser printer and is punched and placed in a small ring binder with the company name on the cover. It makes for a nice presentation. If requested, additional copies are provided for a nominal fee.

QUESTIONS AND ANSWERS

The following are some of the most common questions that investigators who conduct these sweeps get asked.

Q: Are you 100 percent sure there are no surveillance devices in this area?

A: You should answer something along these lines: "Using our equipment and knowledge, we cannot find any surveillance devices at this time. There are no indications that the area has been penetrated." That says a lot: the way my team works, three to six people, all of them very experienced, have gone over the area for about eight hours and checked every inch of it. More than $100,000 in electronic equipment was used, again, by experts. That is as much as anyone can do.

Q: What type of devices are usually found?

A: Again, most sweeps are negative, but of the devices that are found most are rather common and readily available: inexpensive microphones that have been wired to the listening post and transmitters that operate on or slightly outside the FM broadcast band or at about 300 MHz. Occasionally a remote-control transmitter, one that the eavesdropper can turn off and on from the listening post, is found, but the exotic types such as spread-spectrum and burst transmitters are very rare. And the X-Band transmitter that operates at 10.525 GHz, which has been available on the open market for about two years, has, to my knowledge, never been found in a sweep.

Other devices that are fairly common are citizen band transmitters and baby monitors that have been removed from their cases to reduce the overall size and installed where a constant supply of power is available, such as in table lamps.

Q: What about outside devices, such as a laser?

A: Lasers are very iffy. Sometimes they work, sometimes not. Anything in the air between the listening post and the target (e.g., dust, rain, fog) will interfere, as will anything that vibrates the target windows (e.g., street traffic, passing aircraft, construction equipment, air conditioners, fans, elevators). To defeat lasers, just close the drapes.

Q: What about directional microphones?

A: With the windows closed, they are virtually useless.

Q: What about downline phone taps?

A: Anything beyond the point of demarcation is, as you read in Part 1, very difficult to install. It is possible to have the telco disconnect your lines at the CO end and to make impedance and TDR measurements, but this too is iffy. There just isn't much you can do about a downline tap unless you can get access and physically search the lines. And you already know how difficult that can be.

Q: What if you miss something?

A: It is possible to miss an RF transmitter with the electronic equipment and then find it in the physical search. Although it is unlikely, if it happens, do you tell the client? My firm keeps no secrets from the client—tell him.

CHOOSING A SWEEP TEAM

If you are considering hiring a sweep team, I can arrange the initial contact, per the beginning of this chapter. All that is required is a phone number; I don't need to know, or want to know, who you are. If you want to hire someone else, then what you have read here will enable you to tell a professional from an amateur—who knows the business and who does not. Don't be afraid to ask questions. A professional team will expect this; it's part of the job. You will be paying out a fair amount of money for the sweep, and you have the right to get what you are paying for.

In addition to references, ask to see a sample copy of the report the firm provides to its clients. Ask about the equipment to be used, whether its employees have a spectrum analyzer and if they know what an X-Band bug is? Ask whether you will be allowed to watch, to see for yourself. A professional company will insist that some responsible person be there at all times and will explain what each piece of equipment is and what it does. This is called *tradecraft*. But if you do go on the search, do try to stay out of the way.

With what you have read in this chapter and perhaps in *The Bug Book* and *Don't Bug Me*, and what you will read in the rest of the book, you will have no trouble finding someone who will do the job right. The first time.

PART 7

APPENDICES

CELLULAR
FREQUENCIES

In this appencix are listed all 832 cellular channels. The first group is non-wireline; the second group is wireline. As you will recall from the text, they are in 21 sets, each with one control channel, and seven groups, each with three sets. The 832 channels could be listed, sorted, in four ways: by frequency, channel, set, and group. But this would tak upa a lot more pages. So I have sorted them by frequency only.

The total range is 869.040 to 893.970 as follows:

    869.040–879.360 NML Voice
    879.390–879.990 NWL Data Ch **313–333**
    880.020–889.980 WL Data Ch **334–354**
    890.010–981.480 NWL Voice
    891.510–893.970 WL Voice

    Grp = Group, A to G
    Ch = Channel 001 to 1021
    Freq = Frequency 869.040–893.970
    Se = Set, 1 to 21

Channel numbers 800 to 999 are not used. Control channels are in **bold**.

NON-WIRELINE FREQUENCIES

Grp	Ch	Freq	Set	Grp	Ch	Freq	Set	Grp	Ch	Freq	Set
[A]	001	870.030	01	[A]	008	870.240	08	[A]	015	870.450	15
[B]	002	870.060	02	[B]	009	870.270	09	[B]	016	870.480	16
[C]	003	870.090	03	[C]	010	870.300	10	[C]	017	870.510	17
[D]	004	870.120	04	[D]	011	870.330	11	[D]	018	870.540	18
[E]	005	870.150	05	[E]	012	870.360	12	[E]	019	870.570	19
[F]	006	870.180	06	[F]	013	870.390	13	[F]	020	870.600	20
[G]	007	870.210	07	[G]	014	870.420	14	[G]	021	870.630	21

Grp	Ch	Freq	Set	Grp	Ch	Freq	Set	Grp	Ch	Freq	Set
[A]	022	870.660	01	[E]	068	872.040	05	[B]	114	873.420	09
[B]	023	870.690	02	[F]	069	872.070	06	[C]	115	873.450	10
[C]	024	870.720	03	[G]	070	872.100	07	[D]	116	873.480	11
[D]	025	870.750	04	[A]	071	872.130	08	[E]	117	873.510	12
[E]	026	870.780	05	[B]	072	872.160	09	[F]	118	873.540	13
[F]	027	870.810	06	[C]	073	872.190	10	[G]	119	873.570	14
[G]	028	870.840	07	[D]	074	872.220	11	[A]	120	873.600	15
[A]	029	870.870	08	[E]	075	872.250	12	[B]	121	873.630	16
[B]	030	870.900	09	[F]	076	872.280	13	[C]	122	873.660	17
[C]	031	870.930	10	[G]	077	872.310	14	[D]	123	873.690	18
[D]	032	870.960	11	[A]	078	872.340	15	[E]	124	873.720	19
[E]	033	870.990	12	[B]	079	872.370	16	[F]	125	873.750	20
[F]	034	871.020	13	[C]	080	872.400	17	[G]	126	873.780	21
[G]	035	871.050	14	[D]	081	872.430	18	[A]	127	873.810	01
[A]	036	871.080	15	[E]	082	872.460	19	[B]	128	873.840	02
[B]	037	871.110	16	[F]	083	872.490	20	[C]	129	873.870	03
[C]	038	871.140	17	[G]	084	872.520	21	[D]	130	873.900	04
[D]	039	871.170	18	[A]	085	872.550	01	[E]	131	873.930	05
[E]	040	871.200	19	[B]	086	872.580	02	[F]	132	873.960	06
[F]	041	871.230	20	[C]	087	872.610	03	[G]	133	873.990	07
[G]	042	871.260	21	[D]	088	872.640	04	[A]	134	874.020	08
[A]	043	871.290	01	[E]	089	872.670	05	[B]	135	874.050	09
[B]	044	871.320	02	[F]	090	872.700	06	[C]	136	874.080	10
[C]	045	871.350	03	[G]	091	872.730	07	[D]	137	874.110	11
[D]	046	871.380	04	[A]	092	872.760	08	[E]	138	874.140	12
[E]	047	871.410	05	[B]	093	872.790	09	[F]	139	874.170	13
[F]	048	871.440	06	[C]	094	872.820	10	[G]	140	874.200	14
[G]	049	871.470	07	[D]	095	872.850	11	[A]	141	874.230	15
[A]	050	871.500	08	[E]	096	872.880	12	[B]	142	874.260	16
[B]	051	871.530	09	[F]	097	872.910	13	[C]	143	874.290	17
[C]	052	871.560	10	[G]	098	872.940	14	[D]	144	874.320	18
[D]	053	871.590	11	[A]	099	872.970	15	[E]	145	874.350	19
[E]	054	871.620	12	[B]	100	873.000	16	[F]	146	874.380	20
[F]	055	871.650	13	[C]	101	873.030	17	[G]	147	874.410	21
[G]	056	871.680	14	[D]	102	873.060	18	[A]	148	874.440	01
[A]	057	871.710	15	[E]	103	873.090	19	[B]	149	874.470	02
[B]	058	871.740	16	[F]	104	873.120	20	[C]	150	874.500	03
[C]	059	871.770	17	[G]	105	873.150	21	[D]	151	874.530	04
[D]	060	871.800	18	[A]	106	873.180	01	[E]	152	874.560	05
[E]	061	871.830	19	[B]	107	873.210	02	[F]	153	874.590	06
[F]	062	871.860	20	[C]	108	873.240	03	[G]	154	874.620	07
[G]	063	871.890	21	[D]	109	873.270	04	[A]	155	874.650	08
[A]	064	871.920	01	[E]	110	873.300	05	[B]	156	874.680	09
[B]	065	871.950	02	[F]	111	873.330	06	[C]	157	874.710	10
[C]	066	871.980	03	[G]	112	873.360	07	[D]	158	874.740	11
[D]	067	872.010	04	[A]	113	873.390	08	[E]	159	874.770	12

Grp	Ch	Freq	Set	Grp	Ch	Freq	Set	Grp	Ch	Freq	Set
[F]	160	874.800	13	[C]	206	876.180	17	[G]	252	877.560	21
[G]	161	874.830	14	[D]	207	876.210	18	[A]	253	877.590	01
[A]	162	874.860	15	[E]	208	876.240	19	[B]	254	877.620	02
[B]	163	874.890	16	[F]	209	876.270	20	[C]	255	877.650	03
[C]	164	874.920	17	[G]	210	876.300	21	[D]	256	877.680	04
[D]	165	874.950	18	[A]	211	876.330	01	[E]	257	877.710	05
[E]	166	874.980	19	[B]	212	876.360	02	[F]	258	877.740	06
[F]	167	875.010	20	[C]	213	876.390	03	[G]	259	877.770	07
[G]	168	875.040	21	[D]	214	876.420	04	[A]	260	877.800	08
[A]	169	875.070	01	[E]	215	876.450	05	[B]	261	877.830	09
[B]	170	875.100	02	[F]	216	876.480	06	[C]	262	877.860	10
[C]	171	875.130	03	[G]	217	876.510	07	[D]	263	877.890	11
[D]	172	875.160	04	[A]	218	876.540	08	[E]	264	877.920	12
[E]	173	875.190	05	[B]	219	876.570	09	[F]	265	877.950	13
[F]	174	875.220	06	[C]	220	876.600	10	[G]	266	877.980	14
[G]	175	875.250	07	[D]	221	876.630	11	[A]	267	878.010	15
[A]	176	875.280	08	[E]	222	876.660	12	[B]	268	878.040	16
[B]	177	875.310	09	[F]	223	876.690	13	[C]	269	878.070	17
[C]	178	875.340	10	[G]	224	876.720	14	[D]	270	878.100	18
[D]	179	875.370	11	[A]	225	876.750	15	[E]	271	878.130	19
[E]	180	875.400	12	[B]	226	876.780	16	[F]	272	878.160	20
[F]	181	875.430	13	[C]	227	876.810	17	[G]	273	878.190	21
[G]	182	875.460	14	[D]	228	876.840	18	[A]	274	878.220	01
[A]	183	875.490	15	[E]	229	876.870	19	[B]	275	878.250	02
[B]	184	875.520	16	[F]	230	876.900	20	[C]	276	878.280	03
[C]	185	875.550	17	[G]	231	876.930	21	[D]	277	878.310	04
[D]	186	875.580	18	[A]	232	876.960	01	[E]	278	878.340	05
[E]	187	875.610	19	[B]	233	876.990	02	[F]	279	878.370	06
[F]	188	875.640	20	[C]	234	877.020	03	[G]	280	878.400	07
[G]	189	875.670	21	[D]	235	877.050	04	[A]	281	878.430	08
[A]	190	875.700	01	[E]	236	877.080	05	[B]	282	878.460	09
[B]	191	875.730	02	[F]	237	877.110	06	[C]	283	878.490	10
[C]	192	875.760	03	[G]	238	877.140	07	[D]	284	878.520	11
[D]	193	875.790	04	[A]	239	877.170	08	[E]	285	878.550	12
[E]	194	875.820	05	[B]	240	877.200	09	[F]	286	878.580	13
[F]	195	875.850	06	[C]	241	877.230	10	[G]	287	878.610	14
[G]	196	875.880	07	[D]	242	877.260	11	[A]	288	878.640	15
[A]	197	875.910	08	[E]	243	877.290	12	[B]	289	878.670	16
[B]	198	875.940	09	[F]	244	877.320	13	[C]	290	878.700	17
[C]	199	875.970	10	[G]	245	877.350	14	[D]	291	878.730	18
[D]	200	876.000	11	[A]	246	877.380	15	[E]	292	878.760	19
[E]	201	876.030	12	[B]	247	877.410	16	[F]	293	878.790	20
[F]	202	876.060	13	[C]	248	877.440	17	[G]	294	878.820	21
[G]	203	876.090	14	[D]	249	877.470	18	[A]	295	878.850	01
[A]	204	876.120	15	[E]	250	877.500	19	[B]	296	878.880	02
[B]	205	876.150	16	[F]	251	877.530	20	[C]	297	878.910	03

Grp	Ch	Freq	Set	Grp	Ch	Freq	Set	Grp	Ch	Freq	Set
[D]	298	878.940	04	[D]	677	890.310	12	[A]	997	869.220	16
[E]	299	878.970	05	[E]	678	890.340	13	[B]	998	869.250	17
[F]	300	879.000	06	[F]	679	890.370	14	[C]	999	869.280	18
[G]	301	879.030	07	[G]	680	890.400	15	[D]	1000	869.310	19
[A]	302	879.060	08	[A]	681	890.430	16	[E]	1001	869.340	20
[B]	303	879.090	09	[B]	682	890.460	17	[F]	1002	869.370	21
[C]	304	879.120	10	[C]	683	890.490	18	[G]	1003	869.400	01
[D]	305	879.150	11	[D]	684	890.520	19	[A]	1004	869.430	02
E]	306	879.180	12	[E]	685	890.550	20	[B]	1005	869.460	03
[F]	307	879.210	13	[F]	686	890.580	21	[C]	1006	869.490	04
[G]	308	879.240	14	[G]	687	890.610	01	[D]	1007	869.520	05
[A]	309	879.270	15	[A]	688	890.640	02	[E]	1008	869.550	06
[B]	310	879.300	16	[B]	689	890.670	03	[F]	1009	869.580	07
[C]	311	879.330	17	[C]	690	890.700	04	[G]	1010	869.610	08
[D]	312	879.360	18	[D]	691	890.730	05	[A]	1011	869.640	09
[E]	**313**	**879.390**	01	[E]	692	890.760	06	[B]	1012	869.670	10
[F]	**314**	**879.420**	02	[F]	693	890.790	07				
[G]	**315**	**879.450**	03	[G]	694	890.820	08	[C]	1013	869.700	11
[A]	**316**	**879.480**	04	[A]	695	890.850	09	[D]	1014	869.730	12
[B]	**317**	**879.510**	05	[B]	696	890.880	10	[E]	1015	869.760	13
[C]	**318**	**879.540**	06	[C]	697	890.910	11	[F]	1016	869.790	14
[D]	**318**	**879.570**	07	[D]	698	890.940	12	[G]	1017	869.820	15
[E]	**320**	**879.600**	08	[E]	699	890.970	13	[A]	1018	869.850	16
[F]	**321**	**879.630**	09	[F]	700	891.000	14	[B]	1019	869.880	17
[G]	**322**	**879.660**	10	[G]	701	891.030	15	[C]	1020	869.910	18
[A]	**323**	**879.690**	11	[A]	702	891.060	16	[D]	1021	869.940	19
[B]	**324**	**879.720**	12	[B]	703	891.090	17	[E]	1022	869.970	20
[C]	**325**	**879.750**	13	[C]	704	891.120	18	[F]	1023	870.000	21
[D]	**326**	**879.780**	14	[D]	705	891.150	19				
[E]	**327**	**879.810**	15	[E]	706	891.180	20				
[F]	**328**	**879.840**	16	[F]	707	891.210	21				
[G]	**329**	**879.870**	17	[G]	708	891.240	01				
[A]	**330**	**879.900**	18	[A]	709	891.270	02				
[B]	**331**	**879.930**	19	[B]	710	891.300	03				
[C]	**332**	**879.960**	20	[C]	711	891.330	04				
[D]	**333**	**879.990**	21	[D]	712	891.360	05				
[A]	667	890.010	02	[E]	713	891.390	06				
[B]	668	890.040	03	[F]	714	891.420	07				
[C]	669	890.070	04	[G]	715	891.450	08				
[D]	670	890.100	05	[A]	716	891.480	09				
[E]	671	890.130	06	[B]	991	869.040	10				
[F]	672	890.160	07	[C]	992	869.070	11				
[G]	673	890.190	08	[D]	993	869.100	12				
[A]	674	890.220	09	[E]	994	869.130	13				
[B]	675	890.250	10	[F]	995	869.160	14				
[C]	676	890.280	11	[G]	996	869.190	15				

220

WIRELINE FREQUENCIES

Grp	Ch	Freq	Set	Grp	Ch	Freq	Set	Grp	Ch	Freq	Set
[A]	334	880.020	01	[C]	378	881.340	03	[E]	422	882.660	05
[B]	335	880.050	02	[D]	379	881.370	04	[F]	423	882.690	06
[C]	336	880.080	03	[E]	380	881.400	05	[G]	424	882.720	07
[D]	337	880.110	04	[F]	381	881.430	06	[A]	425	882.750	08
[E]	338	880.140	05	[G]	382	881.460	07	[B]	426	882.780	09
[F]	339	880.170	06	[A]	383	881.490	08	[C]	427	882.810	10
[G]	340	880.200	07	[B]	384	881.520	09	[D]	428	882.840	11
[A]	341	880.230	08	[C]	385	881.550	10	[E]	429	882.870	12
[B]	342	880.260	09	[D]	386	881.580	11	[F]	430	882.900	13
[C]	343	880.290	10	[E]	387	881.610	12	[G]	431	882.930	14
[D]	344	880.320	11	[F]	388	881.640	13	[A]	432	882.960	15
[E]	345	880.350	12	[G]	389	881.670	14	[B]	433	882.990	16
[F]	346	880.380	13	[A]	390	881.700	15	[C]	434	883.020	17
[G]	347	880.410	14	[B]	391	881.730	16	[D]	435	883.050	18
[A]	348	880.440	15	[C]	392	881.760	17	[E]	436	883.080	19
[B]	349	880.470	16	[D]	393	881.790	18	[F]	437	883.110	20
[C]	350	880.500	17	[E]	394	881.820	19	[G]	438	883.140	21
[D]	351	880.530	18	[F]	395	881.850	20	[A]	439	883.170	01
[E]	352	880.560	19	[G]	396	881.880	21	[B]	440	883.200	02
[F]	353	880.590	20	[A]	397	881.910	01	[C]	441	883.230	03
[G]	354	880.620	21	[B]	398	881.940	02	[D]	442	883.260	04
[A]	355	880.650	01	[C]	399	881.970	03	[E]	443	883.290	05
[B]	356	880.680	02	[D]	400	882.000	04	[F]	444	883.320	06
[C]	357	880.710	03	[E]	401	882.030	05	[G]	445	883.350	07
[D]	358	880.740	04	[F]	402	882.060	06	[A]	446	883.380	08
[E]	359	880.770	05	[G]	403	882.090	07	[B]	447	883.410	09
[F]	360	880.800	06	[A]	404	882.120	08	[C]	448	883.440	10
[G]	361	880.830	07	[B]	405	882.150	09	[D]	449	883.470	11
[A]	362	880.860	08	[C]	406	882.180	10	[E]	450	883.500	12
[B]	363	880.890	09	[D]	407	882.210	11	[F]	451	883.530	13
[C]	364	880.920	10	[E]	408	882.240	12	[G]	452	883.560	14
[D]	365	880.950	11	[F]	409	882.270	13	[A]	453	883.590	15
[E]	366	880.980	12	[G]	410	882.300	14	[B]	454	883.620	16
[F]	367	881.010	13	[A]	411	882.330	15	[C]	455	883.650	17
[G]	368	881.040	14	[B]	412	882.360	16	[D]	456	883.680	18
[A]	369	881.070	15	[C]	413	882.390	17	[E]	457	883.710	19
[B]	370	881.100	16	[D]	414	882.420	18	[F]	458	883.740	20
[C]	371	881.130	17	[E]	415	882.450	19	[G]	459	883.770	21
[D]	372	881.160	18	[F]	416	882.480	20	[A]	460	883.800	01
[E]	373	881.190	19	[G]	417	882.510	21	[B]	461	883.830	02
[F]	374	881.220	20	[A]	418	882.540	01	[C]	462	883.860	03
[G]	375	881.250	21	[B]	419	882.570	02	[D]	463	883.890	04
[A]	376	881.280	01	[C]	420	882.600	03	[E]	464	883.920	05
[B]	377	881.310	02	[D]	421	882.630	04	[F]	465	883.950	06

Grp	Ch	Freq	Set	Grp	Ch	Freq	Set	Grp	Ch	Freq	Set
[G]	466	883.980	07	[D]	512	885.360	11	[A]	558	886.740	15
[A]	467	884.010	08	[E]	513	885.390	12	[B]	559	886.770	16
[B]	468	884.040	09	[F]	514	885.420	13	[C]	560	886.800	17
[C]	469	884.070	10	[G]	515	885.450	14	[D]	561	886.830	18
[D]	470	884.100	11	[A]	516	885.480	15	[E]	562	886.860	19
[E]	471	884.130	12	[B]	517	885.510	16	[F]	563	886.890	20
[F]	472	884.160	13	[C]	518	885.540	17	[G]	564	886.920	21
[G]	473	884.190	14	[D]	519	885.570	18	[A]	565	886.950	01
[A]	474	884.220	15	[E]	520	885.600	19	[B]	566	886.980	02
[B]	475	884.250	16	[F]	521	885.630	20	[C]	567	887.010	03
[C]	476	884.280	17	[G]	522	885.660	21	[D]	568	887.040	04
[D]	477	884.310	18	[A]	523	885.690	01	[E]	569	887.070	05
[E]	478	884.340	19	[B]	524	885.720	02	[F]	570	887.100	06
[F]	479	884.370	20	[C]	525	885.750	03	[G]	571	887.130	07
[G]	480	884.400	21	[D]	526	885.780	04	[A]	572	887.160	08
[A]	481	884.430	01	[E]	527	885.810	05	[B]	573	887.190	09
[B]	482	884.460	02	[F]	528	885.840	06	[C]	574	887.220	10
[C]	483	884.490	03	[G]	529	885.870	07	[D]	575	887.250	11
[D]	484	884.520	04	[A]	530	885.900	08	[E]	576	887.280	12
[E]	485	884.550	05	[B]	531	885.930	09	[F]	577	887.310	13
[F]	486	884.580	06	[C]	532	885.960	10	[G]	578	887.340	14
[G]	487	884.610	07	[D]	533	885.990	11	[A]	579	887.370	15
[A]	488	884.640	08	[E]	534	886.020	12	[B]	580	887.400	16
[B]	489	884.670	09	[F]	535	886.050	13	[C]	581	887.430	17
[C]	490	884.700	10	[G]	536	886.080	14	[D]	582	887.460	18
[D]	491	884.730	11	[A]	537	886.110	15	[E]	583	887.490	19
[E]	492	884.760	12	[B]	538	886.140	16	[F]	584	887.520	20
[F]	493	884.790	13	[C]	539	886.170	17	[G]	585	887.550	21
[G]	494	884.820	14	[D]	540	886.200	18	[A]	586	887.580	01
[A]	495	884.850	15	[E]	541	886.230	19	[B]	587	887.610	02
[B]	496	884.880	16	[F]	542	886.260	20	[C]	588	887.640	03
[C]	497	884.910	17	[G]	543	886.290	21	[D]	589	887.670	04
[D]	498	884.940	18	[A]	544	886.320	01	[E]	590	887.700	05
[E]	499	884.970	19	[B]	545	886.350	02	[F]	591	887.730	06
[F]	500	885.000	20	[C]	546	886.380	03	[G]	592	887.760	07
[G]	501	885.030	21	[D]	547	886.410	04	[A]	593	887.790	08
[A]	502	885.060	01	[E]	548	886.440	05	[B]	594	887.820	09
[B]	503	885.090	02	[F]	549	886.470	06	[C]	595	887.850	10
[C]	504	885.120	03	[G]	550	886.500	07	[D]	596	887.880	11
[D]	505	885.150	04	[A]	551	886.530	08	[E]	597	887.910	12
[E]	506	885.180	05	[B]	552	886.560	09	[F]	598	887.940	13
[F]	507	885.210	06	[C]	553	886.590	10	[G]	599	887.970	14
[G]	508	885.240	07	[D]	554	886.620	11	[A]	600	888.000	15
[A]	509	885.270	08	[E]	555	886.650	12	[B]	601	888.030	16
[B]	510	885.300	09	[F]	556	886.680	13	[C]	602	888.060	17
[C]	511	885.330	10	[G]	557	886.710	14	[D]	603	888.090	18

Grp	Ch	Freq	Set	Grp	Ch	Freq	Set	Grp	Ch	Freq	Set
[E]	604	888.120	19	[B]	650	889.500	02	[F]	746	892.380	14
[F]	605	888.150	20	[C]	651	889.530	03	[G]	747	892.410	15
[G]	606	888.180	21	[D]	652	889.560	04	[A]	748	892.440	16
[A]	607	888.210	01	[E]	653	889.590	05	[B]	749	892.470	17
[B]	608	888.240	02	[F]	654	889.620	06	[C]	750	892.500	18
[C]	609	888.270	03	[G]	655	889.650	07	[D]	751	892.530	19
[D]	610	888.300	04	[A]	656	889.680	08	[E]	752	892.560	20
[E]	611	888.330	05	[B]	657	889.710	09	[F]	753	892.590	21
[F]	612	888.360	06	[C]	658	889.740	10	[G]	754	892.620	01
[G]	613	888.390	07	[D]	659	889.770	11	[A]	755	892.650	02
[A]	614	888.420	08	[E]	660	889.800	12	[B]	756	892.680	03
[B]	615	888.450	09	[F]	661	889.830	13	[C]	757	892.710	04
[C]	616	888.480	10	[G]	662	889.860	14	[D]	758	892.740	05
[D]	617	888.510	11	[A]	663	889.890	15	[E]	759	892.770	06
[E]	618	888.540	12	[B]	664	889.920	16	[F]	760	892.800	07
[F]	619	888.570	13	[C]	665	889.950	17	[G]	761	892.830	08
[G]	620	888.600	14	[D]	666	889.980	18	[A]	762	892.860	09
[A]	621	888.630	15	[E]	717	891.510	06	[B]	763	892.890	10
[B]	622	888.660	16	[F]	718	891.540	07	[C]	764	892.920	11
[C]	623	888.690	17	[G]	719	891.570	08	[D]	765	892.950	12
[D]	624	888.720	18	[A]	720	891.600	09	[E]	766	892.980	13
[E]	625	888.750	19	[B]	721	891.630	10	[F]	767	893.010	14
[F]	626	888.780	20	[C]	722	891.660	11	[G]	768	893.040	15
[G]	627	888.810	21	[D]	723	891.690	12	[A]	769	893.070	16
[A]	628	888.840	01	[E]	724	891.720	13	[B]	770	893.100	17
[B]	629	888.870	02	[F]	725	891.750	14	[C]	771	893.130	18
[C]	630	888.900	03	[G]	726	891.780	15	[D]	772	893.160	19
[D]	631	888.930	04	[A]	727	891.810	16	[E]	773	893.190	20
[E]	632	888.960	05	[B]	728	891.840	17	[F]	774	893.220	21
[F]	633	888.990	06	[C]	729	891.870	18	[G]	775	893.250	01
[G]	634	889.020	07	[D]	730	891.900	19	[A]	776	893.280	02
[A]	635	889.050	08	[E]	731	891.930	20	[B]	777	893.310	03
[B]	636	889.080	09	[F]	732	891.960	21	[C]	778	893.340	04
[C]	637	889.110	10	[G]	733	891.990	01	[D]	779	893.370	05
[D]	638	889.140	11	[A]	734	892.020	02	[E]	780	893.400	06
[E]	639	889.170	12	[B]	735	892.050	03	[F]	781	893.430	07
[F]	640	889.200	13	[C]	736	892.080	04	[G]	782	893.460	08
[G]	641	889.230	14	[D]	737	892.110	05	[A]	783	893.490	09
[A]	642	889.260	15	[E]	738	892.140	06	[B]	784	893.520	10
[B]	643	889.290	16	[F]	739	892.170	07	[C]	785	893.550	11
[C]	644	889.320	17	[G]	740	892.200	08	[D]	786	893.580	12
[D]	645	889.350	18	[A]	741	892.230	09	[E]	787	893.610	13
[E]	646	889.380	19	[B]	742	892.260	10	[F]	788	893.640	14
[F]	647	889.410	20	[C]	743	892.290	11	[G]	789	893.670	15
[G]	648	889.440	21	[D]	744	892.320	12	[A]	790	893.700	16
[A]	649	889.470	01	[E]	745	892.350	13	[B]	791	893.730	17

Grp	Ch	Freq	Set	Grp	Ch	Freq	Set	Grp	Ch	Freq	Set
[C]	792	893.760	18	[F]	795	893.850	21	[B]	798	893.940	03
D]	793	893.790	19	[G]	796	893.880	01	[C]	799	893.970	04
[E]	794	893.820	20	[A]	797	893.910	02				

PLACES TO
GET THINGS

Listed here are the sources of the products, services, and information mentioned in the text. Wherever possible, I have listed the original manufacturer rather than a reseller. Most of these products are made in the United States. Please note that some of them are tagged with the word *restricted*. This means that they may not be available to the general public. These providers may deal only with law enforcement and government agencies, cellular telephone service providers and repair facilities, or corporate security personnel. Please respect their wishes and don't contact them if you are not qualified.

I do not receive any form of compensation for sales resulting from the products and services listed in this book, but please mention that you read about manufacturers in this book if you contact any. They would like to know how you learned of their products. This list is in eight parts:

- *Electronic equipment*—ESN readers, DTMF decoders, frequency counters
- *FCC records*—CD-ROM, floppy disk, printed or disk, microfiche
- *Publications*—books, manuals, periodicals, cellular maps, phone-programming instructions, data-encryption programs
- *Secure equipment*—phones and scramblers, cellular fax systems, fax systems, wireless modems, encrypting modems, voice changers, call-screening systems, drop-out relays, long-play recorders, automatic recorders, computers
- *Countermeasures equipment*—bug detectors, countermeasures receivers, phone-line monitors, line trace equipment, answering machine protectors
- *Monitoring equipment*—commercial cellular monitoring systems, fax-interception systems, pager-interception systems, transmitter ID system, answering machine monitors, phone line transmitters
- *Radios and accessories*—scanners and communications receivers, accessories, computer control systems
- *Addresses and phone numbers*

ELECTRONIC EQUIPMENT

Electronic Serial Number Readers

Source: Curtis Electro Devices
(RESTRICTED) Curtis is one of the best-known manufacturers of ESN readers, having been in business for a number of years and widely advertised in cellular trade and law enforcement

publications. This is because Curtis makes a good product, but lately, because of cloning, the company has been under a great deal of fire by the media and the cellular service providers. So Curtis has taken measures to prevent the unlawful use of its readers, as described in Part 2. Sales are restricted to those who have a legitimate use, and this will be verified before any readers will be shipped.

Source: WaveTek Communications Div.
(RESTRICTED) WaveTek is the manufacturer of the Cellular Activation Tester, which, among other things, reads ESNs and has security features built in. The phone to be read has to be in the possession of the person using the system. Sales are restricted to authorized purchasers—those who work in the cellular industry and law enforcement—and the company verifies this.

DTMF Decoders

DTMF stands for dual-tone multifrequency—Touch-Tones. To translate these tones into the numbers they represent, you need a decoder.

Source: MoTron Electronics
MoTron is the manufacturer of a number of products, including the TDD-8X, which decodes all 16 digits (0 to 9, # and *, A,B,C, and D) that are used in some military phone systems. It comes assembled and tested, with a large, bright-red LED eight-digit display, and scroll right and left buttons to view its 104-digit memory. It also has a CLEAR button to erase what is stored. To use it, plug in a 12-volt adapter and a cable from the decoder's audio jack to a scanner or tape recorder. You can also dump its memory to a computer through a serial port. The price for the decoder, software, audio and RS-232 cables, and a nice plastic box to mount it in is about $135. An electronics company I used to work for used this decoder in one of its products. I built hundreds of them and never had a problem with the decoders. MoTron also makes the transmitter identification system described in the text.

Frequency Counters

Frequency counters are just that, devices that count, measure, and display the frequency of a transmitter they receive. They are made by any number of companies and range in price from about $100 to thousands of dollars for laboratory-quality units by Tektronix. The main difference between these models is accuracy. Engineers who have the responsibility for making sure commercial broadcast stations are exactly on frequency, as required by the FCC, need to determine the frequency to within a few cycles, so expensive, high-end equipment is essential. But if one wants only to find the frequency of a transmitter to be able to punch it into a scanner and listen, any of the low-end types will work fine.

Source: Optoelectronics
Opto has portable, pocket-sized counters from about $139 to $349 and bench models to about $700. They also have preselectors, which amplify signals to increase the sensitivity and effectiveness of receivers, and a computer control package for the PRO-2006 scanner.

Source: Startek International, Inc.
Startek makes counters starting at only about $119, the model 1350. It has no bells and whistles, but it covers 1 to 1,300 MHz and has a bright-red LED display. The company also has four "ATH" (auto, trigger, and hold) models from $179 to $339. All are pocket sized, and there are a number of accessories available, including a carrying case, various antennas (including one for cellular), and bandpass filters (see Glossary). They are shipped with built-in nicad batteries and a recharger.

FCC RECORDS

CD-ROM

Source: PerCon Corporation
FCC Master Frequency Database
The PerCon CD system is reviewed in Part 2.

Source: Grove Enterprises
Grove FCC Database
Grove is perhaps best known as the publishers of *Monitoring Times*, an excellent magazine dedicated to all phases of radios and listening. It has something for everyone. The FCC Database is reviewed in Part 2.

Printed or Disk

Source: C.E.T.
This company will make a search of all FCC-licensed transmitters within a specified area. The information is returned either printed or on floppy disk in .DBF or ASCII format. Call for details.

Microfiche

Source: US Department of Commerce
The National Technical Information Services sells FCC records on disk and microfiche to the public. These lists contain license information for the industrial highway maintenance, commercial broadcast, aviation, common carrier, and maritime services, as well as for police and fire.

PUBLICATIONS

Books

Source: Diane Publishing, 600 Upland Ave., Upland, PA 19105
Cryptography and Privacy Sourcebook
Edited by David Banisar
Available from the Electronic Privacy Information Center. This massive work (8 1/2 x 11 inches, 450 pages) contains a great deal of information on U.S. encryption policy, including information on the Clipper chip, the Digital Telephony Act, and ITAR cryptography export restrictions. It includes copies of legislation (Foreign Intelligence Surveillance Act, Omnibus, etc.), press releases, info about the FBI and NSA involvement in Clipper, statements made before Congress, statistics on electronic surveillance, and more. For anyone seriously interested in these subjects, especially researchers, this book is a must. The price is approximately $50 in the United States and $65 elsewhere.

Source: Landau, Susan, et al.
Codes, Keys, & Conflicts: Issues in U.S. Crypto Policy
Publisher: Association for Computing Machinery, Inc.
Available from the Electronic Privacy Information Center, this book has some very useful

227

information on cryptography in general and the Clipper chip in particular. It looks at cryptography from several perspectives, including law enforcement, national security, and privacy. It has a very good bibliography.

Source: EPIC
An Online Guide to Privacy Resources
This is a comprehensive list of information sources, including organizations, reading rooms, Internet file transfer sites, publications, mailing lists, and upcoming privacy-related conferences and events. Send e-mail to alert@epic.org for more information.

Source: The following books are from TSA
The Axnan Attack
This is the story of a team of professional eavesdroppers who are hired to penetrate the corporate headquarters of a medium-sized company in the United States. During the process, they attempt to eavesdrop on a meeting of the target company's regional managers in a hotel in Lake Placid, New York. There are details of how the eavesdroppers plan and operate, as well as their personal feelings during the high-risk parts of the operation. The weaknesses of the defenses that the company maintains against espionage penetrations are examined in a critique at the end of the story. It is instructive and thought provoking. This book fills a gap; where other books tell about surveillance in theory, *The Axnan Attack* puts it in the first person. What is it really like to be a spy? As books go, *The Axnan Attack* is not a literary work; it is not written by a professional writer who has based it on research and rumor. It is written by someone who knows the surveillance business, someone who has been there. It sells for around $32.95 plus $3.95 shipping and handling.

A Guidebook for the Beginning Sweeper
This book will be useful as a thought-provoking reference work for anyone who engages in sweeping or engages sweepers (countereavesdropping specialists). It is not a technical manual but, instead, deals with tactics that can defeat a resourceful and highly professional eavesdropper. Such other things as a sweeper's fee structure, legal considerations, and a glossary of terms are included. There is also a discussion of the eavesdropper's problems and the vulnerabilities that he will display and how he will try to reduce them. One of the book's principal features is a discovery checklist that can be used as a reminder of the things that a sweeper and his client should consider at the time that an eavesdropping penetration is discovered. Do not be deceived by the title. This book is not just for beginners.

This is a comprehensive manual that teaches more than just the fundamentals of countersurveillance. Where *The Bug Book* teaches the basics of surveillance, this book teaches about the details of a sweep. It explains, in plain English, about all the other things that are involved in learning to be a TSCM expert: dealing with a client, setting up a search, researching the legal aspects, assembling the equipment to be used, and a very detailed methodology for conducting a sweep. This is an excellent book for anyone, the private individual or a security type, who wants to learn the business end of countersurveillance. The glossary is excellent, and this book is highly recommended. It sells for approximately $49.95 plus $4.95 shipping and handling.

Source: Frank Terranella
Guide to U.S. Monitoring Laws

Manuals

The following are technical publications, some very technical, about the cellular radio system. They are for those who want a very detailed understanding of how it works. Some of them are expensive but may be available at public library reference sections.

Source: Electronic Industries Association (EIA) at 2000 Eye Street NW, Washington, DC 20006. Write for latest versions and prices.

(IS stands for interim standard; RMS is recommended minimum standard. Dual-mode means both analog and digital phones.)
IS-19-B: RMS for 800 MHz Cellular Subscriber Units
IS-3-D: AMPS Cellular System Mobile-Land Station Compatibility Standard
IS-20-A: RMS for 800 MHz Cellular Land Stations
IS-41-B: AMPS: Cellular Intersystem Operations, 5-Vol. Set
IS-52: Uniform Dialing Procedures . . . in Cellular Radio Telecom
IS-53: Cellular Features Description
IS-54-B: Cellular Dual-Mode Mobile/Base Station Compatibility Standard
IS-55: RMS for Dual-Mode Mobile Stations
IS-56: RMS for Dual-Mode Base Stations
IS-85: Cellular Standards for Full-Rate Speech Codes
IS-553: AMPS Cellular System Mobile-Land Station Compatibility Standard
IS-88: NAMPS System Standards
IS-89: NAMPS System Standards
IS-90: NAMPS System Standards
IS-41, revison B, contains information on how one vendor hands off calls to another and includes subscriber profiles. It is published by AT&T.

Periodicals

Source: Communications Publishing Associates
All in Communications Magazine
This publication is oriented toward those who work in the cellular, pager, and two-way radio industry, in the United States, Europe, and Central or South America. It is also available in Spanish. In its October 1994 issue *All in Communications* had an interesting mix of articles that were informative to both management and technicians; they are not so technical that they are hard to understand and not so general that they are boring. This issue includes a useful glossary of terms and advertisements for some interesting products. For example, it has a well-written article on the RS-232 interface that explains just what it is and what the signals are on each of the pins and what they do. It takes the mystery out of terms such as RTS, CTS, and DTR. There is a general article on how the cellular system works, one on the basics of cellular fraud, and others. If you have an interest in cellular, I think you will find this publication informative and well worth the price.

Source: RSA Data Security, Inc.
Ciphertext, the RSA newsletter
This publication has information on what's new in the world of cryptology and the never-ending battle between the government and the right to privacy (e.g., the latest on the Clipper chip). Some articles are written by people such as Drs. Adi Shamir, Ron Rivest, and Burton Kaliski,

who are among the most brilliant scholars in the field of ciphers, and these articles are not easy to understand by people with IQs under 400. Others are in English (that is, less technical) and are for everyone. Write for subscription information or look for it on the Internet newsgroup sci.crypt.

Source: T&L Publications
Nuts & Volts is a fascinating publication of how-to articles, columns, and advertisements (personal and commercial) for just about anything to do with electronics, computers, and communications. One particular series of articles, by Damien Thorn, presented information on the cellular radio system that is well worth reading. I subscribe to this excellent publication.

Source: Intertec Publishing Corp.
Cellular Business is intended for management rather than technical staff, but it is an excellent source of information and has many ads on new products and services. It costs about $24 per year for 11 issues.

Cellular Maps

Source: International Transcript Services
These maps show the location of cell sites, but as far as I know, only the latitude and longitude are given, no street addresses. This is based on a sample map I was able to look at, but do not have. I do not know if there are restrictions on map sales, as the cell locations are public domain information. If you need locations for only one area, then perhaps this is the way to get them. But the Grove FCC Database and CD mapping program is a better deal if you want locations in many different areas. The price varies from about $15 to $50 per map. Write for details if interested.

Phone-Programming Instructions

Instructions on how to program or reprogram cellular phones are available from many sources. There are at least a dozen files available free on local BBSs and through AFTP on the Internet. There are also books advertised in magazines such as *Nuts & Volts*. Because there are so many different brands, models, and types of cellular phones, no single file or book can contain instructions for all of them. What you get is what you get.

Source: Peregrine Dynamics
Offers a disk with instructions and software for about $17. Write for details.

Source: Busters Electronics
Offers diagnostic and programming information, cables, etc. Write or call for free catalog.

Data-Encryption Programs

Privacy and security in data communications can sometimes be had only with the use of encryption. There are a great many products—hardware and software—that provide this to different security levels, as discussed in the text. Here is where to get some of them.

Source: Everett Enterprises
The Private Line

Source: Digital Crypto
IRIS

Source: PGP, Inc.
As stated, Pretty Good Privacy was first produced by Philip Zimmerman several years ago, using the IDEA cipher and the RSA algorithm. There is a Windows interface available for the earlier versions that makes it menu driven and much easier to use. These three programs are available for downloading on a number of BBSs and Internet Web sites. The new version, PGP Mail, version 4.5, is available from PGP, Inc. It has a Windows interface built in and so is very easy to set up and use. If you have Internet access, check out PGP's site, http://www.pgp.com.

SECURE EQUIPMENT

Phones and Scramblers

Source: Transcrypt International
Transcrypt makes a cellular encryption system that is available for many popular models of transportable and mobile phones, an embedded module for the Motorola Micro-Tac "Flip Phone" and landline phones. Details in the text.

Source: Cylink Corporation
SecurePHONE

Source: Research Electronics, Inc.
The Scrambler

Source: Securicom
The TVS250 is reviewed in the text.

Cellular Fax Systems

Source: Ryno Enterprises
The FaxPak, model FP-180B is discussed in detail in the text.

Fax Systems

Source: The Ricoh Corporation
Model SFX2800M. No details were available when this book was written.

Wireless Modems
One way to keep anyone from intercepting your computer data by tapping your phone line is to not use a phone line. Wireless modems are described in Part 4 on computer security. Some sources are the following:

Source: GRE America, Inc.
GINA—The Global Integrated Network Access system, which uses spread spectrum technology. Details are in the text.

Source: Cylink Corporation
Airlink is a wireless data communications system that can be used between two individual

computers or as part of a network where any number of devices can be linked. This includes voice telephones (single or PBX, landline or cellular) and fax as well as computer data. Different data rates and configurations make this a very versatile system, which, with spread spectrum technology and encryption, provides high security. Operating in the 900 MHz band, the range is advertised as typically 30 miles.

Encrypting Modems

Source: Cylink Corporation
The LSA and LXA are modular plug-in units that go between a computer and modem, using standard RJ-11 modular telephone cables. Their size is 1.6 x 5.4 x 4.8 inches, and they encrypt the data being sent with the DES. They require a 9-volt adapter, which is included, and use the SEEK system for key management.

Voice Changers

Source: Viking International
The Model TVC, which is battery operated, can be used with any phone or two-way radio. The output is through a small speaker that can be placed over the microphone. This model has a variable pitch control, allowing fine-tuning of the sound—from very low to very high. It is so small, you can carry it in a pocket. It sells for under $200.

Source: Shomer-Tec
This company also manufactures the TVC (not the same as the one from Viking), which connects to the handset of any phone and has eight different settings and a built-in amplifier with volume control, and runs on three AA batteries. It sells for about $69.

Source: Akzo Marketing
The present model sold by Azko is a simple, no-frills, one-piece phone made in China. It is a push-button type, but not Touch-Tone; it converts the number key to pulses. It doesn't have last-number-dialed memory. It's just a cheapo phone, but it works. The circuit that does the voice changing is apparently the same one as used in more expensive models, selling in spy shops for about $100. The Azko phone sells for about $19.95. On the panel above the push buttons is a slide switch with three positions. Center is normal, left lowers the sound, and right raises it. There are four settings for each way, or a total of eight. Just slide the switch either way up to four times. Put it back in the center, and your voice returns to normal.

Call-Screening Systems

Source: Shomer-Tec
A Bel-Tronics AD100 Call Screener can be used to screen your calls and avoid being harassed or pestered by telephone solicitors.

Source: Shomer-Tec
This particular model requires that you have caller ID service. It stores up to 100 numbers of people you don't want to talk to, which you can program in manually. Or if someone unknown or not on the list calls, you let your answering machine take the call, and if you push the reject button, and that number is automatically added. The caller's name and

number, date and time are displayed on the LCD screen. This device currently sells for around $99.95.

Drop-out Relays

Source: SWS Security
The #5710 Phone Line/Tape Recorder interface from SWS Security is a low-cost device designed to couple a telephone line to a standard tape recorder to provide highest-quality surreptitious automatic recording. Connecting in parallel to a target phone line at any point between the telephone set and the CO, the #5710 will start and stop the recorder as the phone line is used. Audio from both sides of the telephone line is shaped, filtered, impedance and level matched, and sent to the audio input of the tape recorder. Recorder switching is accomplished by a connection between the #5710 and the recorder remote jack.

Significant benefits of the #5710 include fail-safe operation over a wide range of on- and off-hook line voltages, superb audio quality limited only by the characteristics of the phone line and recorder used, phone line filtering for virtually noise-free recording, hum filter of 60/120 (50/100) cycle, a very high input impedance to make the unit virtually undetectable by standard countersurveillance measures, extremely rugged watertight construction, and extremely reliable operation. No batteries are required, making the unit maintenance free and usable in remote areas or countries.

The #5710 was designed specifically for use with the Marantz PMD series of recorders (most similar devices will not activate the Marantz because of its electronic switching) and also works well with virtually any remote-start recorder or other device. Additionally, the #5710 is hardened to withstand lightning strikes or repeated high-voltage attacks that are sometimes used to destroy surveillance devices connected to the phone line.

The #5710 includes circuitry to prevent it from being defeated by "spyproof" telephones used by the criminal element. The unit will switch loads of several amps. This means that the #5710 can be used to switch devices other than tape recorders, giving capability for very high-powered parallel phone line transmitters.

Specifications of the #5710

Input impedance	40 MΩ (essentially invisible to countermeasures sweeps including TDR)
Audio bandpass	300 Hz to 10 kHz (greater than that of a phone line), 50/60 Hz notch (hum) filters
Switching time	Less than 50 mS
Audio output impedance	10kΩ
Telephone line connection	Standard modular plug or alligator clips (specify)
Recorder audio output cable	3.5mm miniphone plug, 5-ft. (1.5m) cord
Recorder switching output cable	2.5mm subminiphone plug, 5 ft. (1.5m) cord
Size	3 x 2 1/2 x 1 1/2 (75mm x 63mm x 38mm)
Weight	11 oz. (300g)
Construction	Blue-finished, waterproofed, cast-aluminum box, encapsulated circuitry

Source: Viking International
The TA229 starts any tape recorder that has a remote-control jack (most models do) whenever the phone or any extension is lifted off the hook. The recorder stops when it is replaced. It

complies with FCC regulations and will not interfere with the phone. It is completely automatic and requires no power source other than the phone line. It costs about $25.

Source: Shomer-Tec
Shomer-Tec sells the Model TRD-12, which does the same as the TA229, but costs about $19.

Long-Play Recorders

Source: Viking International
There are probably a number of places to get these recorders, but the only one I know of that makes a high-quality unit is Viking. They range from five to ten hours recording time per side and from about $150 to $300 in price. All are available with VOX for another $30. They have all of the features you would expect, plenty of audio power and a large speaker, remote control jack, automatic record level, record level indicator, tape counter, etc. Viking has other interesting products. Write or fax for its latest free catalog.

Automatic Recorders

Source: Shomer-Tec
One of the problems with recording telephone calls is that you have to remember to turn the recorder on. But this recorder is automatic. No external dropout relay is required.

Computers

Source: B.C.C.
B.C.C. is the original equipment manufacturer (made in the United States) of a notebook computer that has a DES encryption chip built in. Everything that is entered into this attractive portable is scrambled automatically unless you tell it otherwise. So if you use it to send data over a modem, you don't need to be too concerned about anyone outside the government reading it.

COUNTERMEASURES EQUIPMENT

Bug Detectors
If a phone line transmitter has been installed, you may be able to find it with this equipment. But keep in mind that no matter how good the device, the skill of the operator will probably make the difference between success and failure and also that the physical search is much more effective than any electronic device. *The Bug Book* has a lot of information on finding surveillance devices, which will help, but if at all possible, consult a professional. Finding surveillance devices can be a very complicated process, particularly if they were installed by an expert.

Source: Sheffield Electronics
The Model 262

Source: Lorraine Electronics
Model RFD-X and others

Source: Technical Services Agency, Inc.
The Eagle Plus

Source: Information Security Associates
The DAR-3

Source: Kaiser Electronics
The 2057-A

Phone-Line Monitors

There are dozens of products that fit this category, ranging in price from about $30 for a "tap alert" to thousands for some of the most sophisticated types. A tap alert will indicate that an extension phone has been picked up by flashing an LED. But it will not detect series or parallel taps, infinity devices, a capacitor-coupled listen-down amplifier, or even a lineman's test set in listen mode. Only something that would by itself take the line to off hook will trigger it.

Source: Lorraine Electronics
The TA 900 features a current meter as well as a volt meter. It checks for RF on the line (indicating a surveillance transmitter) and features a listen-down amplifier with volume control. Write for current price.

Source: Capri Electronics Corp.
Capri is the original equipment manufacturer of a number of midrange self-defense products. They are better than most of the cheap stuff found in spy shops but not as good as professional equipment that sells for 10 times as much. Capri is a small company that makes good equipment and doesn't misrepresent it. Write or call for a free catalog.

Line Trace Equipment

Source: Information Security Associates
The WT-1 Wire Tracing Kit is for use when you are searching a phone line for taps. A signal is injected at one end of the line, and the sensing unit picks up the signal to make following it easy.

Answering Machine Protectors

Source: Shomer-Tec
The Ampro can be used to protect your answering machine against intruders. Just plug in between the wall jack and the machine, and if someone tries to break in by sending a tone burst, such as from the Answering Machine Intruder, this little device will disconnect the intruder. It will not prevent you from being able to access your machine, is completely automatic, includes a power adapter and instructions, and sells for about $129.

MONITORING EQUIPMENT

Commercial Cellular Monitoring Systems
NOTE: Possession of these devices is a violation of federal and local law.

Source: Cellular Evaluation Systems
CES sells a computer interface system for the Oki 900 cellular phone that makes it into a monitoring system. This device is detailed in the text.

Source: Custom Computer Services
CCS manufactures the Digital Data Interpreter, also reviewed in the text.

Fax Interception Systems

Source: PowerFax, Inc.

Pager Interception Systems

Source: SWS Security
The Beeper Buster

Source: PowerFax, Inc.
The Pager Monitor

Transmitter ID System

Source: Motron Electronics
The TxID-1 is described in Part 2 of this book. This computer-aided system can positively identify a particular radio transmitter, including cordless and cellular phones.

Answering Machine Monitors

Source: Shomer-Tec
With the Answering Machine Intruder, as it says in Part 1, it is indeed possible to crack the code and get into these infernal devices, to listen to messages, erase them, and even change the message. "We're sorry. The number you have reached . . ." Just plug the Answering Machine Intruder in to a modular phone jack (RJ-11) and a cassette recorder. The included tape has instructions on using it. Once it has found the access code, you have control of the machine. The price is about $149.

Source: Xandi Electronics
Phone Line Transmitters
The XSP250 phone transmitter is about the size of a dime, making it one of the smallest types available to the general public. It sells for $34.95, and transmits on the standard FM radio band. I am not convinced that it has the advertised range of a quarter mile, but it is of interest because it can be easily hidden behind the phone's modular connection block. It is line powered, so no batteries are required. The transmitters are available only in kit form.

Xandi has a number of other products of interest here: a frequency converter for scanners that do not cover cellular, voice changers, and a bug detector. I built the bug detector and found that it works. Although experience in soldering is required, the manual makes putting it together easy enough that little knowledge of electronics is needed, mainly the ability to identify the different components. I would not hesitate to buy Xandi's products.
NOTE: Xandi is no longer selling transmitters. As with most other retail/mail order sources, the feds have stopped this.

Source: Sheffield Electronics
Model TEL-11KP
This is a combination phone and room audio transmitter. Normally it transmits room conversations from its built-in microphone, but switches automatically to the phone line whenever the phone is used. It is the only transmitter that I know of that transmits both sides of the conversation. It is available in kit form only, but it is partly assembled and takes only 10 minutes to complete, at least according to the ad. It currently sells for under $75, but may no longer be available when this book is published.

Source: SWS Security
The 5790
Details about this device can be found in Part 2.

Source: Deco Industries
Deco made a dozen or so surveillance transmitters, both variable frequency and crystal controlled, before it stopped production in 1997. Its Model VT-75, which can be used either for room audio or on a phone line, has become somewhat of a standard, because it is an excellent product. Assembly, which requires the ability to use a soldering iron, takes all of five minutes and consists of attaching two wires that go to the phone line, two resistors, and the antenna wire. I have built a number of these transmitters and found it to be one of the best models available. The audio is good, and the range, depending on conditions, can be several blocks or even, under perfect conditions, more than a mile (of course, this depends on many things). The VT-75 covers 70 to 130 MHz and was reviewed in *The Bug Book*. It is a good product. Thousands of these transmitters were sold, so there are still some available if you look in the right places.

Source: Electronic Rainbow
This company sells mostly kits, all of which are inexpensive. One is a phone transmitter for about $12.95, which makes it the lowest priced model I know of. Electric Rainbow also sells the Telephone Monitor, model TM-1, described in this *Nuts & Volts* ad as follows:

1. *Records outgoing calls:*
   Date and time of each call
   Length of the call
   What number was dialed
   Automatic recording of credit card numbers
2. *Records incoming calls:*
   Date and time of call
   How many times phone rings
   If answered, the length of call
3. *Records any DTMF tone:*
   Detects any tone on line sent by phone company or any other source.

The unit plugs into a parallel computer port and the phone line. Software is included. In kit form it is about $99.95; assembled, approximately $169.95. Just one more way to make your phones more secure, as you can tell when long-distance calls were made without waiting for the bill. Since similar products sell for several hundred bucks, this seems like a good deal to me.

RADIOS AND ACCESSORIES

Scanners and Communications Receivers

Source: Electronic Equipment Bank, Inc.
EEB is one of largest resellers of radios in the country. Located a few miles from Washington, D.C., this company sells every major brand and some you may never have heard of: ICOM, Yaesu, Japan Radio, Kenwood, Sony, Motorola, Grundig, GE, and, for those to whom money is no object, Watkins-Johnson. EEB also carries accessories, books, antennas, converters, pre-amplifiers—everything that has to do with radios. The company also sells transmitters, as well as doing custom work, modifications, and repairs. Its catalog is 92 pages filled with everything you can think of.

Source: Ham Radio Outlet
HRO specializes in ham radio equipment, but also has a large selection of communications receivers, such as ICOM, Yaesu, and other brands. HRO is an old, established company. The staff members are experienced and professional. Whatever you need, HRO has it or can tell you where to get it.

Source: Grove Enterprises
Grove has a large selection of scanners, communications receivers, accessories, books, antennas—everything to do with monitoring. Its prices are competitive. Write for a catalog and see for yourself.

Recorder Activator

Source: Capri Electronics
Capri sells the SR-09 ScanRecord, which is a "dropout relay for scanners." It automatically turns the recorder on when a signal is heard. It operates on either one 9-volt battery or an external adapter and comes with all connecting cords and instructions. It requires a recorder with remote-control jack and sells for about $50.

Computer-Aided Scanning

Source: Scan Star
This is one of the better programs with which a computer can control a scanner or communications receiver. It has many features and unlimited channels and banks. Call the BBS for a free demo. Also, a review will be on my Web site one of these days.

Source: Optoelectronics
The Optoscan 456 interface for the PRO-2006 scanner. See the short review in Part 3.

Source: DataMetrics
DataMetrics' Communications Manager program lets you monitor any number of frequencies in whatever way you set the system up. It works with the ICOM R7000, PRO-2006, and probably other radios; the information I have is several years old. The demo disk, also several years old, shows what a powerful program this is. I suspect this product has been improved on, so you might write to see what is new.

ADDRESSES AND PHONE NUMBERS

All entries are in alphabetical order. Some suppliers have requested that their phone numbers not be listed.

All Ohio Scanner Club
50 Villa Road
Springfield, OH 45503

AMC Sales Inc.
193 Vacquero Dr.
Boulder, CO 80303
303-499-5405
800-926-2488

ANARC Publications
P.O. Box 462
Northfield, MN 55057

AT&T Secure Communications Products
P.O. Box 20046
Greensboro, NC 27420
800-243-7883

Akzo Marketing
111 East 14th St., Ste. 311
New York, NY 10003
800-379-2515

BCC
1610 Crane Court
San Jose, CA 95112
408-944-9000

Busters Electronics
2039 Civic Center Dr. #176C
N. Las Vegas, NV 89030
702-642-00325

Capri Electronics Corp.
P.O. Box 589
Bayfield, CO 81122
303-884-9084

Communications Engineering Technology
1001 S. Ridgewood Ave.
Ridgewood, FL 32132
800-445-0297
Fax 904-426-0099

Communications Publishing Associates, Inc.
175 Fontainebleau Blvd., Ste. 1-A2
Miami, FL 33172
305-229-9992

Communications Sources
Mobile Services
1919 M St. NW, Room 628
Washington, D.C.

Computer Professionals for Social Responsibility
P.O. Box 717
Palo Alto, CA 94301
415-322-3778
Managing Director: Kathleen Kells
E-mail: cpsr-info@cpsr.org

CSE Associates
P.O. Box 297
Walkersville, MD 21793
http://www.cse-assoc.com

Curtis Electro Devices
4345 Pacific Street
Rocklin, CA 95677
916-632-0600

Custom Computer Services
P.O. Box 11191
Milwaukee, WI 53211
414-781-2482

Cycomm Corporation
6665 Hampton
Portland, OR 97223
Fax 503-620-8089

Cylink Corporation
910 Hermosa Ct.
Sunnyvale, CA 94086
408-735-5800

Cypherpunks
E-mail: majordomo@toad.com

DataMetrics
2575 S. Bayshore Dr., Ste. 8A
Coconut Grove, FL 33133

Datotek, Inc.
3801 Realty Road
Dallas, TX 75234
214-241-4491

Digital Crypto
P.O. Box 1
Penarth
South Glamorgan
UNITED KINGDOM CF6 2WB

Electronic Equipment Bank, Inc.
516 Mill St. NE
Vienna, VA 22180

Electronic Frontier Foundation
1667 K St. NW, Ste. 801
Washington, D.C. 20006
202-347-5400
Director: Andrew Taubman
E-mail: info@eff.org

Electronic Industries Association
2000 Eye Street NW
Washington, D.C. 20006

Electronic Privacy Information Center
666 Pennsylvania Ave SE, Ste. 301
Washington, D.C. 20003
202-544-9240
Director: Marc Rotenberg
E-mail: info@epic.org

Electronic Rainbow
6254 La Pas Trail
Indianapolis, IN 46268
317-291-7262

Everett Enterprises
7839 Vervain Court
Springfield, VA 22152

GRE America, Inc.
425 Harbor Blvd.
Belmont, CA 94002
Fax 415-591-2001

Grove Enterprises
P.O. Box 98
140 Dog Branch Rd.
Brasstown, NC 28902
704-837-9200
Fax 704-837-2216
BBS: 704-837-9200

Ham Radio Outlet
510 Lawrence Expressway
Sunnyvale, CA 95051
408-736-9496

Index Publishing Group
3368 Governor Dr. #273F
San Diego, CA 92122

Information Security Associates
350 Fairfield Ave.
Stamford, CT 06902
203-357-8051

International Transcript Service
2100 M St. NW, Room 148
Washington, D.C. 20037
202-857-3800

Internet Society
12020 Sunrise Valley Dr., Ste. 270
Reston, VA 22091
703 648-9888
Executive Director: Anthony Rutkowski
E-mail: isoc@isoc.org

Intertec Publishing Corp.
9800 Metcal
Overland Park, KS 66212

Lorraine Electronics
716 Lea Bridge Road
Leyton, London
ENGLAND
E10 6AW

Martin Kaiser Electronics
P.O. Box 171
Cockeysville, MD 21030
http://www.marti-kai.com

Mobile Radio Resources
1224 Madrona Ave.
San Jose, CA 95125
Fax 408-269-5811

Motorola Secure Telecommunications
8820 E. Roosevelt St.
Scottsdale, AZ 85257
602-441-8541

MoTron Electronics
310 Garfield St., Ste. 4
Eugene, OR 97402
503-687-2118
Fax 687-2492

Murray Associates
Box 668
Oldwick, NJ 08858
908-832-7900
http://www.spybusters.com
E-mail: murray@spy.busters.com

MVS
Box 994
Merrimack, NH
508-792-9507

Naval Electronics
5417 Jet View Circle
Tampa, FL 33634
813-885-6091
Fax 885-3789

Nuts & Volts
T & L Publications
430 Princeland Court
Corona, CA 91719
909-371-8497

Optoelectronics
5821 NE 14th Ave.
Ft. Lauderdale, FL 33334
800-327-5912

PerCon Corporation
4906 Maple Springs/Ellery Road
Bemus Point, NY 14712
716-386-6015
Fax 716-386-6013

Peregrine Dynamics
720 Portage Trail
Cuyahoga Falls, OH 44221

PGP, Inc.
2129 S. El Camino Real, Ste. 902
San Mateo, CA 94403
415-631-1747
http://www.pgp.com

PowerFax, Inc.
P.O. Box 9436
Lyndhurst, NJ 07071

Privacy Rights Clearinghouse
5998 Alcala Park
San Diego, CA 92110
619-260-4806
800-773-7748
Director: Beth Givens
E-mail: prc@teetot.acusd.edu

Research Electronics, Inc.
1570 Brown Ave.
Cookeville, TN 38501

Ricoh Corporation
703-525-3234

RSA Data Security, Inc.
10 Twin Dolphin Dr.
Redwood City, CA 94065
415-595-8782

Ryno Enterprises
711 Boston Post Rd., Ste. 168
Marlboro, MA 01752

ScanStar
Signal Intelligence
408-926-5630
ScanStar BBS
408-258-6462

Scanware Associates
7910 NE Double Hitch Court
Bremerton, WA 98310
206-698-1383
Fax 698-8207
BBS 206-871-4228

Securicom
P.O. Box 5227
Chatsworth, CA 91313
818-710-0110

Sheffield Electronics
P.O. Box 377940
Chicago, IL 60637

Shomer-Tec
P.O. Box 28070
Bellingham, WA 98228
360-733-6214

Society for Electronic Access
P.O. Box 7081
New York NY 10116
212-592-3801
E-mail: sea@sea.org

Startek International, Inc.
398 NE 38th St.
Ft. Lauderdale, FL 33334
305-561-2211

SWS Security
1300 Boyd Road
Street, MD 21154
http://www.swssec.com

Technical Communications Corp.
100 Domino Dr.
Concord, MA 01742
508-862-6035

Technical Services Agency, Inc.
10903 Indian Head Highway, Ste. 304
Ft. Washington, MD 20744

Telecommunications Advisers, Inc.
722 SW Second Ave., Ste. 200
Portland, OR 97204
503-227-7878

Transcrypt International
4800 NW First St.
Lincoln, NE 68521
402-474-4800
Fax 402-474-4858

U.S. Department of Commerce
National Technical Information Service
703-487-4630

U.S. Privacy Council
P.O. Box 15060
Washington, D.C. 20003
202-829-3660
Director: Evan Hendricks
E-mail: privtime@access.digex.net

Viking International
150 Executive Park #4600
San Francisco, CA 94134
Fax 415-468-2067

Voters Telecom Watch
E-mail: shabbir@panix.com

Wavetek Communications Div.
5808 Churchman Bypass
Indianapolis, IN 46203-6109
317-788-9351

Will's BBS
303-343-4053

Xandi Electronics
P.O. Box 25647
Tempe, AZ 85285

TELEHONE CABLE COLOR CODES

What does BOGBS-WRBYV mean?

To find a particular pair in a cable, it is necessary to know the telco color codes. BOGBS-WRBYV are the first letters of the standard colors used. These 10 colors are paired in such a way that they can identify 25 pairs of wires and are arranged in two groups. The first is blue, orange, green, brown, and slate; the second is white, red, black, yellow, and violet. To standardize them, they are abbreviated as follows:

Blue	BLU	White	WHT
Orange	ORG	Red	RED
Green	GRN	Black	BLK
Brown	BRN	Yellow	YEL
Slate	SLT	Violet	VIO

The 25 combinations are as follows:

01	BLU-WHT	14	GRN-YEL
02	BLU-RED	15	GRN-VIO
03	BLU-BLK	16	BRN-WHT
04	BLU-YEL	17	BRN-RED
05	BLU-VIO	18	BRN-BLK
06	ORG-WHT	19	BRN-YEL
07	ORG-RED	20	BRN-VIO
08	ORG-BLK	21	SLT-WHT
09	ORG-YEL	22	SLT-RED
10	ORG-VIO	23	SLT-BLK
11	GRN-WHY	24	SLT-YEL
12	GRN-RED	25	SLT-VIO
13	GRN-BLK		

The first color of the first group is used with the first color of the second group. BLU is paired with WHT, which is called BLU with a WHT mate. This continues with the first color of the first group and the second color of the second group which is BLU with a RED mate. Then the first color of the first group and the third color of the second group, BLU-BLK, then BLU-YEL and BLU-VIO. Then it is repeated using the second color of the first group, ORG, paired with each of the five colors from the second group. This makes 25 pairs.

A larger cable is made up of a series of smaller, inner cables, each containing 25 pairs, color coded as above, which are called *binder groups* or *pair units*. Each of them is tagged with a colored string inside the outer insulation. The tags use the same format as the pairs—the first binder group is tagged BLU-WHT, the second BLU-ORG, etc.

TO FIND THE PAIR BY NUMBER

Now suppose you had the pair number. How would you find it? Let's say the number is 168, or the 168th pair in the cable. Since there are 25 pairs in each binder group, divide 168 by 25 and get 6.72. The 168th pair will be in the 6th binder group. Next, take the remainder of 0.72 and multiply it by 25. This equals 18, so it is the 18th pair in the 6th binder group. Refer to the chart of the 25 color combinations and you see that the 6th binder group is ORG-WHT, and the 18th pair is BRN-BLK.

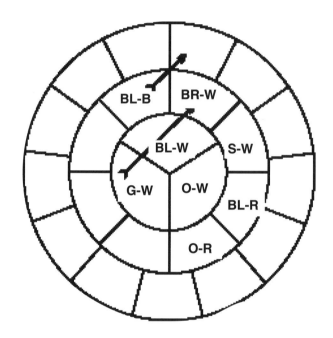

This is the way AT&T and the Bell System coded them, but with so many new companies handling telephone traffic, one may encounter cables that use a completely different system. Cables are not limited to 600 pairs, and while this is one the most common sizes, there are "super" cables that have as many as 3,900 pairs. Getting access to any cable is difficult, and opening the cable to find, and tap, a particular pair is much easier said than done, but this is how the right pair is located.

The drawing shows how the binder groups are arranged in a 360-pair cable. Starting in the center with BLU-WHT, go clockwise to ORG-WHT, then to GRN-WHT, on around the second layer to BLU-BLK, and then to the outer layer starting with ORG-BLK.

FIBER-OPTIC CABLES

Most of the new cables that are being installed use fiber optics, which is also replacing some of the old copper-wire cables. The use of fiber optics has increased from about 20,000 miles in 1985 to more than 100,000 in 1993, and although it makes up only about 6 percent of the total, there are many reasons why it will increase in the future.

- A copper wire can normally carry only one conversation.
- A copper wire is easier to tap.
- A copper wire is expensive.
- A copper wire is heavy.

• A copper wire is more subject to noise, such as crosstalk from other lines.

The term *fiber optic* refers to a thin strand, or fiber, of plastic that has strong light-conduction properties. Light travels through it similar to the way that electricity flows through a wire, except that with fiber optics photons rather than electrons carry the messages. It is not subject to corrosion, whereas copper is, especially in areas near the ocean where salt in the air collects on the bare terminal connections. And since one fiber can carry many conversations, the cable size is much smaller.

The actual fibers, referred to as "light guides," are composed of three parts: the core, which carries the light; the cladding, which surrounds the core and prevents light from leaking out (eliminating crosstalk interference); and a protective coating. A fiber that is capable of transferring more than a gigabyte of information per second and is a mile in length weighs about 2 ounces. The equivalent in copper wire weighs more than 30 tons.

Fiber-optic cables do not connect individual phones; they are used as trunks to connect one facility to another. This could be one CO to another or to a microwave tower. At one end of the cable, the copper wires of the individual phone lines feed into electronic equipment that mixes (multiplexes) all of the messages they carry together, so that they can be transmitted over a single strand. Then the signals are converted into light using a laser. At the other end, the process is reversed.

Tap a Fiber-Optic Cable?

Forget it. First, you would have to be able to access the cable in a junction point or at the CO. Then you have to open the cable, which may set off an alarm. And then you would have no way of knowing which strand carries the line you want to tap. But even if you did, you would need some sophisticated and expensive equipment to extract a conversation from that strand. This could be done by cutting the strand and inserting your own multiplexing equipment (should you have plenty of time and money), or it is possible to extract some information without cutting the strand.

After separating it, you bend it into a U-shape and insert it into a clamp. Some of the laser light escapes the strand, where it is detected by a photoelectronic device built into the clamp and then amplified. Then it feeds into a demultiplexer. Only an expert with this expensive equipment could tap a fiber-optic strand, which a pro would not do anyway, because it is easier to install the tap at a place on the line where copper wire is used.

This is part of the technology (mentioned in Part 1) that government agencies, mainly the FBI, claim has made them unable to install legal, court-ordered taps. So they pushed the Digital Telephone Act (Senate Bill 266) through Congress. It was sort of sneaked through with no discussions or arguments in just a few minutes, and President Clinton signed it into law.

GLOSSARY

In this section are listed the technical terms used in the text, with an explanation of what they mean. It is in four parts, which (I hope) makes it easier to find what you are looking for: (1) landline telephone systems; (2) cellular telephone number assignment module (or NAM) data; (3) cellular radio; and (4) basic electronics, computer science, data encryption, surveillance, and everything else. Some terms have more than one definition, in which case I have used what seems to best apply here. Also, some terms apply to more than one of the four parts. They are listed in the part that seems the most relevant.

LANDLINE TELEPHONE SYSTEMS

aerial: The name given to phone wires that are above ground, not in underground conduits. Also another name for antenna.

ANAC: Automatic number announcement circuit; the computer-synthesized voice that "speaks" the numbers. Part of the ANI system.

ANI: Automatic number identification ("Annie"); a service of telco that will identify the number of a line. Call the ANI number and a computer voice will read back the number you are calling from. This is one way that wiretappers find the right pair.

avantriculator: See *framistat.*

B-box: (Bridging box); a large metal cabinet, usually on street corners, where the underground phone lines "surface" so telco workers can access them.

blue box: A device that generated a 2,600-cycle audio tone, plus Touch-Tones. It was used to make free toll calls before the installation of outband signaling.

box: Any of a number of devices with colors as names, used to do things with phone systems, most of which people are not supposed to do—or be able to do. There are red, blue, mauve, silver, gold, and whatever else. *Mauve?*

busy line verification: A service of the telco where a caller can request an operator to determine whether a particular line is actually busy or out of order. The operator accesses the line in question through a special BLV trunk to check the status. An actual connection is made, which the person using the phone may hear as an audible *click*, but the operator hears the conversation through a frequency inversion scrambler. That way the operator can determine if there is conversation on the line without being able to tell what is being said. See also *frequency inversion*.

BY: ("B-Y"); an old telco term for a line that is busy.

cable: Any number of electrical conductors together, usually inside an insulating sheath. It may contain from two to thousands of individual wires.

CAMA: Centralized automatic message accounting, sometimes called "caller log." This is a system that records call details. Long-distance and local calls are logged, including the number called, date and time, and duration. It is used from a centralized location, usually a tandem office. CAMA is similar to LAMA (local automatic message accounting), except LAMA is localized in a specific CO and CAMA is not.

Centrex: A type of electronic phone system available from the telco. The actual equipment is at the telco switching office, rather than at the place of business. Centrex can work with as few as two lines and as many as 200. It is similar to Comstar.

cheese box: Also called a gold box, this device is believed to have been invented by "Cheesebox" Callahan, one of the all-time great wiretappers. It was a call-forwarding system set up in a warehouse or vacant apartment.

COCOT: Customer-owned coin-operated telephone; a pay phone owned and operated by a private business and not the local telephone company, such as Pacific Bell. Its programming, rates, synthesized voice, etc., all originate from within the phone and are controlled or modified by calling its internal modem from the owner's offices.

cracker: Hacker, cracker, phreaker—semantics . . .

customer premise equipment: (CPE); data or voice communications equipment, computers, telephones, etc., located inside the customer's office rather than at another location, such as with Centrex, which uses equipment located at the telco.

DA: ("D-A") old telco term for "don't answer," as in there is no answer.

distribution closet: An area in a bulding set aside for incoming phone lines. The lines connect to a panel, sometimes called a 66 block, and from there they lead to individual offices or apartments or sometimes to a floor closet.

drop wire: (Drop line); the phone wire that leads from a telephone pole to a house or building.

DTMF: Dual-tone multi-frequency; Touch-Tones. The audio tones used by telephones to dial numbers and other functions. The standard phone has only 12—0 through 9, *, and #. Some phones, such as used by the military autovon system, also have a, b, c, and d, which have special functions.

floor closet: A telephone line distribution area on some or all floors of large office and apartment buildings.

fortress: The name given to pay phones made for the Bell system, because they are very hard to break into. COCOTs are less secure—and less dependable.

framistat: See *gullible*.

ground detect: A function of pay telephones that supposedly defeats red boxes by physically detecting whether coins have been inserted. Some phones have this, but others do not.

hack: The definition depends on whom you ask. To hack something usually means to get access to it by breaking in to it (computer systems, telco-restricted information, cellular systems, whatever) "because it's there." To hack something does not mean that it is done with the intent of causing damage, destroying data, crashing systems, or stealing information. The notion that hackers are necessarily destructive is nothing but hype, created by the media.

hacker: Someone who hacks. What else?

horizontal frame: (HF); one of two large steel racks where incoming lines are connected. From the HF the lines (pairs) go to the vertical frame.

junction point: An underground room, usually entered through a manhole cover at a street intersection, where telco lines are accessed for splicing, repairs, and sometimes tapping. See also *bridging box*.

leased line: A dedicated telephone line leased from the telco for a specific purpose, such as for surveillance or the silent alarm systems at ATMs.

local loop: The loop of wire that connects an individual telephone to the CO.

MDF: Main distribution frame; this is the area where all cable pairs of a certain office meet and a third wire, the sleeve wire, is added. The sleeve wire is used in gathering ANI information, as well as determining a called line's status (off/on hook) in certain switching systems by the presence of voltage. If voltage is present, the line is busy; if there is no voltage, the line is idle.

off hook: The condition of a telephone line when it is in use. Lifting the receiver of a phone causes this condition. The line voltage (normally about 48 volts, but it may be as low as 32 drops to about 10 or 12. If you had a meter connected to the line, you would see the change in reading, and, if an extension is picked up, it would drop an additional 2 to 4 volts.

PABX: Private automatic branch exchange, usually called PBX (private branch exchange).

point of demarcation: The point at which phone lines become the property of the telco, usually beyond the 66 block in an office building or SPSP in a private residence.

provisioning: A function of the telco ESS whereby a line can be protected from REMOBS or SAS. It is believed to be for the lines to law enforcement and federal intelligence agencies, but Pacific Bell will not comment on this.

red box: A device that duplicates the tones generated by a pay telephone when coins are inserted. If you hold the unit to the microphone and press a button, the telco system is fooled into believing money was deposited. These devices still work with some telco systems, but may require that a real coin is first deposited to open the microphone.

REMOBS: Remote observation. See also *switched access service*. Remote observation is a function of the telco ESS with which authorized personnel can monitor any phone line in the system that does not have special protection such as provisioning.

seizing: Answering a phone line; picking up the receiver; causing it to be busy or in use, in an off-hook condition.

66 block: The generic name for the electrical panel used for connecting incoming phone lines to the cables leading to offices or apartments. It was so named because of its capacity of 66 lines, but it also applies to panels of other sizes. It is also called a "punch-down" block from the type of connectors used.

social engineering: Various definitions apply, but here it refers to the process of obtaining information that one is not supposed to have from someone who is not supposed to give it out—e.g., obtaining unlisted telephone numbers from the telco.

SPSP: Single-pair station protector; a small metal or plastic can or box where an incoming phone line connects to the phone cable, like a small 66 block. It contains fuses to protect the telco lines and CO equipment.

SS-7: A simplified explanation is an outband or out-of-band system wherein signaling information is sent through a different line than voice transmissions. This system was developed in the 1960s to prevent toll fraud abuse by the use of blue boxes.

switched access service: See also *REMOBS*. A feature of the ESS through which a phone line can be tapped from a remote location.

telco: A generic term for any telephone company.

television: The inverse square of intelligence.

trap: The name for a feature of the telco system computer that can make a record of all calls made to the "trapped" number. It is used to find prank or obscene callers. It is the same principle as the pen register.

unlisted number bureau: The name varies from telco to telco, but it is the department that keeps records of unlisted numbers and addresses to provide to authorized telco employees or unauthorized hackers who know how to ask for the information.

vertical frame: See *horizontal frame*.

WATS: Wide area telephone service; an old telco term for 800 numbers.

CELLULAR NAM DATA

ACCOLC: A four-bit field designating the overload class for the cellular phone. The intention of this entry is to allow the cellular system to be able to determine priority in the event of a system overload; however, it is currently useless because the system operators have generally not provided guidance for their installers. The usual (and correct) system now in effect (in the United States) is to use a zero plus the last digit of the phone number. Test phones should be set at 10 and emergency vehicles at 11. The numbers 12 through 15 are reserved (a class 15 system is supposed to be for police, fire, or military agencies).

E.E.: A one-bit flag designating that end-to-end signaling is enabled. End-to-end signaling means that the DTMF tones will be transmitted on the voice channel as well as being echoed on the handset. This feature in necessary for such services as banking by phone, activating answering machines, and using third-party long-distance services, such as Sprint and MCI. A 1 enables the flag. Usually set to 1.

GIM: A four-bit field designating the group identification mark. This number tells the cellular system how far to look in the SIDH to determine if a phone is roaming in a system that may have a roam agreement with the phone system. It is usually set to 10.

HA: Horn-alert feature. When enabled, the vehicle horn beeps repeatedly, advising the owner of an incoming call and irritating the neighbors.

IPCH: Incoming page channel, an 11-bit field designating the initial paging channel to be used if in the home system. Normally, it is 334 for wireline systems and 333 for nonwireline systems.

LD: Lock digit; a feature of a cellular phone that allows the owner to lock it, thus making it inoperative. In some systems, this can be done by calling the phone from any other phone, as well as from the keypad. It is useful if a phone is lost or stolen.

MIN mark: A 1-bit flag designating that MIN2 (area code) is always sent when making system access. 1 enables the flag. It is usually set to 1.

MIN1: A 24-bit field representing the mobile telephone number. MIN2 plus MIN1 equals MIN, the 10-digit phone number.

MIN2: A 10-bit field representing the area code of the mobile ID number.

NAM: Number assignment module; a chip in a cellular phone that contains various items of information about that phone, most of which are in this section of the Glossary.

REP: Repertory memory (speed dialing) in the cellular phone.

SCM: A 4-bit field designating the station class mark. This represents information about the phone, such as its type and power output level (portable, transportable, mobile) and whether or not it can access all 832 channels. When a phone is cloned and this field is not correct, the cellular system computer will recognize it as not being a legitimate phone.

SIDH: A 15-bit field in the NAM designating the system identification for the home system; the area where the phone was activated.

CELLULAR RADIO

A carrier: The nonwireline cellular vendor, e.g., CellularONE.

A/B switch: A switch on a cellular phone with which the user can select the cellular vendor.

access fee: A fee that landline telcos can charge cellular customers for connecting with their systems.

air time: The time a cellular phone is being used, usually in increments of one minute, meaning that if you make or receive a call that lasts only 10 seconds, you still have to pay for one minute.

AMPS: Advanced mobile phone service; the standard for cellular phone systems in the United States and other countries, including the United Kingdom, Canada, Australia, Mexico, and South America. The term was originated by AT&T in 1975, and the AMPS system first used in Chicago in 1982.

B carrier: The wireline cellular vendor, e.g., GTE Mobil Net.

blocking: Making a channel unavailable in the cell it is normally used in, when it has been borrowed by a nearby cell.

borrowing: Reassigning one or more channels in a cell to another cell when needed in times of heavy use.

CDMA: Code-division multiple access; a fairly new type of cellular phone standard that uses spread-spectrum (direct-sequence) technology and very low power. It is in use in only a few areas of the United States, but it is being considered in many others.

cell: Cell site; one of the divisions of a cellular radio system. Cells are generally 3 to 5 miles in diameter but can be as many as 40 and have one radio transmitter receiver setup, which may use one to three if the 21 available channel "sets."

Cell-Tell: A single-cell monitoring system built into an attaché case. It includes a DTMF display, VOX, and cassette recorder for taping intercepted calls.

cell splitting: Splitting one cell into two cells to increase the capacity in an area of heavy cellular phone use.

CGSA: Cellular geographical service area; the area in which a cellular vendor provides telephone service. See also *MSA* and *RSA*.

channel: A frequency used by the cellular system to send and receive data and voice conversations. There are two types of channels: data (control) and voice. Data channels carry electronic signals that control the cellular phones. Voice channels carry the conversations. Forward channels (both data and voice) are from the cell site equipment to the cellular phone. Reverse channels (both data and voice) are from the cellular phone to the cell site equipment. So, there are forward voice channels, reverse voice channels, forward data channels, and reverse data channels. The cellular system uses a total of 832 channels. Each of the two vendors is assigned half of them, or 416. Of these 416, 21 are data, and 395 are voice. They are divided into 21 sets, each of which is controlled by one of the 21 data channels. These sets are assigned to the cells in groups of seven, with each cell using one group, and a group consists of three sets—3 x 7 = 21. Because there are only 395 voice channels and they must serve thousands of cellular phones, the channels are reused in different cells. To prevent interference, they are assigned in such a way that no adjacent cells use the same group. (See text for details.) See also *frequency*.

clone: The process of changing the ESN of a cellular phone to a different number. This may be done to have two legal phones with the same number or to make calls that are billed to someone else.

CMC: Cellular mobile carrier; the vendors of cellular radio service such as GTE, Cellular-1, etc.

co-channel cell: The term used for cells that use the same channels. They are separated from each other by at least one other cell that uses a different set of channels. This is to prevent interference.

control channel: This is also called data channel. It is a frequency used only for sending control, or data, signals between cellular phones and the cell site equipment.

COW: Cell on wheels; a portable cellular radio system that can be towed to any location to provide service during an emergency overload or general increase in use or pending the installation of a permanent site.

DDI: Digital data interpreter; a device that interfaces a receiver and computer. It controls the radio for cellular monitoring or test purposes and decodes the Manchester data sent on the control channels, which is displayed on the monitor.

forward data channel: See *channel*.

forward voice channel: See *channel*.

group: Unofficial term for the channels used by one cell. A group usually consists of three sets. They are designated A through G.

gullible: See avantriculator.

hand-off: The process of changing the channel being used by a particular cellular phone to another channel. This is usually done when the signal from the phone drops below a certain level and is received at a higher level by a different cell. The hand-off is transparent to the user and takes about one-third of a second.

lifetime phone: A cloned cellular phone that contains a modified NAM chip into which different ESNs can be entered from the keypad. No computer, no software, no cables, no disassembly required. Batteries included.

Manchester: The code used in the transmission of data on cellular control channels.

MIN: Mobile identification number; the telephone number assigned to the cellular phone.

MSA: Metropolitan service area; an FCC designation of cellular service areas. See also RSA.

MTSO: Mobile telephone switching office; the site of the computer that controls the cellular system and connects it to landline phones. It monitors calls, keeps track of the location of phones, records billing information, and arranges hand-offs.

NAM: Number assignment module; the chip in a cellular phone that stores the MIN, ESN, SCM, and other information.

NAMPS: Narrow (band) AMPS; a recent development in cellular radio that uses a narrow-band signal so that one channel can handle three conversations.

pigtail: The type of antenna used on vehicles. It is recognizable by the loading coil.

PIN: Personal identification number; a "secret" password such as is used with bank ATM cards and now with some cellular phones. For the latter use, if the PIN is not entered, the system will not place the call. As the pin is not intercepted by ESN readers, the ESN cannot be used for cloning.

power: As used in cellular phones, there are different levels. Pocket types are limited to 0.6 watts and transportables to 3 watts. The MTSO can control the power output of a phone. If the signal from a phone is too weak, the computer increases it; if it is too strong, it lowers it. with the new CDMA system, the power is considerably lower because less is needed.

reverse data channel: See *channel*.

reverse voice channel: See *channel*.

RSA: Rural service area; an FCC designation of cellular service areas. See also *MSA* and *CGSA*.

SAM: System access monitor; a device used to monitor the data sent to and from a cellular phone for testing and repair purposes. Sometimes called an ESN reader, it intercepts the ESN, MIN, AND SCM from cellular phones.

set: A number of voice channels, up to 20, that are controlled by one particular data channel.

SSD: Shared secret data; it is defined in interim standard IS-54. This is part of a digital system that encrypts the ESN so that it cannot be intercepted with an ESN reader. The scrambled ESN and a random number are combined to make the SSD. This is an oversimplification, and there is a lot more to it.

TDMA: Time-division multiple access; a system where cellular phone conversations are converted to digital form. This increases the capacity of the cellular system and provides protection against eavesdroppers with scanners or communications receivers. See also *multiplexing*.

test mode: The mode that programmers and technicians enter to activate or test a cellular phone. It is through this mode that phones can be reprogrammed with stolen ESNs. The test mode is accessible by connecting the phone to a computer through a cable. The cables and instructions for using the test mode are available to anyone who wants them.

transmobile: A type of cellular phone used in vehicles through a cigarette lighter cable. It does not have a battery pack so it is not portable.

transportable: A type of cellular phone that can operate with a built-in battery pack, in a vehicle with a cigarette lighter cable, or from a fixed location with a battery eliminator.

tumbled phone: A cloned phone that is capable of storing and using a bogus ESN; a number that does not exist or has not been assigned. At one time, it was possible to fool the system by using a bogus number to get at least one "free" call from outside the area where it was activated, or its SIDH. But with the nationwide database of cellular numbers, which can be checked in real time for stolen or bogus numbers, these phones may no longer work. Also, a cellular phone that fell out the window of a vehicle on the freeway. It also may no longer work.

BASIC ELECTRONICS, COMPUTER SCIENCE, DATA ENCRYPTION, SURVEILLANCE, AND EVERYTHING ELSE

AC: Alternating current; an electric current that starts, as it comes from an AC generator, at what is called the baseline. At this point it is zero volts. It increases to its maximum value—say, 60 volts, which it its "positive peak," and then drops in intensity back to zero. At this point, it flows in the opposite direction to a negative value, the same as the maximum in the other direction, which is the "negative peak," and then back up to zero volts at the baseline. This change, from zero to max to zero, is one cycle, or 360 degrees.

accumulator: One type of register.

AF: Audio frequency; the range of sound that people can hear. It is usually stated as 20 to 20,000 cycles per second, though few people can hear this entire range.

active component: An electronic component that "does something," sort of. A diode rectifies or detects a signal. A transistor amplifies, among other things. An active component by definition "does something." A resistor, capacitor, and inductor, though they actually do things also, are not considered active.

algorithm: A set of instructions used by a computer to accomplish a certain task; a program.

AM: Amplitude modulation, a radio signal that uses changes in its amplitude (intensity) to carry intelligence, or in the case of television lack of intelligence.

amplitude: The relative magnitude or strength of a radio wave or other signal.

antenna: Also sometimes called "aerial"; anything used to radiate a signal from a transmitter to increase its range or the ability of a receiver to "hear" a signal. An antenna may be as simple as a piece of wire or as complicated as a multielement array.

analog: A system wherein values are represented by a varying level. For example, the sound from the speaker of a radio is analog, as it contains many different values of tone, timbre, strength (loudness), etc. See also *digital*.

ASCII: American Standard Code for Information Interchange.

asynchronous: Without sync; without being controlled by a clock. Computers are controlled by an internal clock that regulates the speed at which data is processed. An asynchronous device is not. For example, when transferring data through a modem, the blocks of data are sent on the basis of a signal from the other end (DTR) saying that it is ready to receive.

bandwidth: The width of a transmitted signal, radio or data. Most two-way radios have a signal that is 10,000 cycles (10 kilocycles) wide. Television stations transmit a signal that is 6 megacycles wide; it occupies that much of the radio spectrum, e.g., TV channel 2 is from 54 to 60 mHz. Surveillance transmitters may have a bandwidth of from 6 (narrow band or NB) kHz up, depending on how they are made.

baud: The speed at which data is sent through phone lines or from a computer to a printer or other device.

bipolar: A type of transistor consisting of three elements called base, emitter, and collector.

birdie: An internal signal generated by some scanners and communications receivers, which it "hears" as a station. It is usually a low hissing sound. The newer scanners have eliminated most birdies, but all have a few. To tell a birdie from a real signal, disconnect the antenna, and, if it is still there, it is a birdie.

bit: Binary digit; a one or a zero as used by computers and other digital devices. Eight bits = one byte, which = one letter or number. See also *ASCII*.

boilerplate: Parts of a document, such as the letterhead, address, ZIP code, greeting, salutation, etc., that can be searched for when trying to break an encrypted message. The person attempting to break the code will look for "Dear Mr." and "Very truly yours," and other strings, which if they can be decrypted, can be used to help decode the rest of the document.

bridge rectifier: See *rectifier*.

bug burner: A device used for destroying phone transmitters by sending an electrical charge through the phone lines. This device should be used only by someone who knows what he is doing because there is the danger of both getting shocked and damaging the telco equipment.

bug detector: A device used for finding a bug by tuning in on the signal it transmits, which may be RF, visible, or infrared light. It is not to be confused with pest control.

burst: A transmitter that converts sound to digital form, stores it, and then transmits it in a short, high-speed burst. This makes it more difficult to find with electronic equipment. When searching, look for the batteries, which will probably be larger than the transmitter.

capcode: The unique address of a pager, similar to the MIN of a cellular phone.

capstone: A microcircuit (chip) akin to the Clipper chip in that it is based on the secret Skipjack algorithm (and also designed by the National Security Agency), but which is intended principally for use in secure data transmissions and for the secure storage of data rather than for voice communications. Capstone is also tamper resistant.

capture: Capture effect; a characteristic of frequency modulation receivers that causes them to lock on to the strongest signal they hear, blocking out the others. This is why you may hear two different stations at once on the AM band, but not on FM.

carbon microphone: A microphone that uses small carbon granules inside a "diaphragm." As sound strikes it, the carbon vibrates, which changes the resistance, and these changes are heard by a telephone receiver as sound. It requires a DC voltage to make it work, which is why phone lines have DC on them.

Clipper: A microcircuit (chip) designed by the National Security Agency to implement the Skipjack algorithm to encrypt telephone communications. Voice and other sounds are first converted to digital format, the Skipjack algorithm is then applied, the resulting scrambled data stream is sent over the telephone line to another Clipper-equipped telephone, the receiving unit decrypts using Skipjack, and the resulting data is finally converted into voice or other sounds in the receiver. To protect the secrecy of the Skipjack algorithm itself, as well as certain other elements of the operation of the Clipper chip, each chip is tamper resistant.

coaxial cable: A cable consisting of an inner conductor surrounded by a wire braid, usually grounded. The braid shields the inner wire, which carries the signal, from outside interference, as well as preventing the signal from causing interference. It is used in some LANs and as a transmission line between transmitter/receiver and antenna.

contact microphone: A special microphone used to pick up physical vibrations, such as from, or through, a wall. It is sometimes called an electronic stethoscope. Such a device is easily defeated by taping a small transistor radio to the wall.

CPSR: Computer Professionals for Social Responsibility.

crystal: A small piece of quartz used to set the frequency of a transmitter. Quartz vibrates at a very precise rate and can thus keep the transmitter on frequency. The action is by the piezoelectric effect—if an electric current is applied, the quartz vibrates; if it is bent or twisted, it generates a tiny electric current.

cyphertext: Messages that have been encrypted or scrambled.

Damocles, sword of: Something that materializes out of thin air and hangs over the head of a writer as a deadline approaches.

decibel: dB; a unit used to determine the relative strength of an audio or RF signal. It was named after Alexander Graham Bell, the inventor of the telephone.

decomposition: The breakdown of chemicals in a battery. They can be analyzed to determine the approximate time period in which the battery was functional and a surveillance transmitter was operating. Part of "damage assessment," this can help determine what information may have been compromised.

demodulator: A circuit in some RF transmitter detectors that detects the signal and feeds it into a speaker, so the operator can identify transmissions and eliminate false signals such as commercial radio and television stations.

digital: A system where values or quantities are represented by only two quantities, such as the ones and zeros used in digital devices. For example, in CDs digital audio consists of only ones and zeros stored on the disk that are converted back to audio when played.

direct listen: A method of eavesdropping by using either a microphone hidden in the target area or a phone tap, where wires lead directly to the listening post.

downline: Downline tap; a location along a phone line that is between the point of demarcation and the telco central office. Anywhere on a phone line outside the house or building; on a telephone pole, or in a telco junction point, etc.

drop: Make a drop; plant, hide, or install a bug or listening device.

DTR: Data Terminal ready.

dual conversion: A receiver that has two IF frequencies rather than one. The signals received are amplified by one IF stage and then by the second, which uses a different IF frequency. This helps to eliminate image reception.

DVP: Digital voice protection; a method of digital encryption of audio (voice) signals transmitted over radio or telephone systems. Produced by Motorola, it is believed to be unbreakable with today's technology.

EAROM: Electrically alterable read-only memory, a memory chip that can be reprogrammed from the keyboard.

ECPA: Electronic Communications Privacy Act; a federal law that, among other things, restricts which radio signals one can legally listen to.

EEROM: Electrically erasable read-only memory; a memory chip that can be erased with a command from the keyboard of the device it is placed in, such as a cellular phone.

EFF: Electronic Frontier Foundation.

EPIC: Electronic Privacy Information Center. EPIC, CPSR, and EFF are organizations concerned with the right to privacy in electronic communications.

EPROM: Erasable, programmable read-only memory; a chip that can have information entered into it using a "burner." This is permanent unless it is erased by a high-intensity ultraviolet light.

eavesdropping: Any method (electronic or otherwise) of secretly listening to people's conversations.

elements:
- *Antenna:* the parts of a beam, or yagi, antenna
- *Directors:* the parts that concentrate the signal in one general direction
- *Driven element:* the part that is connected to the transmitter
- *Reflector:* the part that reflects to the signal from the driven element in the desired direction, where it is concentrated by the directors
- *Also the parts of a vacuum tube such as filament, cathode, grid, and plate*

exclusive-or: See *XOR.*

FCC: Federal Communications Commission; the U.S. agency responsible for issuing licenses to amateur and commercial radio and television stations and granting (or refusing) the right to manufacture or import electronic equipment if said equipment complies with its regulations. This was originally to prevent the use of equipment that could interfere with other equipment, but in recent years the FCC has used its regulatory power to prevent the import and manufacture of "noncomplying" equipment that the government doesn't want us to have.

fiber optics: A way of sending information, digital or analog, through a thin strand of glass or plastic.

field effect transistor: FET; one type of transistor. Bipolar is another. Both have three parts, or elements. In the FET, the parts are the gate, source, and drain.

field strength meter: An electronic device that can detect the RF signals from transmitters, bugs, etc. It can be as simple as a small meter with a diode across it and a length of wire for an antenna or as sophisticated and expensive as the models made by Simpson and others, which are used to detect leakage in cable television lines.

filter: An electronic circuit or device that affects sound or RF signals. Filters can be used with audio to block out interference when used with a bug or shotgun microphone. For example, the equalizer on a stereo system is a filter. Some types are these:
- *Bandpass*—allows a certain range or band of frequencies to pass through it and blocks all others
- *Band stop*—the opposite of band pass; a certain range is blocked, all others pass
- *T-notch*—an adjustable filter that can be tuned to block certain frequencies, like an adjustable bandpass filter
- *High pass* and *low pass*

FIPS: Federal Information Processing Standard; e.g., FIPS 185. Also known as the escrowed encryption standard, it is the formal administrative action by the U.S. Department of Commerce that established Clipper as a standard for use by federal agencies.

FM: Frequency modulation; an RF signal that uses changes in frequency to carry intelligence as opposed to changes in amplitude. Also the FM commercial broadcasting band, so named because the stations operating there use frequency modulation transmitters.

frequency counter: A device that measures and displays the frequency of a radio transmitter.

frequency hopping: The technique of changing frequencies quickly from one to another to prevent the transmission from being intercepted.

frequency inversion: A low-security method of scrambling speech used in landline, cordless, and cellular telephones. It will defeat the casual listener but not a pro.

full duplex: A radio or radio-telephone system where both parties can talk and listen at the same time. Cellular telephone, for example, is full duplex.

full quieting: The condition where the signal from a transmitter is heard by the receiver at such a level, or signal strength, that it blocks out all background noise.

gold box: A device for call forwarding. It requires two lines: a person can call in on one line and call out on the other. It is also known as a "cheesebox." A gold box can also be used as a remote-controlled phone tap by connecting it to the target line. It is sometimes called a "slave."

ground: Something that lawyers, politicians, writers, and other undesirables often don't have their feet on. Also the earth, to which one side of electrical circuits may be connected. House wiring, for example, has one side of the line (actually the center of a three-wire, single-phase 220-volt system) connected to ground.

harmonic: A multiple of a given frequency. If the base or original frequency is 10,000 cycles, the second harmonic will be 20,000, the third 30,000, etc.

harmonica bug: See *infinity transmitter*.

hazard: A term used in sweeping for bugs; any place a listening device could be hidden.

hazard chart: A diagram of the area(s) to be searched that shows possible hiding places for surveillance devices; hazards.

hertz: Cycle per second. Same difference.

hook switch bypass: A switch that defeats or "bypasses" the cradle or hook switch in a telephone to turn the microphone on.

hot: The condition of a microphone being activated or turned on.

IDEA: International Data Encryption Algorithm; a very strong cipher developed in Switzerland and implemented in Phil Zimmerman's Pretty Good Program software.

IF: Intermediate frequency; the signal into a receiver (radio, TV, scanner, etc.) is too weak to hear, so it has to be amplified. Before superheterodyne receivers, each amplifier had to be manually tuned to the frequency that was being received. This meant that there were three or four knobs to adjust to get a good signal. To eliminate this problem the "superhet" was developed. Whatever the frequency being received, it is converted to a single IF frequency, typically 10.7 MH, which is then amplified in the IF stages. See also *dual conversion*.

image frequency: A side effect of superhet radios is that signals are sometimes received at a frequency other than what the radio is tuned to. This is because of the local oscillator (LO) that generates a weak signal used to convert the received frequency to the IF for amplification. The image is twice the IF, subtracted from the tuned frequency. If it is tuned to 460.075, and the IF is 10.7, the image will be 460.075 - (10.7 x 2) = 438.675.

IMHO: In my humble opinion; an abbreviation used in electronic mail messages.

infinity transmitter: A device installed on a phone line or inside a phone, used to secretly listen to conversations in the area. See also *hook switch, bypass,* and *harmonica bug.*

information superhighway: Once the generic term for a network the government wanted to create (at an estimated cost of $500 billion), while not realizing that it (the Internet) already existed.

infrared transmitter: A device that uses invisible infrared light to transmit intelligence, much like a TV remote control. It is sometimes used as a surveillance device.

intelligence: A fancy term for information, sometimes used by people who are trying to impress others.

intercept: To overhear, in any of several ways, conversations without the subject's being aware that it is being done.

jammer: A device that generates ultrasonic sound (USS), which causes some but not all microphones to vibrate or oscillate and makes them "deaf." Also a transmitter used to interfere with a receiver to prevent it from receiving.

kilocycle: (kHz); 1,000 cycles. Also called kilohertz.

LAN: Local area network; a system that connects computers and peripherals together. This can be something as simple as hooking up several computers to one printer so they can share it or as sophisticated as dozens of computers (more correctly, terminals) tied together. A large manufacturing company that has several buildings at one site could use a LAN to transfer data back and forth from one office to another. A LAN can use ordinary copper-wire telephone lines, coaxial cable, or a wireless system such as infrared or RF transmissions. See also *WAN.*

LEAF: Law enforcement access field; part of the communication between two Clipper chips. It is used by law enforcement to decrypt a scrambled conversation.

line powered: A phone bug that draws power from the phone line and thus does not need a battery.

listen-down amplifier: Listen down the line amplifier; an audio amplifier connected to a phone line. It amplifies any sound on the line, such as an infinity transmitter, without taking it to an off-hook condition. It lets you hear anything happening without lifting the receiver.

listening post: The physical location of equipment used for surveillance monitoring.

megacycle: MHz; a million cycles per second. Also called megahertz.

mixer: A stage or circuit in a receiver that combines the incoming signal frequency with the local oscillator to produce the intermediate frequency, or IF.

modem: An acronym for modulator-demodulator; a device used to convert computer data to sound so it can be sent through the phone lines, LANs, etc.

multiplexing: "Many into one"; the technique of combining a number of telephone conversations into one signal and transmitting through one wire or fiber-optic strand.

nonlinear junction detector: An electronic device used for finding surveillance devices by flooding an area with microwaves and listening for a return signal that changes phases when in the presence of a semiconductor-transistor or integrated circuit. This device does work, but is easily defeated by using a metal shield around the surveillance device or placing a large quantity of cheap diodes in an area that may be searched. It is also given to false signals.

Omnibus: The Omnibus Crime Control and Safe Streets Act of 1968.

penetrate: To physically enter the target area to place a listening device.

phantom line: Also phantom pair; the process of using one wire from one cable or pair and one from a different cable or pair in wiretapping.

phone tap: Connection of a wire to a phone line, or placement of a coil of wire on or near a line to intercept conversations.

photocell: An electronic component that changes light into electricity, the opposite of a light bulb.

physical search: The process of physically searching for listening devices, lost car keys, etc.

plaintext: Information, documents, or files in unencrypted plain English. See also *cyphertext*.

POCSAG: One of the protocols used in pager message transmissions. Others are Golay and Motorola.

prime number: A number that can be evenly divided only by one or itself. For example, the digit nine is not prime because it can be evenly divided (no remainder) by not only one and nine, but also three. Eleven is a prime number because it can be evenly divided by only one and eleven.

profile: The composite information one might obtain about a person who has installed a surveillance device, based on the type, location, and other factors. See *The Bug Book*.

polarization: The way an antenna is positioned in relation to the earth, either vertically or horizontally. For best reception, the antenna should have the same polarization as the transmitter.

radio spectrum: That part of the electromagnetic spectrum where RF transmitters operate.

RAM: Random-access memory; temporary computer memory that uses chips rather than magnetic media such as a tape or disk.

reflectometer: Literally, to measure (meter) a reflection. A sophisticated electronic device that can measure the distance, along a wire or cable, to where a break or tap is located.

rectifier: A device that converts AC to DC, which can be a vacuum tube or semiconductor, such as a diode or bridge. A bridge is four diodes in one package. AC flows in two directions, and DC in only one; so a rectifier prevents the flow of current in one direction and lets it flow in the other. Also, the result of having eaten too many chili peppers.

remote control bug: An RF surveillance transmitter that can be turned off and on from a distant location. This makes it harder to find and conserves battery life. If someone is listening and hears the sounds of a search, he can turn it off until the search is over.

register: A temporary storage place for data, usually a chip or part of another larger chip. For example, you type the digit 2 on your keyboard and hit the < <ENTER> > key. The keyboard encoder converts this to an eight-bit binary ASCII number and sends it to a register, sometimes called an "accumulator." Enter another digit (e.g., 6) and it goes to another register. When the computer receives a command to do something with these numbers, such as add them, it sends them to a memory location in RAM. Registers have names that indicate how the information flows in and out, such as FIFO (first in first out); FILO (first in last out); LIFO (last in first out); and LILO (last in last out). When data are lost, they go to a big register in the sky called LaLa or "the bit bucket."

repeater: A system that uses a larger, higher-power transmitter to relay a signal from a smaller one, thereby increasing the range. Also an amplifier placed along telephone lines to boost the signal when it gets weak

RF: Radio frequency; an area of the electromagnetic spectrum used for radio and TV transmissions.

selectivity: The extent to which a receiver can tune in on one signal without hearing other unwanted ones. It is not the same as capture.

simplex: A radio system where both parties cannot talk simultaneously. One talks and the other listens, and then they switch.

snuggling: The process of tuning a bug to transmit near the frequency of a powerful station, such as commercial radio or TV. This makes it more difficult to detect with countermeasures equipment.

spade clip: A type of electrical connector that fits under a screw without having to remove it.

square wave: A time-varying electrical signal that looks on the screen of an oscilloscope like a square or rectangle.

synthesis: The process of generating different frequencies without needing crystals for each one. It is based on a voltage-controlled oscillator (VCO).

spectrum analyzer: A special radio receiver that displays the waveform of a received signal on a screen, similar to an oscilloscope. It is useful in finding surveillance transmitters because they have a higher frequency limit, up to about 40 GHz, compared with about 2 GHz for countermeasures receivers. The only device that will detect the X-band transmitter.

subcarrier: The principle used in wireless intercoms to send audio through the electrical wiring. Also a method of transmitting information inside the carrier of a commercial radio or TV station. Closed captioning, Muzak, video-text are examples.

subcarrier detector: A device for finding a hidden subcarrier surveillance device.

subcarrier extension: An extension telephone that uses the same method as wireless intercoms. The conversation can be intercepted with a similar device in the area served by the same pole transformer. Contrary to what some advertisements promise, they are not secure.

SVX: A digital voice encryption system similar to DVP but more secure.

sweep: The use of electronic equipment and a physical search to find surveillance devices.

target: The area to be bugged or line to be tapped.

TDMA: Time-division multiple access; a cellular radio standard in which voice transmissions are in digital form and sent in blocks over short periods. This allows a number of users to operate on the same channel at the same time.

TDR: See *reflectometer*.

telemonitor: A device similar to the infinity transmitter, except it does not prevent the phone from ringing.

TEMPEST: Transient Electromagnetic Pulse Emanation Standard; a U.S. government standard that has to do with the amount of RF energy radiating from a computer. See *Digital Privacy* for details.

tessera: (name changed to fortessa); a circuit board intended for insertion in personal computers that implements the capstone chip and its key escrow system for secure transmission and storage of data. See also *Clipper*.

timbre: The combination of frequencies, harmonics, and subharmonics that gives sounds their unique qualities. For example, in musical instruments it is timbre that allows us to tell the difference between a violin and a cello, even when they both play a note of the same frequency. The same is true of human and animal voices.

Torx screw: A special fastener used to lock some telco connection blocks, TV cable converters, etc. It can be removed with a Torx wrench.

transducer: A device that changes energy from one form to another. For example, a microphone changes mechanical energy (the movement of the diaphragm) to electrical energy. A photocell changes light energy to electricity.

tube mic: A microphone with a small, usually plastic, tube attached. It can be inserted into the target area through a small hole, such as a wall plug, from an adjoining room.

UART: Universal asynchronous receiver-transmitter; a chip used in transferring data to and from a computer.

vacuum tube: (simplified explanation) a glass envelope that contains various elements used for control and amplification. The elements and their functions are as follows:
- *Filament*—similar to the filament in a light bulb, except that its purpose is to radiate electrons rather than photons; it is sometimes coated with the element thorium
- *Plate*—also called anode, it attracts the electrons flowing from the filament or cathode
- *Cathode*—an element in some tubes that is heated by the filament to emit electrons, instead of electrons being emitted by the filament
- *Grid*—an element placed between the cathode and plate that controls the flow of electrons

Van Eck: The first person to demonstrate TEMPEST. See *TEMPEST*.

voice print: A "fingerprint" of a particular human voice that can be compared to other recorded voices to determine if they are the same.

voice recognition: A system that analyzes the human voice and makes a record of its unique characteristics. This record can be used to positively identify a person. Oki Telecom, a manufacturer of cellular phones, is developing a voice-recognition system to be built into its phones. If someone other than the registered owner of a phone attempts to use it and the voice print does not match the one registered to the owner, the cellular system will not place the call. See also *voice print*.

VOX: Voice-operated relay; an electronic device that senses audio input and automatically activates a tape recorder or other device.

WAN: Wide area network; essentially the same as a LAN but larger.

wireless intercom: An intercom that uses the power lines instead of ordinary wires to send the sound back and forth.

wireless microphone: A transmitter that usually operates on the commercial FM broadcast band. It is used to eliminate the problem of long microphone cords used by stage entertainers and for surveillance.

ZIF: Zero insertion force; a chip socket used in devices where the chips are frequently changed, such as an EPROM burner. It has large openings for the pins so the chip can quickly and easily be inserted; then a little lever is turned, which closes the contacts onto the pins.